Asha Bhosle

Asha Bhosle

A Life in Music

RAMYA SARMA

An imprint of Manjul Publishing House Pvt. Ltd.
• C-16, Sector 3, Noida, Uttar Pradesh 201 301, India
Website: www.manjulindia.com
Registered Office:
• 2nd Floor, Usha Preet Complex, 42 Malviya Nagar,
Bhopal 462 003 – India
Distribution Centres
Ahmedabad, Bengaluru, Chennai, Hyderabad,
Kochi, Kolkata, Mumbai, Noida, Pune

Asha Bhosle: A Life in Music by Ramya Sarma

Published by Amaryllis, an imprint of Manjul Publishing House in 2025

ISBN 978-93-5543-681-8

Cover design: Neelima P Aryan
Photographs: Yogen Shah

To Papa – always
and Mumma – wish you were here

Ken Hunt: It's all about the music
Lesle Lewis: It's all about the song

Contents

Introduction

A few years ago, I was asked if I was interested in writing a book. Being a bit of a masochist and willing to try and do more than I was already squishing into a workday, I agreed, albeit cautiously, since the still sane voice of reason did occasionally wander in and slap me on the head. Before I knew what was happening, I not only had a literary agent, but also a book contract. The book that I had so rashly signed on to write was aimed to be a profile of the well-known singer, Asha Bhosle.

After a first rudimentary attempt at writing a few chapters, I had to have a deep think and get to a more sustained and determined exploration of my subject. I would write about Asha Bhosle as seen by people who had worked with her or knew her, I decided, thereby profiling her through her career and her music, especially the non-filmi version. The process, I assumed, would not be that difficult.

It was not that hard, indeed; it became almost impossible, frustrating, annoying and even funny at times. There were people who agreed to talk to me and then either vanished or were stricken with sudden illness. An infamously outspoken filmmaker agreed to chat and then refused to remember that he had spoken with me. A composer was enthusiastic and set a date and time for a meeting and then changed his phone number. A well-known poet refused me a conversation when he learned that I had not met or interviewed the subject of the book, who was very dear to him. There were some who, although not willing to talk to me themselves, were kind enough to suggest someone else, and give me their contact details. Hilariously, a famous ghazal singer in Pakistan responded amiably, but wanted me to renew his Tata Sky account before he would talk to me! And as all this was happening, I was reading – interviews, articles, news reports, social media – anything that popped up on Google, in conversation with people, in magazines and newspapers, on TV or even on the radio. I heard more film music than I had ever done and developed a weird taste for Indi-pop that I never thought I would. My driver, a fan, diligently listened to a radio show on which he had heard a story about Asha that he told me about; wherever he drove me to, we listened to that particular show and learned a lot from it about people I was never going to write about.

Then there were people who were friendly, communicative and extraordinarily helpful. Lesle Lewis talked to me for hours about Asha, let me put my sore feet up on his studio couch and sang songs from a still-to-release album for me. Atul Churamani not only gave me the information I needed, but gave me lunch and something I cherish far more – a friend. Shujaat Khan flew in to the city for a concert, spent time with me talking about Asha, put me in touch with his delightful wife Parveen – who told me about shopping trips and junk food she shared with the diva – and agreed to be interviewed again for a new website on music without asking what happened to the book. Usha Uthup came out of the recording studio, agreed to be spoken to, said a few apropos words and then disappeared, appearing again to ask a couple of years later why I had not done a full interview and got more from her. Sonu Nigam was strangely elusive and then made me change my fulminating mind on his professionalism by responding to my questions and singing for me, all on WhatsApp! Boy George, from whose album covers I had learned to use eye make-up, replied to my email and told me about his experience with Asha – I was so excited by this unexpected response that I woke up various people in various parts of the world to tell them about it! And then, a man whom I consider a friend even though we have never met: Ken Hunt. He was generous in his sharing and even more so in his caring. He talked to me – mostly on email and WhatsApp, a couple of times on the phone – about Asha, his own work with her, his writing, his music, his cooking, his family, even his tortoises. There were so many more like this, giving, encouraging, hugely helpful, from Poonam Dhillon, Mahesh Kodiyal and Ameen Sayani to Hrishikesh Kannan, Ken Ghosh, Sumit Dutt, Rajan Shahi, Aman Arora, Anjali Mathur, Brahmanand Singh, Hariprasad Chaurasia, Kumar Sanu, Longinus Fernandes, Madhulika Liddle, Mandar Bichu, Manish Purohit, Manohar Iyer, Mukesh Batra, Narendra Kusnur, Parveen Khan, Rajeev Masand, S. Ramachandran, Satish Chopra, Shamir Tandon and Yogen Shah. There were others who helped with phone numbers, contacts, suggestions and chocolate, like Aditya Raj Kapoor, Ananth Padmanabhan, Dhiren Trivedi, Dominic Ferrao, Indu Mirani, Krithika R, Letty Maria Abraham, Neeta Kolhatkar, Nina Rao, Prathamesh Jadhav, Rachana Parekh, Ritu Ferrao, Rocky Mohan, Roshmila Bhattacharya, Suresh Gopale, Suresh Nair and Vivek Kapoor.

Along the way, I learned a great deal about writing, about people, about friendship and about Asha Bhosle. I found out that not only was she a good cook, she often went to the market to buy pots and pans, to poke the eggplants, snap the beans and feel the tomatoes with her own hands, instead of trusting anyone else to choose for her. She could be a child, I heard, taking a day off from a concert tour to go to Disneyland, dancing under a waterfall in the middle of the road, or suddenly getting fed up of being a professional on a recording and wanting to go home. The diva was vain, I discovered, wanting to look her best and even suggesting a touch of computer magic to make a bulge disappear or a wrinkle – God forbid! – vanish. She watched soap operas on television and even came up with new plot lines and suggestions for characters, telling the producer what he should do to make it better. Ice cream was a favourite food, but she rarely ate any, and she could giggle like a teenager making up stories. She could break in grief, but also pull herself together almost immediately and get back to work. People liked her, when they did, but were generally wary of her and the power she and her sister wielded in the music world, especially in Hindi films.

It was a study in contrasts – the people with whom the singer was most friendly, those with whom she worked very closely, they were not forthcoming. Those who knew her as a singer rather than a playback artiste may have been cautious and censoring themselves, but they were willing to recall memories of working with her. The many who did talk, did so at length and told me stories that showed me who Asha was – and still is. She acted in a lead role in a film, but some of her best scenes were cut out because her family was made uncomfortable by the honesty and openness of her acting – did they coddle and cosset her to the point where she refused to meet people outside her own small circle? Was she afraid to step outside that charmed bubble and be an ordinary woman

– obviously not, since she went to the vegetable market and slaved over a hot stove cooking for family and friends! Or was it a well-learned caution that kept her protected? After years of media speculation and truckloads of gossip about her relationships, her rivalries and her insecurities, she might, in fact, have been justified in doing so. But then who was the woman who adventurously sang into a microphone in a recording studio on the other side of the world, far away from the music director for whom she was singing? The voice that played with notes in songs like '*Aaja aaja*' and '*Duniya mein logon ko*' and also sang '*Mera kuchh samaan*' and '*Dil cheez kya hai*' belonged to the same person, the one who was game for a challenge and is still able to rise to one at ninety-plus years of age! My voyage of discovery had so many diversions and detours that I found an Asha not often seen, with music that slid off the big screen and into homes, studios and discos all over the world.

So who is Asha Bhosle? This book is an attempt to find out.

The History of Film Music

De de khuda ke naam pe pyaare
Taaqat ho agar dene ki
Kuchh chaahe agar toh maang le mujhse
Himmat ho agar lene ki!

A song from the film *Alam Ara* (1931)

On 14 March 1931, *Alam Ara* was released at the Majestic Cinema in Bombay. The novelty of a film with sound and, more interestingly, songs, had the cash registers ringing. The film was so popular that 'police aid had to be summoned to control the crowds', it was reported. Ardeshir Irani, its producer, was hailed as the father of modern Indian cinema, the progenitor of the Sound Era who worked on synchronising running pictures with sound. The film made history.

Soon after, cinematic productions such as *Laila Majnu*, *Shakuntala*, and *Shirin Farhad*, all of which were released in 1931, caused a buzz not just for their story and music, but also for their actors. In those days, the actors were the singers, and if they could carry a tune, the film usually did well. *Shirin*

Farhad had Jahanara Kajjan and Master Nissar, who were good-looking, could sing well and delivered impeccable Urdu dialogue, making them the 'hit pair' of the 1930s.

Alam Ara had seven songs orchestrated with only three instruments: the violin, the tabla and the harmonium. It included the first song in the history of Indian cinema: '*De de khuda ke naam pe pyaare*'. Sung by Muhammad Wazir Khan, the song was recorded live, with just a harmonium and tabla for accompaniment. The music was composed by Ferozshah M. Mistry and B. Irani. As director Shyam Benegal once said, 'It was not just a talkie, but a talking and singing film with less talking and more singing. It set the template for the kind of films that were made later.'

In the same year came Jamshedji Framji Madan's *Shirin Farhad*, which had a whopping forty-two songs. *Indrasabha*, released a year later, directed by J.J. Madan and V. Shantaram, had an astonishing seventy-one songs! Soon enough, the trend faded out, and there came to be on average less than a dozen such musical numbers in the movies that followed.

Indian (especially Hindi) films without music would be like a meal without salt. Music is often almost a character playing an independent role in a story. Sometimes it is a device to take the plot to the next chapter. Once in a while it is a break in the tension, adding a lightness before the tone is heightened again. And frequently, it becomes a crowd-puller. The incorporation of music probably began as a background effect, a way to create a mood and fill the gaps between dialogues, or as a way of communicating to the audience the dynamic between characters. But soon the talkies were all about songs, often accompanied by dance.

It was rare that a film was made without songs – such movies were often labelled 'art' or 'parallel' cinema, a tag deliberately fostered by some, like Satyajit Ray. The film song, especially in Hindi cinema, became a staple. It cut across linguistic, religious, and, as the popularity of the medium grew across the world, ethnic barriers. Composers brought in new sounds, new singers, and, as technology evolved, new sound effects, making the process of creation easier, more eclectic, more foolproof. The image of R.D. Burman innovating with bottles, flowing tap water, or squeaking balloons is evocative – much more so than the vision of contemporary music directors working in studios with a stunning array of machines around them.

What makes film songs special is that they are most often sung by professional playback artistes and given a different life when they are lip-synced on the screen by the actors playing that particular character. Frequently, the songs mouthed by one character on screen are sung by different singers, making the finished product a trifle incongruous.

Once upon a time, it was the actor who did the singing, but that soon gave way to a more behind-the-scenes approach, with playback singers and actors each holding their own; and it seems to be coming full circle lately, with stars now singing their own screen songs.

But in between came a time when playback singers started ruling the musical roost. It started at the big production houses that had built a reputation during the silent era and stood by their conviction that sound was the next step towards a new and truly exciting future in cinematic history.

There was Ardeshir Irani and R.S. Choudhury's Imperial Studios; Himansu Rai, V. Shantaram and Master Vinayak in Prabhat Films; B.N. Sircar in South Calcutta founded New Theatres; Homi Wadia established Wadia Movietone; Chandulal

Shah set up Ranjit Studios. Perhaps it was New Theatres in Calcutta that used the first song recorded with playback, as far back as 1934, in the Bengali *Bhagya Chakra*, directed by Nitin Bose; it was remade as *Dhoop Chhaon* (also released in 1935) in Hindi, with the same crew, and is very likely the first Hindi film to feature a playback song.

Most singers – and actors who sang – were trained in classical or folk music, and stayed true to their genres. Many had a family tradition of music, and maintained the norms of the gharana in the new medium. If they were novices, the music was composed more simply, allowing the untrained voice to sing nevertheless. That suited the tastes of the audience well enough at the time. But there was change in the air.

For one, the insidious influence of the West was filtering into India and Indian films in many ways, from music to fashion to technology. And then there was a kind of pan-Indian wave, with sounds from various parts of the country adding heft to the music that was gradually becoming identified as 'Bollywood'. And those at the helm of so many memorable compositions stayed associated with specific studios for decades, as in-house musicians who were deeply and inextricably identified by the production house they worked with. Prabhat talent came in the form of Master Govindrao Tembe, Keshavrao Bhole, Krishnarao Phulambrikar, and Vasant Shantaram Desai, while New Theatres fostered Pankaj Mullick, Raichand Boral, and Timirbaran Bhattacharya. Bombay Talkies hitched on Khorshed Homji and Ramchandra Pal, while Himansu Rai's British Production Company depended on foreign talent, and Imperial Studios trusted its Parsi patrons who were fans of Western music. Ranjit Studios used the classical sounds of Jhande Khan, Banne Khan, and Rewashankar Marwari; Ashok Ghosh and Pransukh Nayak helmed the tunes at Sagar and National Studios.

How did it all lead to where movie music is today? Perhaps the beginning came with the vision of Ram Daryani, a financier, who took a calculated risk and brought a twenty-year-old tabla player called Anil Biswas to Bombay from Calcutta to work with composer Ashok Ghosh as part of the Sagar Movietone orchestra. It was Biswas who decided to tap the collective talents of the members of that musical group to work as a team on one song. Around the same time, Bombay Talkies was launched by the husband–wife duo Himansu Rai and Devika Rani, with Saraswati Devi, who believed in the use of an entire orchestra in every composition, to take songs to a new and comparatively more Western realm which the Hindi film industry was not very familiar at the time. It was possibly the studio's best-known film, *Achhut Kanya* (1936), starring Devika Rani and Ashok Kumar, that was the first to make any noise as a 'musical', with songs sung by the stars themselves.

But a much bigger noise came soon after at New Theatres. The Calcutta-based production company harnessed the skills of a young man who would rule the airwaves for much longer than anyone could have foreseen: Kundan Lal Saigal from Jalandhar in Punjab. The singer was hired with a contract of ₹200 per month and played a role in three films – *Mohabbat Ke Aansu*, *Subah Ka Sitara* and *Zinda Laash* – all released in 1932 and none successful. And then in 1933, the following year, *Puran Bhagat* became a rage and Saigal's four bhajans brought him a huge fan following across the nation. *Yahudi Ki Ladki* (1933), *Mohabbat ki Kasauti* (1934), *Karwan-E-Hayat* (1935) and *Chandidas* (1934) made him a star. In fact, the story goes that after Lata Mangeshkar watched *Chandidas*, she insisted that she would marry the handsome hero with the seductive voice! It has been said that Saigal was so successful mainly because of the recording technology of the time. Songs were recorded in one take, orchestral support and all, on 78 RPM discs made of lac, with players that used needles on the stylus.

There was much more going on in showbiz. Perhaps it was Lahore-based businessman Dalsukh Pancholi who gave this new wave the creative impetus it deserved when he produced *Gul-E-Bakawali* (1939) and then *Khazanchi* (1941), both with music by Master Ghulam Haider. He was perhaps one of the first of a new generation of composers who combined the pure and classical sounds heard until then with the more populist, pan-Indian and Western-influenced music that was filtering into films. Orchestration was becoming trendier and more modern, while songs were evolving to being lighter and more listener and amateur-singer friendly. Ghulam Haider used the dholak and dhol, duff and matka to add much-needed energy. His *Gul-E-Bakawali* was a pre-Partition Punjabi film with the voices of Saigal and Noor Jehan; *Khazanchi* was a musical 'experiment' in which Haider combined Indian classical ragas with Punjabi folk music to create mega-hits sung by Noor Jehan, Shamshad Begum and others. The music of *Khazanchi* was described as 'defying the very structure of the modern Hindi song', composed by the 'father of the age of modern Hindi music'. And it made Haider rich. He charged over ₹25,000 per film and got it! But he is perhaps best known for the singers that he introduced the world to: Shamshad Begum, Noorjehan and Lata Mangeshkar.

This was the time that the movies were starting to become accessible to the general public. It was not all joy. J.B.H. Wadia could have been the first to discover exactly what songs in a film meant to the audience flocking to the cinema halls to watch and listen to them. In 1937, he produced *Naujawan*, India's first song-less talkie, directed by Aspi Irani, produced by Wadia Movietone, J.B.H. Wadia. To quell protests and keep people buying tickets, he had to explain why he had released a silent movie when the age of the talkie (and the screen song) had already arrived, before he was allowed to continue screenings. It was an experiment in making a fast-paced thriller that could not be punctuated by song and dance, he said, but it was one that failed miserably.

So back to music it was, with a horde of new composers, new sounds and new singers. Punjabi folk music was a huge source of inspiration: Pandit Amarnath, Husnlal Bhagatram, Hansraj Behl, Pandit Gobindram, G.A. Chishti and others brought in the *tappa* in a stylised and stylish manner. Uttar Pradesh was represented by Naushad, who drew from his roots for films like *Andaz*, *Anmol Ghadi*, *Dillagi*, *Mela*, *Rattan*, *Shah Jahan*, et al. Anil Biswas and S.D. Burman channelled their Bengali heritage, bringing in the sounds of Rabindra sangeet and Baul and Bhatiyali music. Khemchand Prakash and Ghulam Mohammed reflected Rajasthan in their compositions and S.N. Tripathi and Vasant Desai brought in more purely classical ragas and *bandish*es. Inspired by the struggle for Indian independence and coloured by patriotic fervour came lyrics that spoke to and of the revolutionary spirit even as they sang of love and romance, written by poets like Kidar Sharma, Pradeep, Bharat Vyas and others.

While hordes flocked to the cinema halls and producers smiled all the way to the bank and back, not everyone was happy. Much of the money used to finance the movies being made came from the purses of those who had made profits by wheeling and dealing during World War II, the long battle for Indian independence, and the Bengal famine. But they provided beleaguered audiences with an escape. The magical world of films was taking over the vast wage-earning population of the nation. And hardest hit by this new wave of entertainment was theatre, especially the traditional forms like Natya Sangeet. Many stage artistes who had no other skills save acting and performing had nowhere to go except to the big screen. Several who couldn't make the transition or did not manage to find work outside their own genre gave in to frustration. Alcoholism was rampant, theatre companies were going bankrupt and ticket sales were falling.

One of those badly affected was Deenanath Mangeshkar, who had made his name as a stage performer and had a young wife and five children to support. Suddenly, after many years of being the darling of theatre-goers, he found himself out of work. Frustrated and desperate, he allowed his eldest daughter Lata, a well-trained and talented singer, to look for assignments. Lata was blessed with a sweet voice, and at just twelve years old she won the National Level talent contest, then called the Khazanchi Competition, becoming the first Marathi-speaking singer to do so. People sat up and took notice, Ghulam Haider among them. While some said her voice was 'too thin' and too heavily Marathi-accented, Haider insisted that very soon filmmakers would 'fall at Lata's feet and beg her to sing' for them. With his '*Dil mera toda*' (*Majboor*, 1948), she became seen and heard, and wanted. In 2013, Lata said, 'Ghulam Haider is truly my godfather. He was the first music director who showed complete faith in my talent.'

In the 1940s there was astonishing growth in the world of film production all over the country. Bombay was the hub of cinematic progress. The studio system itself was evolving, with most employees choosing not to work for a fixed salary, preferring to freelance or work film by film. And the production houses could opt for top-billed talent. Composers and singers were possibly the most fortunate, since fans wanted more of their favourites in every movie. In fact, some people bought tickets only to hear that one song over and over again! The old order started crumbling. Bombay Talkies, once the top dog in the business, was gradually losing ground to the new and more progressive and risk-taking studios. And then Anil Biswas and his brother-in-law, Pannalal Ghosh, stepped in to give it a new impetus. Abdul Rashid Kardar from Lahore arrived in Bombay and soon established Kardar Studios and Kardar Productions, harnessing the talents of music mavens like Naushad, Majrooh Sultanpuri, Suraiya and Mohammad Rafi – whose first big success came with '*Suhani raat dhal chuki*' from *Dulari* (1949). Kardar also started the Kardar–Kolynos Contest, sponsored by a toothpaste brand, to find new talent – Chand Usmani and Mahendra Kapoor being the brightest of the discoveries. And there were many more who 'arrived' in the city of dreams to seek fame and fortune, just as Noor Jehan, Parul Ghosh, Arun Kumar, Snehprabha, Kanan Devi, Amirbai Karnataki and Zohrabai Ambalewali had done.

Soon after her debut, Khemchand Prakash gave Lata a song that made her a star, even though he was not alive when it was finally released. Bombay Talkies, the studio that was fast fading into oblivion, was taken over by actor Ashok Kumar, who made *Mahal* (1949), a spooky suspense thriller about reincarnation and love. Haider's 'discovery' Lata sang the haunting '*Aayega aanewala*', which captured listeners everywhere and still does today. Lata had arrived. Everyone wanted her voice, from Biswas to Haider to Naushad and C. Ramachandra. She not only grabbed more than her fair share of the playback assignments, she also made it rather more than normally difficult for her younger sister, Asha, to find work in this new and exciting world.

This is when, many believe, the 'golden era' of Hindi film music truly began. The 1950s were alive with the sounds of music by O.P. Nayyar, who never used the talent of Lata, but preferred Asha, with whom he was said to have shared a personal and professional relationship, in films like *Aan* (1952), *Albela* (1951), *Baiju Bawra* (1952), *Daag* (1952), *Naya Daur* (1957) and so many others. Roshan, Madan Mohan, Hemant Kumar, Khayyam, Salil Chaudhury, Ravi, Jaidev and contemporaries composed unforgettable numbers, with lyrics by the likes of Majrooh Sultanpuri, Shakeel Badayuni, Sahir Ludhianvi, Hasrat Jaipuri, Indivar, Shailendra, Kaifi Azmi and their ilk. By the 1960s, Shankar-Jaikishan had taken over the top spot, mentored by Raj Kapoor and composing for romantic heroes Shammi Kapoor and Rajendra Kumar. For them, Lata (a Raj Kapoor favourite) and Mohammed Rafi were the voices that fit. The next decade was the time of musical partnerships; Kalyanji-Anandji and Laxmikant-Pyarelal rose stratospherically.

And then there was R.D. Burman. The son of S.D. Burman brought in youth and trendiness, channelling influences from the West and using rhythms and sounds rarely heard in the Hindi film world up to that point.

Teesri Manzil (1966) made him a star composer, with Asha Bhosle and Mohammed Rafi belting out songs like '*O mere sona re*', '*O haseena zulfonwali*', '*Aaja aaja*' and '*Deewana mujhsa nahin*'. *Aradhana* (1969) cemented his success and is still known for its songs '*Roop tera mastana*', '*Mere sapnon ki rani*' and '*Kora kagaz thha yeh mann mera*'. Asha, who married R.D. Burman in 1980, sang only one song in the film: '*Gunguna rahe hai bhanware*', a duet with Rafi.

The following decade was far less romantically musical. Films such as *Sholay* (1975), *Don* (1978) and *Mera Gaon Mera Desh* (1971) featured angry young men (Amitabh Bachchan, in particular, and Vinod Khanna) who wanted to change the world with violence, which left little scope for song and dance. In contrast to this came films like *Abhimaan* (1973), *Amar Prem* (1972), *Chitchor* (1976), *Pakeezah* (1972) and *Kabhi Kabhie* (1976), which highlighted love lost, found and cherished. But there was a place for almost everyone. Singing and dancing in films became an extension of the emotive process, taking the story forward or revealing plotlines.

Indian film music, especially in Hindi movies, is subtle even as it is robust, hearty, enthusiastic, exuberant. Even the most *dhinchak* of disco tunes can have its base in a raga. Some scores could be background music, showing light and moody effects with subdued reticence; a theme song might be reprised to emphasise the core of the story, be it a revenge drama, a classic good versus evil conflict or a simple love story. Then there are mirrors of feeling: the quick patter of drumbeats as the heroine's heart beats faster, the sonorous thump of a bass as the villain approaches, the rapid flutter of the flute as children run…

It was all part of the world of Hindi cinema – the *masti*, the masala, the magic. And it always will be the gateway to a world that is exciting, enchanting, inspiring.

1

The One and Only

The Marathi Brahmin family of Pandit Deenanath Mangeshkar hailed from a small village in Maharashtra in Sangli district over eighty years ago. Deenanath's mother, Yesubai Rane, belonged to the Devadasi community of Goa, now called the Gomantak Maratha Samaj, and sang at temple festivals. She was well-known for her mastery over music. His father was Ganesh Bhatt Abhisheki of the Hardikar family, who had the ancestral right to bathe (i.e. perform *abhisheka to*) the linga idol of Lord Shiva at the Mangeshi temple in Goa. Proud of his heritage, Deenanath added Mangeshkar to his name after he grew up, signifying that he was from the village of Mangeshi, about 560 km from Mumbai.

When Deenanath was just five years old, he was sent to Shri Baba Mashelkar to learn music. A few years later, he started studying in the Gwalior gharana, one of the oldest schools of khayal, its most famous disciple being Miyan Tansen. The young Deenanath also studied under Pandit Sukhdev Prasad of the Kirana Gharana in Bikaner, and became the *gandabandh shagird* of Gayanacharya Pandit Ramkrishna Buwa Vaze to learn the aggressive and varied style the guru practised. At just eleven years of age, he became part of the Kirloskar Natak Mandali, a local drama group, but branched out to form Balwant Mandali with his friends, becoming well known with his masterful presentation of Vaze's compositions and the patriotic themes he favoured. Deenanath could sing, making him so popular that Bal Gandharva, himself a history-maker in Marathi theatre, wanted him to be a part of his group, promising to welcome him to it 'by throwing a carpet of rupee coins under his feet'. In those days, a single rupee was worth a fortune!

Deenanath Mangeshkar's personal life, too, was fairly dramatic. He first married Narmada, who became 'Shrimati' to her in-laws. She was the daughter of a rich businessman of Thalner, and gave him a daughter: Latika, or Hridaya. Unfortunately, the child died young and Shrimati passed on soon after. Then Deenanath then married his first wife's sister, Shevanti, also called Shudhmati. He had several children with her: a son named Hridaynath, and four daughters: Lata (originally 'Hridaya' in memory of that first child), Asha, Usha and Meena. Music was in every brick in the small house they lived in, and the eldest daughter, Lata, was soon singing with her father at home and on stage.

The onset of the movies had affected the theatre, and the once-adored stage artistes were now struggling. Those who could transition to movies were few, and artistes who knew only their trade fell victim to the loss of work, money and adulation, many resorting to alcoholism to cope with their misfortune. Deenanath's untimely death in April 1942 at the age of just forty-one hit the family hard. Asha was only nine years old at the time. 'Our financial position was not good, but we children were too young to be much affected,' says Asha. 'We would have one cup of tea or a handful of peanuts, and then go off to play.' In those days, there was not much else to do.

There was no radio, but there was always music. All the children sang, encouraged by their mother. 'My mother was a very clever lady,' Asha says, pride and love colouring her words. 'She took care of five children alone, with no income.' The family tapped into their family tradition of music and theatre to make a living. Apropos, when Asha was learning classical vocal music from Navrang Nagpurkar, he reportedly told her to focus on the popular rather than the traditional, saying that she could make more money that way.

The Mangeshkar children had to make a better life, to find work, to earn money, but it was not possible in the village, where opportunities were few, if any. The family left Goa for Pune, and soon moved to Kolhapur and from there to Bombay. In the big city, a new world opened up for them.

Shudhmati Mangeshkar believed in thinking positive. She would tell her children: 'You are the children of a very big man. You will do something big. You cannot live in poverty. After all, God has given you beauty and this voice.' She backed her daughters all the way, as she did her son. Asha acknowledges her for her strong support:

> *The one gift that my mother gave me was the gift of self-confidence. She always told us to forget about household chores and focus on music. She also told us that there was no one more talented and that we should be so proud of who we were. That self-confidence and a very strong willpower have stood me in good stead.*

Shudhmati was a good mother and a superb one-woman cheering squad. None of the Mangeshkar girls could be called traditionally 'beautiful', but there was incredible beauty and brilliance in what they had inherited from their parents:

music. 'We loved her a lot and we still do. Had my mother not been there, you would not have heard Lata Mangeshkar, Usha Mangeshkar, Hridaynath Mangeshkar or Asha Bhosle. It is because of her that we pursued music and singing.'

Lata, the eldest, had already performed with her father and her talent was not unknown. She started working in films as an actor, not just a singer, her dark complexion, solid build and two long, tightly braided plaits fast becoming almost iconic representations of a girl who could sing anything. Hridaynath, who was only five when his father passed away, started singing too, and was soon a lauded performer and composer. Lata, whom he thought of as his guru, sang some of his best semi-classical songs, including '*Nis din barsat nain hamare*', a Surdas bhajan, and Meerabai's '*Barse boondiyan sawan ki*', as well as the bestselling albums *Chala Des Wahi* and *Meera Soor Kabira*. Both sisters maintain that he is a difficult taskmaster who composes music that is spiritual and heavenly.

While Lata could sing almost anything, she preferred more classical tunes, with devotional songs being a favourite. Asha has said of her sister, 'From as far back as I can remember, I saw my father and sister singing. We owned a theatre, with about 200 employees. It was the death of my father at a very early age that pushed Lata didi, who was not yet fourteen, to go out and sing to make ends meet.' Asha herself sang her first song at the age of ten. But even while music played such a leading role in the Mangeshkar household, the goal for the girls was one which every girl, then and now, was and is expected to attain: marriage, a new home, a new family.

In 1949, Asha, at about sixteen years of age, eloped with Ganpatrao Bhosle, a man who was twenty years older than she was. For her, it was all about love, a romance that, unfortunately, went painfully sour very quickly. But with her perhaps hasty, perhaps exciting, perhaps fated, runaway marriage she lost something far more valuable and meaningful than just her singlehood. She lost her eldest sister. 'It was a love marriage, and Lata didi did not speak to me for a long time. She disapproved of the alliance.' Was this because Bhosle had been Lata's personal secretary? Did the elder sister feel guilty for having allowed her younger sibling to meet a man so unsuitable for her? That might never be spoken of, but the elopement caused a rift that lasted for many years.

The marriage was a painful one for Asha, but it instilled steel into her spine and made her a strong, resilient woman. It would logically have put emotion into her voice too, adding pathos, sorrow, depth and empathy to her music. Rumour has it that Ganpatrao was a drunkard who beat his wife even when she was pregnant, very often resulting in her needing hospitalisation. Asha explains, 'The family was very conservative and they could not handle a singing star for a daughter-in-law. My husband was short-tempered. Maybe he liked to inflict pain, maybe he was a sadist. But no one would hear about it outside. I gave him respect, never questioned what he did. I just did my duty as per Hindu dharma.'

There was continuous abuse and ill-treatment and finally Asha was asked to leave, 'when I was expecting my youngest son, my third child, Anand. I went back to my mother, sisters and brother.' There were thoughts of ending the torment for good. 'On one occasion I felt I should kill myself. I was ill. I was four months pregnant and found myself in hospital where the conditions were so bad that I thought I had landed in hell. I was in mental agony. So I swallowed a bottle of sleeping tablets. But the love I had for my unborn child was so strong that I did not die. I was dragged back to life, to living.'

Some say her in-laws were responsible for the abuse; others maintain that it was Bhosle who beat her. But Asha firmly states, 'I do not blame anyone and have no ill will. I feel if I had not met Mr Bhosle, if I hadn't got married, I wouldn't have left home, I wouldn't have become a singer, I wouldn't have had such wonderful kids, such great grandchildren.' She pauses for a moment. 'If I had not met Bhosle, I wouldn't have become Asha Bhosle.' For her, 'Life turned out okay.'

Music provided solace. Asha had already begun singing playback for movies. When her teacher asked her whether she wanted to sing classical or light music, she wanted to know which one paid more?

'I thought once my husband set up a business, became stable, I would quit singing. But once I started, it was difficult to quit. I thought, God has sent me for this job, I should not go against his wishes.' It was not easy, nothing like the dream scenario in the movies that she sang for. 'I believed that one could survive on love and fresh air, but that is only possible in films. In real life, when poverty hits you, it is very difficult to cope.

But I'm someone who has learned to laugh through all the troubles. My husband had a salary of merely ₹100 and we stayed in a small one-room tenement in the northern-most suburb of Borivali. Only I know how I struggled in those years. I used to travel in crowded local trains across Mumbai from one rehearsal to another, one recording to the other, with my small child. But throughout that difficult period, there was a perseverance, a belief in myself that I had to give my children a better life.'

Even today, so many years after that bitter separation, Asha does not badmouth her former husband or his family or let her children do so. At most she has said, 'I did not move on from that relationship. I was removed from it.' And she gives no explanation besides: 'Singing in films was okay, but he (Ganpatrao Bhosle) was suspicious. He threw me out.' But any allegations of leaving her marriage for someone with more money are met with fierce defence. 'If I was money mad, I would not have married Mr Bhosle, who was earning ₹100 a month – I'd have married a *lakhpati* (millionaire)!'

Bhosle died in 1966, but 'till 1970, as long as his mother was alive, I supported the family,' she says. 'It is because I have gone through so much that even today I have respect for every human being, no matter from which stratum of society they are. My children do not like it when I speak to my watchman or the gardener, but I tell them that that is the way I am,' she said. 'It is dangerous to be complacent. I am *moohphat* (straightforward).'

It was only when Asha left the Bhosle household that the cold war with her sister Lata ended. The rivalry that had always been extensively speculated on – to the extent of a film (*Saaz*, 1998) being made based on the two – did not exist, Asha insists. 'I gave her the *izzat* (respect) that is due to an elder sister. Ours was a blood relationship that can never be altered. And when we did meet, we never discussed the music business!'

Lata was a silent pillar of support, but a lot of the resilience her younger sister has shown in facing all the vicissitudes her life has handed her came from her mother. 'I would inform my mother about every little thing that happened to me,' Asha explains. 'If she couldn't hear what I was saying, I would write it down on a piece of paper and show it to her. I would pour my heart out to her, especially when I was not getting much work, and she would say in her usual sweet way, "Asha, there is no one else like you. There isn't even any heroine who can be like you!"

Before she died, she said to me, "Don't ever worry, God is always with you.'"

2

Asha and Lata

The story of the singer sisters, Lata and Asha, is a special one. For over six decades, the sisters maintained their own space and enjoyed a fan following beyond compare, an enormous portfolio of work, a reputation untainted by stories of rivalry, politics, and scandal, and voices that still mesmerise.

Rumour has it that the sisters monopolised the world they ruled, not allowing anyone else who could match them to last beyond a song or two, even deliberately sabotaging the competition. Is there any truth in this? Asha has said, 'Neither didi nor I had the time to go to a music director and ask them not to take any other singer, new or not. So I am puzzled why we were accused of monopolising the music scene. Our life experience added to our work, and every music director wants a playback singer they can vibe with on a professional level.'

Singer Alka Yagnik, who slid into the space that Asha was eased out of as age and contemporary music started ruling in the early 1980s, and then stayed there for over thirty years, had this to say to the *Times of India* when asked if it was difficult being pitted against the Mangeshkars:

> When a new artiste comes in, people want to find out if they can outdo the seniors. Everybody has their own place. Nobody can take Lataji's and Ashaji's place. When I started, people used to say that it is difficult for a newcomer to break through because the two sisters were ruling the industry with their voices. But whenever I met them, they were nice and affectionate. People say that they resented it when someone new came, but honestly, I never felt it.[1]

Speaking to singer Sonu Nigam for a special interview for *Stardust* magazine[2], Asha said,

> *Rumours were being spread that the Mangeshkar sisters have monopoly in the music industry. They were spread by a music director who then introduced new singers in the industry, but nobody could become, or was even a close competitor to, Lata Mangeshkar then. And nobody can be Lata Mangeshkar even today. I never liked anybody speaking against us.*

When these rumours were doing the rounds, all I said was, '*Hum hatt jaate hain, aap gaaiye*' *(We will step aside, you sing).* And then many music directors said that when we have singers like Lata Mangeshkar, why we would want anyone else to sing, and take efforts to make them practice. When Asha Bhosle can sing cabaret numbers, qawwalis and classical, then why find new singers to replace them? New singers came into the industry, but couldn't make it big immediately. They

---

[1]16 January 2017, Noyon Parasara, TOI

[2]https://stardustcoolbuzz.wordpress.com/2015/09/08/asha-bhosle-i-always-wished-to-have-a-voice-like-lata-mangeshkar-but-i-was-never-jealous-of-her/

managed to get a few songs, but blamed us for not letting them set foot in the industry. To this, I will always say, 'It is only if you sing well that you will survive in the industry.' I always wished to have a voice like Lata Mangeshkar. I thought that even if I had 99 per cent of her voice, I would make it big in the industry. But I was never jealous of her. Nobody should be jealous of others; rather, they should concentrate on what talent they inherit.

There have always been tales told about how other singers would refuse to share a stage or a recording studio with either Asha or Lata, since they would not only be overshadowed but perhaps even pushed out completely. Asha has always insisted that she is not the one who is afraid to sing with those who could outshine her, 'No, it is they who are afraid.' Even if she did agree, as she did on occasion, her favourite singing partner was always the one closest to her: her sister, Lata. 'Yes, it is true that nobody could do it like Lata didi. The pleasure that I got singing with her cannot be matched. Of course, I have sung a lot with Sadhana Sargam, Alka Yagnik and others, but when you sang with Lata Mangeshkar, Kishore Kumar, Rafi sa'ab, *mazaa aata tha* (you enjoyed)! It was like standing in front of a mountain!'

Things are different now. 'That pleasure is missing. Didi and I had not sung together since *Utsav* (1984), mainly because producers couldn't afford us together anymore.' But film music had also changed. Once, movies would run because of their songs. Now, out of fifty films, one song *might* become a hit.

It is not that Asha did not face the same issues that other singers did. Like her peers, she preferred not to make much of it, not in public, at least. Her sister Lata overshadowed her through a great deal of her career, especially in its early stages. Music journalist Narendra Kusnur, who is a self-confessed Lata fan, though he does like Asha's music, explained it as: 'One sister bloomed earlier. She was older, after all. Lata was in her prime by the time Asha really started, with lots of hit songs to her credit already, which was a huge advantage. Her voice was well suited to heroines of the time. I think Asha knew that she could not sing in that style, the same style as Lata, since she would always be poorly compared to her sister if she did. So she started using her own qualities, especially after she met R.D. Burman and went on a different track. That's where she cleverly stayed, in her special groove. Lata was more classically inclined and got more melodic songs. And for a certain period, there would always be at least one standout Lata number in every major film[3].'

Asha once told a reporter, 'There have been only two singers with whom I have always had to be on my guard. One was Kishore Kumar and the other was Lata didi. Didi would not use verbal tricks like Kishore, but she would take the song to such a vocal climax that to rival her in perfection, I had to be really on my toes.' The two women managed to strike a balance in songs like '*Yeh barkha bahaar*' (*Mayoorpankh*, 1954), '*Kar gaya re*' (*Basant Bahaar*, 1956), '*Jab jab tumhein bhulaya*' (*Jahan Ara*, 1964) and '*Main chali main chali*' (*Padosan*, 1968). She will say even today that Lata was not just her favourite singer, but one who inspired her and made her push herself to do better. 'After listening to Lata Mangeshkar, I don't think anyone can touch my heart. Every time I heard her voice, I sensed *chamatkaar*, a miracle.' But it's all about the where and the when. 'Different singers inspire me at different times. I'll listen to Ghulam Ali and suddenly go "*Arre baap re!*", Kishori Amonkar elicits a "*Baap re!*", Lata Mangeshkar an "Oh my

[3]In an interview with Narendra Kusnur

God!" and Kishore da "*Kya boloon?*" Listening to them makes me want to work harder and feel that I still want to carry on singing. This urge inside me to learn and better myself makes me feel good, makes me feel younger.'

Asha knew well that 'Music directors have confidence in me because they know my calibre and the timbre of my voice. Lata didi was five years senior to me in the profession and in age, and I did not have the guts to even think of asking for a song that she was going to sing for someone. That is the way we were brought up.' Even today that respect and a kind of awe hold good. 'We would stand when Lata didi entered the room, and sit down only after she would ask us to, out of respect for her age. It happened with me also. The entire Kapoor *khandaan*, Chintu (Rishi Kapoor), Dabboo (Randhir Kapoor) and the others bowed down and touched my feet whenever I met them at a recording or a function. '

With her control over ragas and the higher octaves, her sweet, high voice, and her willingness to work harder than expected to deliver the musical goods, Lata was the favourite of music directors in the 1950s and '60s – Naushad, C. Ramachandra, Madan Mohan, Chitragupta, Salil Choudhury, Shankar-Jaikishan and others. Occasional rifts did appear in the otherwise harmonious relationships between singer and composer, but they generally did not have a seriously lasting effect. As a result, very few were open-minded enough or even willing to look beyond Lata. And some were even willing to pay her themselves, no matter that the producer did not have the budget to afford her. Asha managed to collect some of her elder sister's rejects, with an occasional special request thrown in, all of which slotted her into what is now called the 'item song'. 'When I began my career as a playback singer, I had to sing in a style that was different from Lata didi's, since there was a danger of being compared to her. I hate to be compared to anyone. I wanted to establish a style of my own and people started calling it the Asha Bhosle style.'

There was a need on the rapidly evolving sets of Bollywood for a different voice, a naughty, light-hearted, sensual, perhaps even younger one. Lata was a soprano – true, clear, shrill, sweet. Asha, on the other hand, was an alto, more *hatke*, more *natkhat*, more *teekhi*. She had that edge, that mischief, that playfulness that could take her into a niche that could be hers alone. What she did sing made an impact, from Madan Mohan's '*Jhumka gira re*' in *Mera Saaya* (1966), which was in a way overshadowed by Lata's '*Tu jahaan jahaan chalega*', to '*Hungama ho gaya*' for Laxmikant-Pyarelal from *Anhonee* (1973), and a whole host of songs that made listeners want to get up and dance. Just as stars like Suraiya, Nargis, Vyjayanthimala, Rakhee and Meena Kumari, Waheeda Rehman, Nutan, Sadhana, Mala Sinha and Saira Banu insisted on having Lata sing playback for them, actors like Helen, Mumtaz, Zeenat Aman, Parveen Babi and Neetu Singh demanded Asha be their voice in chartbusting numbers.

Where more serious, heavy and obviously raga-based songs were concerned, Lata reigned supreme, with Asha singing just a few, among them '*Kaahe apnon ke kaam nahi*' in *Raampur Ka Lakshman* (1972), '*Achche samay pe tum aaye Krishna*' in *Bidaai* (1974), '*Saancha naam tera*' in *Julie* (1975) and '*Tora mann darpan kehlaye*' in *Kaajal* (1965).

Asha came into her own after extensive grooming by R.D. Burman, as well as by O.P. Nayyar. It is said, albeit discreetly, that R.D. Burman actually preferred Lata, but fought with her and had perforce to turn to Asha. With his guidance and allegedly more-than-friendly support, she managed to outdo the then-reigning seductive-voice queen Geeta Dutt. Lata never sang for Nayyar, which helped Asha's career blossom. And when

RDB showcased her abilities in challenging compositions, Asha truly bloomed.

> *It was the time of club songs and dance numbers, vamps and wicked women. And Asha's voice was so beautifully suited to those with spirit, seductiveness, a sexy vibe.*

While Lata did sing for Helen in '*Mera naam hai Jameela*' for *Night in London* (1967), '*Aa jaane jaan*' in *Inteqam* (1969), and '*Iss duniya mein jeena hai toh*' in *Gumnaam* (1965), these were rare moments when she put aside her more sober sensibilities and ventured into her younger sister's realm. She did the occasional song for the more Westernised characters like Zeenat Aman's in *Don* ('*Jiska mujhe thha intezaar*'), Parveen Babi in *Khuddar* ('*Disco 82*'; 1982), and Neetu Singh in *Zinda Dil* ('*Nahin nahin*'; 1975), but could never match Asha's prolific output in the genre.

Perhaps fortunately for Asha, Lata started cutting down on her assignments in the 1990s. But there was still music being made, much of it fresh, exciting, challenging. The composers who never managed to get a rather picky Lata to sing for them found in Asha a far more willing collaborator, and creative souls like Shankar-Ehsaan-Loy, Sandeep Chowta, Viju Shah, Sanjeev-Darshan, Jeet-Pritam, Pritam as a solo composer, and others made music that rang bells at the cash registers. But those like Jatin-Lalit, Vishal Bhardwaj and A.R. Rahman managed a balancing act with the siblings, ostensibly choosing the voice that fit their song. That careful feat of diplomacy only veterans like Kalyanji-Anandji, Ravi, and Hemant Kumar had managed before that. And heroines like Sharmila Tagore, Asha Parekh, Hema Malini, Rekha, and Jaya Bhaduri got the best singer to do playback for them, perhaps because they were tactful or intelligent enough to see the big picture and choose the most appropriate voice rather than the most favoured one. Of course, there were problems, most sorted out by the obvious truth that singers of a particular time could not match the quality of Lata or Asha. One producer even said that 'Vani Jairam has a heavy voice and poor diction. Runa Laila was too modern. Suman Kalyanpur was the most like Lata in voice and range, but lacked staying power. She was called the poor man's Lata.'

But the sisters remained close, physically at least, for many years, living in neighbouring apartments with a connecting door on Pedder Road, in the heart of South Mumbai. Some years ago, Asha moved to a plush high-rise block a fifteen-minute drive away, because 'I needed more space for my son Anand, daughter-in-law Anuja, and my grandchildren,' she reasoned in an interview. 'I still retain the flat where I lived for the best years of my life, right next door to didi. We were always just a doorbell away. I used to visit her at least once a week, if not more, when I was in Mumbai. She would send me photos on WhatsApp and I also sent her pictures that I took on my phone. Sometimes people sent me pictures from our younger days when we were children and we exchanged all that on WhatsApp. She cut down on work, but it was mainly because, like me, she was not inspired by the kind of film songs offered to her. Music *badal gaya hai* – the music made today has changed.'

A director would have hit the jackpot if he or she had managed to capture the two sisters in the same frame, especially if they could be asked about their relationship and the stories surrounding it. Asha always said she would be willing, 'But only if didi is okay with it. Much has been said about our rivalry, but all I can say is, she has her own special style and I have mine.' The movie *Saaz* (1997), made by Sai Paranjpye and starring Shabana Azmi and Aruna Irani, was supposedly based on the story of the siblings, but as Asha reacted, 'To take two women in long plaits, add a few incidents, and stretch them out into a three-hour film is a huge waste of time. You can cook up as many stories as you like. Lata didi and I were successful and were sisters, so they used our name. It would have been good if they had told the truth, though they did make me a star. But there is no point fighting over what they have shown. Time is a big healer; people will forget both *Saaz* and Asha with time.' She told the *Times of India*, 'Sometimes both of us would be at a function and some industry people would ignore me and talk to her only, as if they were showing their loyalty. Later, when we went home, Lata didi and I would have a good laugh!'

Along the way, stories floated through the rarified air of showbiz about how Lata and Asha did not really get along, how they refused to sing with each other, how the antagonism was evident when they did have to share a stage or a microphone, and much more. But the gossip-mongers forgot that the two were sisters, family, and while tiffs and sulks were part of the game, the rules stayed the same, no matter what: what happened in the family stayed in the family and would not be publicly discussed.

So while Asha has often obliquely mentioned how Lata did not help her in her career or how her beloved didi was not as supportive as she could have been, she has never badmouthed her or directly explained whether there was really a problem between the two women that went beyond normal sibling stresses. But she did say that 'In the early days of my singing career, after I separated from my family, I sang with didi in many songs. She would sing for the good girl and I would sing for the bad girl! I never felt bitter towards her, but Mr Bhosle didn't like our interaction. Didi was also okay when we came together for recordings – she would suggest I adjust my pitch if it was too high for her. She was always cordial. But you know, she never displayed any emotion in public.' And there is absolutely no truth in the stories about the sibling enmity, Asha told a reporter. 'There was healthy competition between us, yes. I always wanted to sing better than didi, but never wanted to bring her down in order to reach that level. One should always compete against a stronger opponent. There is no fun competing with someone weaker! That is why I don't enjoy singing these days.' After all, there are no worthy opponents left, no Lata, no Kishore Kumar, no Mohammed Rafi!

Radio personality Ameen Sayani had this to say: 'Asha was always of a very unpredictable nature: one could never know in advance whether she was going to be nice to you or antagonistic. Nevertheless, she has a heart of gold, and has been like a younger sister to me ever since the 1950s, when I became more or less a member of the Mangeshkar family. And, being a younger sister, she often used to shower me with her affection, and sometimes violently pull my leg.' Sayani has not only showcased Asha's songs on his radio shows, *Geetmala* and *Sangeet Ke Sitaron Ki Mehfil*, but has interviewed her too, asking questions that not many would get an answer to. He preferred to be discreet about his interactions with the singer, though he did say, 'I asked her once whether it was true that there was a continuous rivalry between Lata and her, and that Lata often tried to scuttle Asha's progress. This was vehemently denied by Asha. She said that "Lata, being the eldest, was almost like a mother figure to all of us. What people think of as a rivalry between us was just the fact that our voices were fairly different from each other. So, if there's a soft, beautiful tune to be rendered, Lata got chosen for it. And for lively sexy numbers, I usually got the upper hand. That's why people like O.P. Nayyar, for instance, always chose me and never booked Lata." Incidentally, Nayyar himself had mentioned to me that his songs were earthy and sexy, and that was why he always preferred voices like Asha, Shamshad Begum and Geeta Dutt. "But," said Nayyar, "I will always maintain that Lata has always been number one!"'

As children, the sisters were very close. The story goes that Lata would carry Asha all the time, even to school. One day, in class, a teacher remarked that the school could not possibly have two students paying a single fee. From that day, Lata refused to go back to school unless Asha could be with her and ended her formal education. 'Both of us went back home crying, and Lata didi promised never to return to that school. After that, my father decided to tutor us at home. It was because of me that didi stopped going to school. We were so close that we would stand by each other through thick and thin.' But as the two girls grew up, the tensions increased, as was inevitable. It was Asha's elopement with Ganpatrao Bhosle that perhaps caused the rift to show; perhaps because it meant that Lata was left alone to support the family with the only profession she knew: singing. That disapproval, it is often said, coloured the relationship between the sisters again when Asha was involved with O.P. Nayyar, professionally and, though she has never directly said so, personally. When Lata made her feelings clear, Nayyar refused to work with her again, gossip buzzed.

In an interview, Nayyar revealed how the sisters shared a maid who would be the conduit for news between the two apartments. 'The maid just had to tell Asha that Lata had recorded something wonderful and she would lose it and not be able to sing. Her Lata phobia was so strong that it took me months to convince Asha that she had a voice that was individual enough to develop a singing style that was uniquely hers.' Asha has maintained that she worked for years to be different from her sister, carving her own niche in the film world and creating her own identity, not just to be 'Lata's younger sister'. Lata was also staunch in denying any stories of rivalry or that she restricted her sister's career in any way. She told an interviewer, 'If I had stunted her growth, she would not be where she is today, so famous and sought-after. I could not even think of my sister that way, my own flesh and blood. We have always been together! The first thing is that Asha wasn't here. She got married and went away. Secondly, our styles are very different. We are sisters and our voices sound similar, but she has a very different singing style.'

The sibling bond was visible onscreen too. Asha said, 'Do you know I acted in a film with Lata didi? It was *Mazha Bal* (1943), and I also sang several songs, including '*Chala chala nava bala*'. In *Badi Maa* (1945) I acted with Noor Jehan and didi sang. We had met Noor Jehan in 1942, when she came to Kolhapur, where we used to live then. When I was small, I never had any ambitions to be a singer; when I saw a train, I wanted to be the driver, and when I saw a shop with *goli*s, I wanted to be a shopkeeper! I never dreamed that a day would come when I would be famous as a playback singer. Ambition is a never-ending thing; human beings are never satisfied with what they have.' When she was at the top of her game and heard about the singers who cried foul saying that she and Lata were playing politics to stop any competition in its musical tracks, Asha was direct in her own defence. 'The new girls who shouted from the rooftops that Lata didi and I were monopolising the field should at least get a break after some music director listens to a recording of theirs. In our days, no music director would decide on listening to a recording; they had to hear the singer live and only then would make up their minds to give them a break.' She has often talked about how she and her sister sang: 'Lata didi and I had to sing in the studios with a mic. There were no proper acoustics. Today, you can dub six and eight track recordings in a studio, while back then there was no such thing as dubbing at all! When a music director wanted a retake, you had to do the song all over again with the entire set of musicians. And there was no question of any of us cultivating a godfather like the girls do these days in order to survive in this rat race.' Today it's all much easier. 'You need not even sing the whole song at one go if you are in a hurry to leave. You can come back and do another bit when you have the time.' Memories awake with 'Life was not so easy then. Dev (Anand) sa'ab, Lata didi, and Rafi bhai would go to Malad to record their songs by local train since they could not afford cars then. Today, if a new singer doesn't have a car, the producer sends one to drive them to the recording.'

There is one fact that so many people who revelled in the myriad rumours about the sisters being antagonistic slipped up on: Lata Mangeshkar and Asha Bhosle have sung about seventy-five songs together. And that is a fairly large number, especially considering that both had thriving individual careers to keep them busy.

It probably started when Asha was about eighteen years old – she and Lata (then twenty-two) sang '*Yeh ruki ruki hawayein*' for *Daaman* (1951), composed by K. Dutta, with lyrics by Rajendra Krishan. Of course, since records of the time are not accurately maintained, this may not have been their first duet, and it was certainly not one of their most successful.

As matched voices, they were first noticed in the 1955 song '*Manbhavan ke ghar*' from *Chori Chori* (1956), composed by Shankar-Jaikishan. More recently, the sisters sang together '*Aaina hai mera chehra*' in *Aaina* (1993) with Suresh Wadkar providing the male tone, the song composed by Dilip Sen-Sameer Sen for lyrics by Sameer. 'To sing with Lata didi was like attending a grand feast to celebrate a *tyohaar* (festival). She just had to look at me and her expression would tell me whether I am singing properly or not.'

In December 2014, Lata produced the album *Mein Hawaa* under her record label LM Music, for which Asha sang with Shaan. It was significant since it brought together the sisters thirty years after '*Mann kyon behka*' (*Utsav*), a song in which Lata sang for Rekha, while Asha did so for Anuradha Patel. Releasing the album, Lata said, 'It is a pleasure to come together with my sister again. I've always maintained that she is a very versatile and skilled singer. We've sung many songs together. It's always a challenge to sing with Asha.'

There was occasionally a third wheel involved. Shankar-Jaikishan's '*Muqabla hum se na karo*' from *Prince* (1969) had Mohammed Rafi, while Kalyanji-Anandji's '*Pyar zindagi hai*' from *Muqaddar Ka Sikandar* (1978) included Mahendra Kapoor and '*Sun le pyar ki dushman duniya*' from *Pyar Kiye Jaa* (1966), composed by Laxmikant-Pyarelal brought in Kishore Kumar and Manna Dey. Usha Mangeshkar joined in on '*Hamre aangan bagiya*' in *Teen Bahuraniyan*, with music by Kalyanji-Anandji.

Lata and Asha shared a song in Asha's son Hemant Bhosle's debut as a composer, *Taxi Taxie* (1977) with '*Laayi kahaan yeh zindagi*'. While it was not too successful, *Mere Mehboob* (1963) had the hit numbers '*Mere mehboob mein kya nahin*' and '*Jaaneman ek nazar dekh le*' composed by Naushad, while *Utsav* included the popular '*Man kyun behka*' and '*Neelam pe nabh chhaye*' with music by Laxmikant-Pyarelal. Avowed Lata fans like C. Ramachandra roped in Asha too for '*Ae chand jahaan*' for *Sharada* (1957), while Madan Mohan created '*Jab jab tumhein bulaya*' for *Jahan Ara* and Roshan composed '*Pad gaye jhoole*' for the sisters in *Bahu Begum* (1967). There were many others too, from R.D. Burman's '*Mittwa*' from *Shaan* (1980) and Laxmikant-Pyarelal's '*Baandh le man ko*' from *Dil Aur Deewar* (1978) to Hemant Kumar's '*Dabe labon se kabhi jo koi salaam le*' for *Biwi Aur Makan* (1966) and Shankar-Jaikishan's '*Kar gaya re*' from *Basant Bahar* (1956). The good girl–bad girl divide got a sweet new avatar with Asha voicing the boy's part and Lata the girl's in Vasant Desai's compositions for *Do Phool* (1958): '*Roothi jaye re gujariya*' and '*Bachpan ka tera mera pyar*'.

Who was better? Who was more successful? Whose voice will endure through the future? The jury will always be out on that. For the record, one of Asha's happiest moments, she said was when 'Didi put her hand on my head and said that whatever I have achieved in life, I have done on my own. At fifteen, I left home and never asked for financial help from my family. When didi praised me for this, I felt happy, very fulfilled. God has been kind.'

3

Life Is a Beautiful Journey

She describes herself as a 'simple, homely woman' who goes to the market with her daughter-in-law to buy fish and vegetables. She loves to cook, and her life is rooted in home, family and music. She practises singing for 45 minutes every day and has always maintained that 'You sound as old as you feel. I always felt young at heart.' Asha Bhosle believes in destiny and karma and gives credit for her success to her parents, to God and to her children. 'Many people have contributed to my life and my work, but I struggled alone.' But she will never say die. 'Take risks. It worked for me. My priorities were my children and then music. Whatever came my way that could help me, I took; the rest, I dumped ruthlessly. I was treated like the underdog when I first got into the world of music. But I had no choice.' And she has an interesting way of looking at life and the world. 'What I want is not important, what happens, is. I have never planned life because it is not necessary that what I fix will be fulfilled. My life has taken me from one place to another. An ordinary woman like me has got name, fame, family, children, grandchildren, respect, what else can I want! But given a choice: I have twin grandsons; I want to dance at their weddings.'

Music honcho Atul Churamani knows this firsthand. 'She's full of beans, and her whole universe revolves around her son Anand and his twin sons. And her home.' The star singer is indeed that simple. 'She called me one day and asked, "Do you know where I am? I am buying pots and pans!" She was out by herself in a market on Grant Road, buying vegetables and utensils! And she is *Asha Bhosle*!'

Actor Poonam Dhillon has seen that facet of Asha too. 'She is a big fan of Jackie Chan and will behave like a total fangirl when she sees a poster of his film. She's like a child with that kind of thing, not giving any thought to the fact that she is Asha Bhosle!'

While Asha's marriage to Ganpatrao Bhosle didn't last, she acknowledges it with some positivity because it gave her three children: Anand, her youngest son, who studied business and now handles his mother's career; Varsha, a writer and political columnist whose untimely death in 2012 was a shock to the family; and Hemant, who tried his hand at music direction, then chose to become a pilot. Hemant, who passed away in 2015, rarely stepped into his mother's limelight, while Varsha occasionally wrote about Asha, but kept to herself more often than not. Anand speaks of his mother with affection and strength. He said in a joint interview, 'My memories of growing up were happy. We lived in a joint family with my grandmother, aunts and my uncle and cousins, and I was the baby of the family and my grandmother's favourite child. As kids, we had no clue that my aunt (Lata) and mom were famous singers. It was only when I went to school that people around me told me about it. Even then, I did not believe it. I had never seen them sing at home. I think the hours Mom and aunt put in at the recording studios, singing so many songs and rehearsing for them, gave them their practice. To this day, we stay away from the public eye.'

Journalist Anjali Mathur counted Varsha Bhosle among her friends. Mathur remembered, 'I got to know Varsha when I was working with the *Sunday Observer*. At that time, she wrote a column for the newspaper. We became good friends; I got to know her really well, and for some time the relationship continued even after I left the publication.' But time and everyday life managed to fray the bond between them. 'She wanted me to be available and to meet often, but it was not easily possible.' Varsha was 'incredibly intelligent – she would understand so much – and a beautiful writer, a powerful writer. Her columns were outstanding.' Mathur visited her friend at home and found that 'They were a very close-knit family. The impression I got was that Lata was the matriarch of the family and everyone respected her. And there was also a lot of respect for each other. All the tensions that are reported, I did not see in their daily interactions.'

Mathur had several sessions with Asha for an article on the singer for her sixtieth birthday, 'and there was never even the smallest hint of anything negative with her sister. I was completely in awe of Asha when I met her. I love her singing and am a huge fan. What came across is that she was a really friendly person. When I met Lata, I could sense that she was not very outgoing, but very reserved. Asha was completely different, willing to talk and share. Asha was very ahead of her time; she took decisions that as a feminist I thought were great – the way she walked out of her marriage could not have been easy at the time, especially with three small children. She did it! I don't think her children suffered for it; she was a good mother and grandmother.' What Mathur found particularly interesting was that with two very well-known singers in the family, the Mangeshkar-Bhosle clan was 'still rooted in that Maharashtrian family atmosphere, with no glamour'. Affection for Varsha was unanimous. 'Even Lata depended on Varsha's opinion. If she said a song was good, it was the ultimate encomium for all of them. Because she was such an intellectual and had no soulmate in the family from that perspective, that could have caused some angst and loneliness, which is what she kept trying to fill with her friends and relationships. She also had a great imagination and could create fabulous stories.' Mathur knew that Varsha 'was a very good singer. But for some reason she never sang, even though her mother and brother would have liked her to. She was very fond of R.D. Burman. Her respect for him was evident.'

Asha kept her children and their lives private, even as her own was examined and questioned. Her reasons she often has cited as being practical: 'It is a very tough line and the industry is ignorant and fickle. I have discouraged them from entering the field as it can bring them the limelight for a short while and it all depends on sheer luck. And once you fail, people will speak ill of you. To avoid all that, I have not supported them to do music.'

Anand has his take too and once said that his older brother Hemant did some quality work composing music for films, but 'discovered the fact that a lot of producers and directors are tone deaf and would disregard a lot of the wonderful tunes he came up with, sometimes settling on mediocre stuff because they did not understand music. Rather than compromise on creativity and what he had to offer, he quit the scene and became a pilot,' which Asha is extremely proud of. Hemant's son, Chaitanya, also known as Chintu Bhosle, is a pop-rock musician, a member of the group Band of Boys. Meanwhile,

Anand admitted matter-of-factly that 'I had to come into this business in the early 1980s when concert tours were beginning to gain popularity and Mom needed someone to handle the business and management end of things for her; otherwise, I too would not be around.'

Chaitanya has a varied resume – actor, video jockey, programming head for a radio station, and pop star. His music album *Coming Home* also features his famous grandmother in three songs; her voice is used as 'an instrument' in the title track. But it was not like working with a beloved elder, he has said. 'When we were in the studio, she would say, "Now you are the music director and we are no longer related."' Asha insisted her grandson guide her, teach her to sing in his style, to get the nuances of rock and roll right. 'She would call me at 10 p.m. to ask if everything had gone well. And then she would start pointing out her mistakes and say "Can we record this again?" because she felt it was not quite right. Even after singing over 11,000 songs, she goes over how she sang and whether she should do it again! Her dedication to her art is proved by her willingness to learn, always. And her focus was so absolute that she never wanted to leave the studio or even sit down until we were done.'

And Asha would be ever-willing to try something new, her family knew, never giving up until she had managed to master it. Anand proudly stated, 'Mom has amazing will power. The more you tell her it can't be done, the more she will go out and prove that it can.'

Her children could not miss the constant comparisons made between Asha and Lata Mangeshkar. To them, Asha was their mother, and Lata, the fond aunt. As Anand has said, the two women were 'really like the north pole and south pole', a contrast that is especially obvious when they sang together on stage. 'Even as singers, their styles were so different!'

It goes beyond that, into medical history. 'Mom has to be very careful with her throat, while Lataji could eat anything.' According to Anand, Lata would often be unwell, especially with stomach problems, and her propensity for sinus infections was well known. But as a child, a dose of homeopathic medicine for diphtheria was like a life-long preventive: 'It cured her of any throat problems for life!'

Asha takes a different route. 'Mom will deprive herself of ice cream, which she loves, and have just one soft-serve cone when a tour ends, but she is so strong-willed that even if she is not well, it will be business as usual.' Asha's family is all praise for her, saying that, 'As a singer, no one can touch her in terms of talent and versatility. And as a person, she is a wonderful mother, grandmother and mother-in-law, very popular with her grandkids and everyone else.' That enquiring mind, too, won admiration. Anand said, 'She has a child-like curiosity about everything and a great ability to pick up on stuff she hears and sees. But she is such a little girl at heart!'

He remembered the story of how the group had reached Los Angeles during a music tour and Asha wanted to stay a day longer because she wanted to go to Disneyland!

The singer sees herself as honest and true. 'I believe in living life with honesty,' she has said, 'and I have taught my children the same thing. They are more diplomatic, while I take the liberty to say it as it is. I think with my heart and I will not change that.' Her son agreed, and added, 'Maybe that's why she has not received her due from so many people.'

But Asha soldiers on, no matter who has said what to whom about her, or how she has been treated. 'I saw that this world indulges in lies and deceit, and I got very, very angry. I wanted to hit out, get my revenge. But I gradually realised that it would be a waste of my energy and feelings. It has been a great journey,' she once said. 'I am glad I have the ability to never give up, to change with the times, to see the positive in the negative. Now I never get angry, I just have fun!'

Journalist Shekhar Gupta once asked her about the 'naughty songs' she has sung and the 'naughty things' she has done, and Asha's response came quick and fast.

Naughty things, no. Naughty songs, yes. I have done everything with good intentions. I got married. If people think that was naughty, let it be so. I got married on my own terms, a lot of people talk about it, but I have faced the consequences. I believe that if you do something, you should be strong enough to face the consequences.

In every house there is this problem where kids think their parents are crazy if they tell them what to do. Only when they reach a certain age do they realise their parents were right. Children who are a bit naive get in trouble easily and the more they try to get out of the mess they create, the more difficult it gets. But that's also a stage in life. God has been fair to me.

All the while, she seeks new challenges, planning new albums, even working on an autobiography. And there is a film being planned on her life, rumours say, but she insisted that it would be a work of imagination, based on hearsay. 'Who can get to the heart of my life story? Only I know the truth!'

Some of the truth will perhaps never be told. There was involvement, if not love, with various men, some who played an important role in Asha's professional life, for instance, O.P. Nayyar, who has spoken about his relationship with the singer. That he is to a huge extent responsible for her finding her feet and becoming an unassailable success as a playback singer is undoubted. But the romantic partnership they shared has never been confirmed by Asha, who has always been discreet about her personal life with the media and public.

Nayyar and Asha met in 1952 when the music of the Kishore Kumar–Rehana starrer *Chham Chhama Chham* (1952), directed by P.L. Santoshi. 'At that time, she was not only influenced by Geeta Dutt, but she was also under heavy (inferiority) complex of Lata. As if she was torn between their styles. What I did was to give her confidence and to help her come out of that complex,' Nayyar has been quoted as saying. Nayyar had Asha sing three solos for the film: '*Achha woh tum thhe*', '*Yeh zindagi hai jeene ke liye*' and '*Aa pardesi baalma*', duets with Kishore Kumar and Jagmohan, and a trio with Shamshad Begum and Kishore Kumar. More than happy with her voice and singing style, he called her to sing for *Mangu* (1954), gave her a big break with *CID* (1956) and showed the world what they could do together in *Naya Daur*. They became known for flirty, sexy, sensuous songs, a genre that Asha excelled in.

'*Aaiye meherbaan*' (*Howrah Bridge*, 1958), '*Aao huzoor tumko*' (*Kismat*, 1968), '*Yeh hai reshmi zulfon ka andhera*' (*Mere Sanam*, 1965) and '*Yehi woh jagah hai*' for the 1966 spooky *Yeh Raat Phir Na Aayegi* were a few of the many memorable songs that came out of this partnership. And then there was the popular but ill-fated '*Chain se hum ko kabhi*' from *Pran Jaye Par Vachan Na Jaye* (1974). The song became popular, winning the singer a Filmfare statuette, but was not used in the film. Nayyar insisted that it was love that painted the music super-successful. 'Asha's magic came out when she was with me. Now there is no *ras* in her singing. But Asha is Asha – no one can be her.'

Asha has never given Nayyar credit for *Naya Daur*, maintaining that it was the film's producer, B.R. Chopra, who was responsible for that break that made her career soar. As for the composer, it was nothing personal, she has insisted, 'Whichever composer gave me work, it was because my voice was suited to his music at that time.' This could have been because the two parted acrimoniously on 5 August 1972 for reasons that have never been made clear, though rumours abound.

Whatever happened, Nayyar said in an interview when he was seventy-six years old, 'The most important person in my life was Asha Bhosle. She was the best person I ever met.'

Asha seemed to spark something in men that was so clear in her songs. That come-hither, seductive, and flirtatious note that came so easy to her and made so many of her numbers superhits pulled the men in too, in real life, it was said. Her natural charm, outspoken manner, and lack of inhibition was attractive, and when she wanted something – or someone, as gossip would have it – it was hers.

One such association was reportedly with Marathi actor and film producer Krishna Kondke, better known as Dada Kondke, the master of the onscreen double entendre. Born into a mill worker's family in central Bombay, he became astonishingly successful with nine of his films running for twenty-five consecutive weeks in theatres. But before he made it big time as a movie actor, Kondke worked in a band and then on the stage, touring Maharashtra with his *loknatya* (or *tamasha*) troupe. Watching his performance in *Khankhanpurcha Raja* (The Bankrupt King), writer Vasant Sabnis was so impressed that he created a drama for Kondke titled *Vichha Majhi Puri Kara* (*Fulfil My Desires*), which played in over fifteen hundred shows! Kondke was a star and the big screen demanded his presence. Films like *Tambdi Maati* (1969), *Songadya* (1970) and *Ekta Jeev Sadashiv* (1972) cemented his position.

But the popularity of *Vichha Majhi Puri Kara* had a less

public consequence. According to a translation of a chapter by Anupamaa Joshi *The Greatest Show on Earth: Writings on Bollywood* (edited by Jerry Pinto, Penguin Global, 2012) of *Ekta Jeev* (*A Lonely Life*, 2013), the story of the life of the actor as told to writer Anitaa Padhye, Dada Kondke met Asha Bhosle during the staging of the play. 'She liked it so much that she would come for performances regularly. That is how we grew so close to each other. I was not well known then.' And then comes the bombshell: 'It would come as a big surprise to you if I say that back then, Ashabai and I were going to get married!'

Along with everything else that she is known for, '… she's as wicked as they come – she has an amazing sense of humour,' music executive Atul Churamani realised during his association with her. He remembers what happened during the UK tour for *Naina Lagaike*: 'My wife wanted to come to London during the tour. I was reluctant because I was working. It was the last show and she called, saying, "I always knew you would leave me for another woman, but I did not think it would be Asha Bhosle!" I told Ashaji and she said, "Tell her, *bachke rehna* (beware)!" She is such a sweetheart!'

But it is far more than a charming personality that has kept her going for so long. Churamani explained, 'The younger generation has so much to learn from her – her work ethic. She rehearses, asks for the songs in advance, comes to the studio prepared, comes on time. Biddu told me that she told him that people have a problem when they work with her for the first time – "You are Asha Bhosle," they say, and think that she will demand stuff. She always told them, "But you are the boss and it's your call. Ask me to sing and don't worry about me, whether I am tired or slacking; you have to be happy at the end of the session."'

And if you sit with Asha in a room for two minutes, you

will feel like you have known her all your life, he discovered. 'She makes friends with everyone, whether they are fourteen or eighty. There are two artistes in the industry who are very well liked because they are *moohphat*, direct, to your face – she and Jagjit Singh. They will be blunt – do your homework, do your preparation before you come, you're singing off – but there will be no malice. At least in my dealings with her there has been no politics or nastiness. Her heart is clear and clean. What she feels, she says, and it is over. And so professional! She will come on time, stay until work is done. It is a sheer pleasure to work with people like that.' She is a legend for this reason, Churamani insisted: her commitment.

The legend has maintained a working style that has served her well over the years. At eighty-two, she believed, 'One should be moving forward with a lot of love for everything. One should not impose one's opinions on other people just because you have lived longer, or interfere in other people's lives because you are senior. If you don't push others, no one will push you, and you will be at peace.'

What makes her happy is anything that will make her laugh.

> *I love anything and anybody who makes me laugh. I laugh a lot. I have a habit of laughing too much, in fact.* Din bhar hansti rehti hoon aur har cheez ka mazaa leti hoon – *I laugh all day long and enjoy everything.*

What makes her angry is 'anything unhygienic or dirty. If someone does something unclean while cooking, I get really angry – I sprinkle Gangajal (Ganga water, considered pure by Hindus) all over the house. I'm a Virgo, that's why I am obsessed with cleanliness.'

Art is an interest too, her sister Usha being a painter. 'I

too was fond of painting, but couldn't pursue it due to my singing and other work. But I am extremely fascinated with admiring paintings. In my house you will see six or seven paintings put up instead of photographs.' In 2004, she had a bit of a health scare, she told Dr Mandar Bichu, who has written two books on her sister, Lata Mangeshkar. 'A famous doctor had once predicted that I would lose my sight, as I had glaucoma. I was very upset and nervous. Other specialists actually couldn't find any fault with my eyes and they reassured me that nothing would happen. Luckily they were right. Now, my ophthalmologist has diagnosed a cataract, but every six months, he looks at it and says, 'Maybe later you will need it to be removed.' But generally, I am in good health. For my voice, I avoid cold things and sour things like tamarind. Once my blood sugar had gone a little high, but I controlled it with diet. Taking a diet of sprouted moong, repeatedly boiled rice, and apples for a few months, I could avoid diabetes. I also practise the auto-suggestion technique a lot.'

While only a special few visit Asha Bhosle at home these days, one always-welcome guest is Poonam Dhillon. A Hindi film, theatre, and television actress known best for her films with superstar Rajesh Khanna, *Red Rose*, *Dard*, *Nishaan*, to name a few, she first met Asha Bhosle over twenty-five years ago. 'I was doing a couple of films that she had sung for and we were a group of friends including Romesh Behl, Pancham da, Dabboo (Randhir Kapoor), Gulshan Bawra, Ramesh Talwar (I had done *Basera* and other films with him), all very close. We would meet often, not for work, but just to spend the evening together. Ashaji was staying in an apartment then in Santa Cruz with Panchamda. I was the youngest and most timid of the lot; they were all veterans, seniors in their own ways. I was the kid in the group and Ashaji became a mother figure, very protective and affectionate; she would sing and cook. We would all laugh and have a good time. The bonding started at that time! As I grew up, we continued to meet, to bond; I became closer to the whole family. It was a process that happened over the years. I actually lost my own mother many years ago, so Ashaji was like a mother figure to me. I always called her *Aai* (Marathi for mother).'

The relationship now has little, if anything, to do with work. It is all personal, private, but Poonam was given permission by Asha *Aai* to talk about it. 'She normally comes over for most of my birthday parties – she was part of a surprise party too that my sister planned for me. She's always been there for me and I've always been there for her, especially on birthdays. I even surprised her in Goa a couple of years ago. I'm very lucky to have her genuine affection. Sometimes she calls and tells me she is here or there, but when she is back, she will say let's go to Lonavala or somewhere or do something together. Yes, it's nice for her too, she also feels that warmth and love from me. She calls me 'Sundari'. What I discuss with her, I tell nobody else. It's all between her and me.' The private stays inviolate, Dhillon insisted. And much of that very personal, very insider stuff is 'The personal things that happen within the family. That is really the only thing that really hurts her, even though she cloaks it very well. Professionally, she takes everything in her stride.'

While her sister Lata Mangeshkar's voice became shaky with age and the lady herself fragile, at ninety, Asha has not slowed down much, Poonam has found. 'I'm sure in comparison to before, she must have slowed down, but I don't think that in her attitude, she has. She still enjoys work. Her passion for music is prime, and her love for her family is equally paramount. And these things give her so much happiness. She tells me she is still doing *riyaaz* at her age – her voice has not remained what it was without effort, you know. She still does a lot of riyaaz. She is very focused.'

And can the sisters be compared? 'There have been lots of clones of Lataji, but I don't think anybody has been able to be another Asha Bhosle. Her voice is so unique. That is what I think, even to date, keeps her singing with the younger lot, with the same verve and *mazaa*, God bless her! And at her age, how many people can have what she does! She is doing shows, performing, recording, she's done television, she's done a movie! She was so good in the film – she is a natural actor. In fact, at one of her birthday parties, perhaps her eightieth, it was only family, about forty people, and we were all dancing. We would sit down every now and then and she would say, "*Tum log buddhe ho gaye ho kya?*" (Have you guys become old?) Get up and dance!' Her zest for life, her energy is what keeps her going. I think energy comes with a positive mind and unless you stay positive and not say I am old now, I want to sit down, you will not keep it going as long as she has! She's such a strong person!'

As for age catching up with her, Asha scoffs, 'Where is the time for it to catch up with me? I believe that you are as old as you think. And music is like my breathing. The day it stops, my breath will stop too.' Until then, 'There is so much to do and very little time left. I hope I can continue singing in my next birth!'

Sometimes Dhillon is astonished when she considers just how much her friend has actually done through her career. 'She shocks me with the range of things that she has done – from Boy George to Robbie Williams! There is so much that she's done internationally that has not been talked about enough in India, a lot more than any other Indian artiste has done, long before anyone else went West. She was well respected then – everyone wanted to sing with the legendary Asha Bhosle! She is one of a kind; her voice is unique!'

There is the show-girl side to Asha that balances out her home-body avatar and Poonam has seen it. 'When she is doing stage shows, she wears *chham chham*, blingy saris. Sometimes I tell her that I will bum the saris off her, they are so beautiful! But they are appropriate. She dresses as per the occasion. Onstage she is the complete diva, *the* Asha Bhosle. She enjoys it all – the saris, the jewellery, everything. Panchamda gave her that bracelet, the one with the hanging tassels; she wears it for every show. She's a woman of many vibrant colours. She likes jewellery, and examines whatever I wear. She's lived a life to the optimum, be it in her career, her personal life, her children...'

But life has not been all joy for the singer and Poonam has stood by her when things have been bad. 'She's had sad episodes that have shaken her. Varsha's passing away really hurt her a great deal. I don't think she has recovered or will ever recover. Any mother would feel that way. It was very tragic.' Music has helped, the actress explained, but the loss was huge for Asha. 'Singing is her life. I've seen her and Varsha perform together. Varsha also sang and could cook well. I think the mother and daughter were very close. At her age, for her to go through that, it was very sad. As a parent, you don't want to lose your child! And in that way!'

Dhillon's affection for Asha is clarion. 'When I close my eyes and think of Ashaji, I see her smiling with her dimples. She's got these really cute ones. And I always want to see her like that. I'd like to think of her full of *masti* and happiness, that's how she is. She is also very straightforward. There is no guile in her, no tension. If I've put on weight, she'll come right out and tell me that I'm getting fat! She's like that, absolutely upfront with everybody, a very honest, straightforward person. I think that is what makes her so childlike.'

And there is a heartfelt message to the singer from her younger friend. Poonam expressed herself emotionally with: 'I would want to thank her for all that she has given me in terms of love and affection and support. I always want to see her and be with her in happy days, not in sad days. Not when there's stress or pain or grief – those are moments I never want to go through with her again. We've had such happy times together, like once when we went out to lunch, we both wore sunglasses and took selfies! She's a lot of fun that way – we do crazy things together, go to strange *galli*s to buy saris, etc. You can have fun with her, share anything with her, trust her.'

Personal insight also comes from Parveen Khan, wife of sitar maestro and classical singer Ustad Shujaat Khan. Parveen first met Asha at the opening session of her father-in-law Ustad Vilayat Khan's three-day music conference in New Delhi. 'She was so pleasant and down to earth. Our time spent together was brief, but there was a bond that we both enjoyed.' The two women connected over saris and food, sharing a short but enjoyable time together. 'She is very fond of cooking and enjoys good food – I come from that lineage, since my mother was a great cook, specialising in authentic Mughlai dishes. We would be on the telephone exchanging recipes and she would give me tips on cooking.' And when they were in the same city, usually Delhi, 'She would say, "*Chalo ghoomne chalein* (let's go wandering), let's go to Vichitra and buy saris', since she loved Vichitra prints. We would go eat *chana bhatura* at Green Park, and since there was no parking, I would get a packet and sit in the car and eat with her. "*Main toh chali jaungi lekin pehle chana bhatura khayenge*" (I will leave soon, but let's eat some *chana bhatura* first), she would say. She loved gallivanting, shopping, eating ... She loves Bengali sweets and the *namkeens* that I would buy to send to her. We got her a photograph of herself on a plate – she was so happy and excited and said she was going to show it to her grandkids. She loved putting flowers in her hair... These little things gave her a lot of pleasure.'

Asha doing an album with Ustad Shujaat Khan allowed Parveen to see the working side of the singer too. 'She was always very professional as far as work was concerned, very dedicated, always wanting one more rehearsal.' And even while the two rarely meet now, with one in Mumbai and the other in Delhi, 'My association with her is a long one, through my family, since she knew my father's sisters well. She would tell me about them. And then there was always cooking. Actually, the base of everything is good food and recipes! She is projected as distant and starry, but she is really not that way at all. Our relationship is more one-on-one and homely. She is very *bindaas*, but very humble.' Distance and age have become barriers, Parveen said, 'We do call each other occasionally. Email is not easily possible, she does not use the computer, and text messages don't always work. And now that she is older, her family is also protective.'

There is always a reason beyond the obvious for family closing ranks around one of their own. After all, the downtimes for Asha have been bad.

Her daughter Varsha wrote, 'The earliest memory I have of my mother – Mrs Asha Bhosle to you – is a fleeting montage of doorbells rung very late in the night, a sobbing woman hugging me back to sleep, the strains of strange, repetitive ringing emanating from behind a closed door. I bang on the door wanting to go in, but am roughly pulled away by a man when the music threatens to cease. Later, I learned that that was a routine day in the life of my father, guarding my mother against all impediments which may have prevented her from singing for their supper. I have erased my father from my memory, and with him, some of my own childhood – a defence mechanism, people call it. Mother came into her own quite suddenly. One day it struck her that her third and advanced state of pregnancy might not be able to sustain the daily dose of bashing that came her way. She left behind every single paisa that she had earned, her bungalow, her car, even her clothes, and sought refuge with her mother. Of course, there were instant theories in the industry about this "desertion".'

Asha sang her way through and out of the agony, though not without difficulty, and told singer Sonu Nigam in a special interview for *Stardust* magazine that 'It was with great difficulty that I had gone for recording. The song was joyous. I entered the recording room, and as they placed the mic before me, keeping aside all my relations and negative thoughts, I focused on the song. For songs filmed on Helen, regardless of all my sorrows, I had to step into her shoes to get the feel of the song. During that phase, I was so focused on my work that no other thought ever passed my mind.'

More darkness came years later. Her daughter Varsha, known to be suffering from clinical depression, tried to kill herself on two occasions. The third time, she succeeded. It was 8 October 2012. Varsha was fifty-six years old. She shot herself with her brother's licensed handgun, it was reported, and was found dead on the sofa in her mother's apartment in Pedder Road, Mumbai. Most people would have kept this from Asha, who was on a concert tour in Singapore at the time. But she was told and she flew back immediately.

'They didn't want to tell me. But my son Anand thought it was better if I knew. When I was told I just fell to the ground. I wanted to return by the first available flight.' Her sister Lata, who had been in the house when the family and servants found Varsha's body, was reportedly in shock. 'Didi took this very badly. She couldn't stop crying. I wish she had not been told about it. But there were so many people there, and she had to find out.' Asha's own resilience and music helped pull her out of the grief.

Her outpouring of intense sorrow was heard by Poonam Dhillon, when Asha lamented, 'Why did she have to go? It was my time to go!' But the weakness of a mother soon yielded to the strength of the woman who had faced so much. 'But I must not be weak. I cannot cry in front of my grandchildren. I have to keep the flock together.' As Dhillon knew, Asha never pretended that life was easy. 'All the hardships have only made her stronger. They taught her to live life to the fullest. She is like a soldier – she will always fight, but without help. Her problems are her own and she would rather deal with them herself.' About a month later, Asha was on stage accepting a lifetime achievement award, her back unbowed, but with tears in her voice and an unusual frailty in her demeanour.

Varsha and her brothers also saw the flip side of that brave independence. Asha was often labelled as a 'fallen woman' by a film industry 'saturated with prejudices, hypocrisy and factions,' the journalist wrote. And her mother had to face not just competition from her own sister Lata, but also professional politics, but she faced it all with a fearlessness and honesty that her daughter admired. The tag of 'cabaret singer' was quickly replaced with 'versatile' when Asha married R.D. Burman, but Varsha herself would have preferred to have her mother known as being 'wilful' or 'obstinate', though neither quite managed to describe the woman who was all 'shades of determination and readiness to toil. The more formidable the issue, the harder she applies herself to it!'

Ambarish Mishra, a journalist who has known the singer well for two decades or more, has described her as 'made of steel, except for velvet vocal cords.'

As Asha herself said while talking to a journalist a few years ago, 'What I want is not important; what happens *is*. I have never planned life because it is not guaranteed that what I decide will happen. My life has taken me from one place to another. An ordinary woman like me has found name, fame, family, children, grandchildren, R.D. Burman, respect … what else could I desire?'

Even when Asha felt that she had nobody, as she did when R.D. Burman died too early, she had a kind of back-up plan. As she said, 'Our love was on a different plane; music was our life. I don't feel the loneliness that a woman feels when her man goes away. I feel the loneliness when a piece of beautiful music stops playing – the silence remains forever.' But for her, laughter is a way of escaping the dark times.

Shamir Tandon said it well, 'She likes to keep the mood light. She is an optimist. She is *asha* – hope.'

4

Her Music

It all began with Pandit Deenanath Mangeshkar.

Asha Bhosle's initial influencers were the music, theatre, and attitude that Deenanath Mangeshkar nurtured. When he orchestrated his plays, that sound became his signature – unique, significant, and memorable. The young Asha absorbed this, and slowly, through her life, built on it. More layers of influence were added with radio, travel and later television, exposure to the music of Bing Crosby, Carmen Miranda, Gene Kelly, and others, while Bill Haley and Elvis Presley influenced her in singing rock and roll like in '*Eena meena deeka*' (*Aasha*, 1957). Ghazals became a passion, and Punjabi folk added its rambunctious notes when the singer worked with O.P. Nayyar. But something special happened with Rahul Dev Burman.

By her own admission, Asha and Pancham Da would stay up until 5 a.m. listening to world music. 'We cooked together and watched films together, and he would drag me to watch football matches.' And while Pancham did make comparisons between the singer sisters, he maintained that 'Lataji is like Don Bradman – a good batsman', while he described Asha to be 'like Gary Sobers, an all-rounder who can do anything'. The exposure to so many genres of music and singers gave Asha that edge over her peers. It was a purely sensory experience, as well, since 'Different music moves you differently at different times,' she says. Asked to name her favourite songs across genres, she smiles, 'I love '*The Blue Danube*' by Johann Strauss, R.D. Burman's '*Aao na gale laga lo na*', Ali Akbar Khan's '*Udani*', and Mehdi Hassan's '*Gulon mein rang bhare*'. I also like '*Dum maaro dum*' from *Hare Rama Hare Krishna* (1971), '*In aankhon ki masti mein*' from *Umrao Jaan* (1981) and '*Mohe panghat pe*' from *Mughal-e-Azam* (1960), and one of my favourite songs is '*Piya tu ab toh aaja*' from *Caravan* (1971).'

She said, 'I have completed over seventy years in Indian films. My family has been in entertainment for more than a hundred years. And we have given everything we could to the arts. Maybe that's why we have been here so long. It takes hard work – there is no substitute for it. And work is worship!'

It wasn't always easy. There were rejections, often hurtful and demoralising. On one occasion, Asha and Kishore Kumar were all set to sing a duet together, but 'The sound recordist rejected us because we didn't have good voices!' Kishore Kumar was quite upset, and joked that he and Asha should 'become street singers' instead of trying to work in movies. Of course, the duo worked harder and tried again … the rest, as the cliché goes, is history.

She may sound, in her own words, as if she is a *seedha-saadha* (simple) homebody, but Asha is fairly glamorous when she is on stage. Her performance avatar is blingy and the embodiment of granny-gone-glam. Embroidered and zari-worked saris, generally in pale pastel colours, are offset by gorgeous jewellery, her large bejewelled cuff with the long fringe of gems that swing with the movement of her arm a staunch favourite. Her wardrobe is planned as per the location of the concert and the weather. 'I prefer white saris and pearls rather than diamonds.' Her eyebrows are carefully drawn in, her bindi a visible dot of bright colour, her lips painted subtly. 'Artistes must keep reinventing themselves. Whenever I go on stage, my hairstyle, bangles, and sari are appreciated. I started the trend of wearing a coat over my sari,' a style that is still seen on runways at fashion showings today.

Many years ago, when she sang at a concert in London, 'I was referred to as Madonna in a sari!' And there is a fun element too when Asha performs. 'One day I saw a magic show and thought of introducing tricks like the ones in it, into my stage shows. Now I can make handkerchiefs disappear, or make burned cigarettes appear. It's a sleight of hand that I learned!'

And when she is at home, most often making magic in the kitchen, singing as she cooks, she could be just another housewife and grandmother, albeit a glamorous one, from any small Maharashtrian community anywhere. 'I have always been house-proud. Nobody disturbs me when I am singing, but after that there are things to be done, like planning the menu at home.' Her inspiration, she once said, comes often from her home and family.

The story goes that when she was recording Sachin Dev Burman's '*Chhod do aanchal*' for *Paying Guest* (1957), 'I was not getting the right expression in this song. So, Sachin dada told me to imagine that my husband was pulling my sari and how I would react to that. That gave me the right expression!' The ease with which she was able to fit the song with the character it was sung by onscreen made her a musical chameleon, her success, as Ken Hunt, contributor to *Rough Guide to World Music* wrote, is due largely to her uncanny ability to 'change the colour of her voice. She equally is convincing as the ingénue, the matronly woman, or the old lady looking back wistfully.' There is also the willingness to keep learning. She managed to switch from her native language, Marathi, in which she was initially trained, to Hindi. She absorbed enough Tamil to sing in that language, learned English from 'Listen and Learn' books and tapes and when in her seventies, started learning how to play the guitar. 'If you are determined, you can do anything at any age,' she has maintained.

But in carving her niche in the film world, her feet firmly based on the foundation of rather risqué, for the time, songs, there was a touch of discomfort, she has admitted. 'When the lyrics were not in good taste, I felt uncomfortable. But not with the tunes, not ever. A song is a song, after all. If I sing a *tawaif* number, it does not mean I become one, right?' And there is a triumphant feeling that shows when she says, 'The same people who criticised me then now say I sing good numbers.' Astonishingly, 'Those who liked my music then were too young to buy my records. Today they are grown-ups and their children are listening to that music and I am still singing!'

Adaptability has perhaps always been Asha's biggest plus point, apart from her voice. It comes from being aware of what life has to offer. 'My mother used to say that a human being should not be like a frog in a well. The world is a vast place, and I remind myself of that all the time.' Asha was a practical woman. As she told an interviewer, there was not much she could do besides sing to support her family. 'I have not studied, so I couldn't be a writer. I am not beautiful, so I couldn't be an actress. But I could sing – I could sing anything. And all my pain disappears when I am in front of a microphone. Music is my favourite companion; it never lets me down. I may have been very naïve when I started and it was hard to understand how the industry worked. But rejection and ridicule pushed me on and finally I found success.'

Her music is now being heard in forms she could never have expected. The remix wave has taken much of the harmony and lyricism out of music as it had been composed and made it all about rhythm and a dance floor vibe. 'No one can stop anyone from doing a remix,' Asha said a few years ago. 'But please, if you are doing remixes, be cognisant of the original; these days people are changing songs too much. Some remixes are good. The videos are often vulgar, and can change the original meaning of the song. I wish, that the directors would pay more attention to the lyrics before picturising them. The other day, for instance, I saw a remix of my son '*Chhod do aanchal*': the girls were in pants and shirts with no *aanchal* in sight!'

But she always accepted that change meant acceptance and adapting. And for her, that connect with young people is vital. 'I relate more to the younger generation. When I sing, I sing for them. I am one with them.' She experimented with remixes too when she made the album *Rahul and I*. That was the time when the notion of reworking a well-known song was looked down upon, especially by the established big names in the film music world. But as Asha justified at the time, 'Music has the inherent power to bridge the divides of caste, culture, and age. You do not need to try to connect when you have music. But even with music, you cannot hold on to the past. I have always been called 'trendsetter' and 'non-conformist', so jumping on the remix bandwagon was merely a part of that adventurous expressionism, where songs are notes from the heart. There can be no formula or technique for creativity.'

Asha has always been a bit of a maverick, proving to herself and the world at large that nothing could bring her down and, more important, keep her there at the top. 'You can call it the story of a great survivor,' she once joked. 'It is as challenging as it is exciting to adapt to different genres and changing styles. I have lent my voice to a range of films, from mythological films and action-adventures to family dramas and romantic musicals. But the thing is, you cannot enter a studio and just start singing in front of a microphone. You must first understand the mind of the composer, the mood of the song, and the metre of the tune.' Most of all, 'You should make music directors trust your abilities by rising to meet their expectations and the demands of the composition. And good music is about discipline too.' Along the way, there have been ups and downs, even though Asha has maintained her position, more or less, over the decades of her career. 'I never look back – I kept moving ahead and stayed with the times,' she has said, 'I have been lucky.' Luck is one aspect; the other is her own adventurous spirit. 'I am a trendsetter. People try to copy my style in music, fashion, lifestyle…'

It may come as a surprise that Asha's biggest fans are young people, who appreciate her frank and outspoken personality. 'And I identify with them more,' she says. 'I am happy that they do what they say, unlike some of my contemporaries, who prayed during the day and did everything else at night – double standards, which today's generation does not have.' Not too long before she said this, she admitted in an interview that she would be really nervous about singing at a college show, since she believed that twenty-year-olds would not be able to relate to her songs or her style. But she was pleasantly surprised when 'I realised that they knew every word of my hit songs and they kept singing along. When I met a young couple not so long ago, the husband told me that '*O mere sona re*' had played a key role in the girl saying yes to his proposal of marriage. When people from different generations love your songs, what more can you ask for?'

Asha started out as an actor when she was a little girl but 'perhaps I was destined to be a singer,' she said a few years ago. But singing is also a form of acting, she believes. 'Every time I sing, I am also playing the part of the heroine who would just be lip-syncing the song on screen, I am doing the real singing. That makes singing also a form of acting.' But Asha's frank speak comes as a surprise. Music was merely a hobby; Asha wanted to be a wife and a mother rather than a career woman. But recalling when she had her first son Hemant, she says, 'I wanted to give him the best things in life. My husband had a meagre salary, so I decided to sing professionally to make some extra money. And look where it has taken me!' In spite of the hard slog and the competition, she managed to make it big. 'I had my own style and never considered it a numbers game – Lata didi was my sister, after all, and Geeta Dutt was a good friend of mine.' Both were rivals at the time that Asha was fairly desperate for playback work in films. 'I just wanted to do my job and do it well. Each one of us should do that with sincerity and best intentions, without thinking about rewards. If you are sincere, rewards will follow automatically.'

Being a single mother of three young children did not make life easier, never mind that she had her own family as back-up if she wanted. But Asha persevered. 'When your child's innocent face looks at you, you want to do everything in your power to keep him happy. I had to do well in my career and success – my children depended on me. So there was no scope for failure.' That was her motivation. But she does not claim any special credit for doing it all, and making a life for herself and her family. 'Where there is a will, there is a way,' Asha has always said. 'And there are thousands of women like me doing exactly what I did.'

Asha has always believed in the power of women. 'The woman makes the world go round. She is Shakti. If a woman is aware of this inner strength, no man will be able to beat or dishonour her.' Hard-learned lessons that have made her what she is today have made her understand that 'We women should stop bickering and back-biting; only if we can keep our homes intact will others respect us.'

The death of her second husband R.D. Burman spurred her into what could be considered the third phase of her musical career. She started working with renewed interest on private albums and remixes.

Her explanation for this has always been simple: 'I like to work and I always want to take on something new and challenging. I never say die.' And there were enough people ready and willing to help her on this new trip, such as music industry veteran Atul Churamani, for one, who was vice president (Artistes and Repertoire) at Saregama for eight years after working with Magnasound for ten years and EMI Music before that. His reaction to working with Asha in 2010 could be summed up with a tweet: 'atul churamani@anrman: was in the studio with asha bhosle today. every aspiring singer should have the experience. what an extreme talent! a true legend[4].'

Churamani started Magnasound with a few other people and in the process of establishing it and marketing international music in India, moved from New Delhi to Bombay, as it was called then. 'I became general manager of the company, then a director on the board. During that time, we started the whole Indi-pop thing, so I was credited very kindly as

[4]Tweeted in 2010

having created stars like Baba Sehgal, Daler Mehndi and Alisha. But the fact is that it was Magnasound, and I just happened to be the right place at the right time.' When the company started losing ground, as Churamani explains, he moved out to become part of the team that founded Virgin Records India Pvt. Ltd, putting money and more behind artistes like Shaan, Shubha Mudgal, Bhupen Hazarika, et al. From there, HMV took him on to 'sign artistes', but there was a financial glitch and Saregama was his next stop. He focused on doing concerts in the UK. 'We did Sonu Nigam and the Birmingham Symphony Orchestra, with three concerts, a deal with Sony TV, etc. The next year we did Rahat Fateh Ali Khan with the same orchestra as a tribute to the late Nusrat Fateh Ali Khan.' From there, Churamani moved on to working with ringtones with OnMobile. 'I actually quit the music industry in some sense and went on to head content. I wanted to find out how this mobile phone thing worked. If I did only this, I would have lost my standing in the music industry. I was part of various advisory boards and other teams, and I was not willing to stop at any of that. So I was taken on as a consultant.' After a year, frustration and boredom began creeping in. 'I am creative person, so I needed to keep it going. In 2013, I registered a company called Turnkey Music and Publishing Pvt. Ltd, with the idea that I would start taking on publishing people who were not publishing outside India. I had the connections and had built the network. When I went back to the artistes, a few did sign up.'

One of the artistes that Churamani was instrumental in showcasing in a non-film genre was Asha Bhosle. 'It was quite strange, because I would meet her at awards functions and places – she was a living legend! Obviously she had no idea who I was. Once I left Magnasound and joined Virgin, her son Anand called me, saying, 'Let's meet. I've always admired the kind of thing you do,' etc. I met him, we chatted, I would drop by their house and we would be sitting around talking and she would walk by and we would exchange greetings. I was introduced to her, and it was all casual. I never knew her directly or had any conversations with her. I remember once when I was there, the MTV Viewer's Choice Awards were being announced – she won for '*Kambakth ishq*', Sandeep Chowta's song from *Pyaar Tune Kya Kiya* (2001). The drawing-dining room at Asha's home in Prabhu Kunj in South Mumbai is enormous. It was filled with people, 'maybe relatives or friends, all having lunch, and she was serving them. She got a call saying that she had won – she was very excited and was telling everyone. I had my back to the table from where I was sitting and was not really listening to the chatter. And then, she started singing. The sound was like a crystal bell, completely in *sur*. Oh God, that was a defining moment for me – the woman is a legend...amazing!'

Destiny then took over and engineered a series of events that eventually led to Churamani working with Asha. 'A friend of mine, a ghazal singer and composer called Somesh Mathur, was performing in Delhi. I was going to be in the city and he invited me to the concert. It was a simple thing with just one harmonium and a tabla player. Somesh sang a song that I had never heard before. It was an amazing song: '*Aaj jaane ki zid na karo*'. After the concert I told him that the composition was fantastic, but completely new to me.' Churamani learned that it was very well known, having been composed by Wali Mohammed and sung by Abida Parveen. 'I got hold of it – possibly the most romantic song I have ever heard; there cannot be anything better.' Some days later, Mathur called Churamani to ask him to listen to something.

'He had programmed the track and sung the song. My hair stood on end. It was incredible. Somesh has a lovely voice. He lisps and has a limited range, but is super.' It was an 'aha' moment. 'In my mind, that crystal bell rang. I said, "I have to get this lady to sing this." The track was about 13 minutes long, elaborate and complete. The orchestration was amazing. I rang Anand Bhosle and told him I wanted to play him something and wanted his reaction. I told Somesh to dub a vocal and I would get Asha to sing it.' After a minor argument, Mathur gave Churamani the song who took it to Anand. 'In a couple of minutes Ashaji walked in. With no hello or hi, she demanded, *"Yeh kya hai?"* (What is this?) I asked if she liked it. She said it was "very lovely. Whose is it? What is it?" It was then that I was introduced to her. It was 2002.'

Churamani told Asha the backstory and the singer demanded what she should do about it. 'I said I wanted her to sing the song. "*Ek gaana? Kisi aur ke album mein*?" She was sceptical. I said there were other songs as well, but they had not been programmed yet. But if she said so, I could get it done and she could sing all of them. She said she would think about it.' Getting it done was not easy. Why would Mathur give the songs to someone else to sing, since it was, after all, his album. He focussed on Jagjit Singh's next instead, after programming and adding his vocals to the songs that Asha would sing. 'She listened to it and agreed to do it.' Once the money talks were done and the deal was signed with Saregama HMV, with whom he worked by then, Churamani was set to take things forward. He knew the secret to getting the best out of Asha. 'Ashaji is probably one of the most competitive people in the world. She had two huge idols – her sister Lata Mangeshkar and Ghulam Ali. She is always seeking the approval and praise of her sister in anything that she does. So when she hears an original vocal, she wants to sing it better; she will try and go one up on all the nuances that the original singer had.' The treatment the album needed, the kind of singing it merited, was different. 'So it didn't come out exactly as planned, but it is an outstanding piece of work. It is still magical, so many years later. Anyone I gave it to fell in love with it.'

The relationship, such as it was, continued. Churamani remembers that 'She wanted to do an album on her seventy-fifth birthday, anything she wanted, I was more than happy to do for her, because in my mind she's a legend. The more you have of her in your catalogue, the richer it is going to be and whether it is successful or not today does not matter. We did the album *Precious Platinum*.' The videos were done by Sumit Dutt, who shot them in Lonavala. For the album, Asha, Dutt and Mathur collaborated on re-creating classics, from '*Aaj jaane ki zid na karo*', made so popular by the honey-voiced Farida Khanum, and '*Rafta rafta*' by Mehdi Hassan to the crowd-pleaser from her idol Ghulam Ali, '*Chupke chupke*', Jagjit Singh's '*Ahista*' and others. She said to *The Record* when the album was released, 'Initially I was a bit scared of doing these songs, as they had already worked before. I hadn't recorded them ever, but I was extremely fond of some of them. I never imagined I would sing them some day! I decided to take this up as a challenge. Somesh Mathur worked on some fresh arrangements and I tried to balance their style and mine.' Since ghazals focused on the words and the emotions they carried, Asha says, 'I had to put myself into those words so I could express myself better. Whether I am singing '*Aaj jaane ki zid na karo*' or '*Chupke chupke*', I have to convey their meaning and mood, but that's true for any song in any genre. Whether I sing classical-based songs, love songs or cabaret numbers, I have to change myself accordingly.'

It was the age of music videos, when the visuals could capture the mood of a song even when a voice didn't quite do the trick. Add cinematographic skill to an emotional rendering and there is magic, a whole story told in sound and light. So when Asha's voice met Sumit Dutt's directorial vision, a spell was cast. The first short film, which is essentially what a music video is – was for '*Aaj jaane ki zid na karo*'.

'She was in all white – even the set was white. My take was that she is an icon, a living legend, so I wanted to present her like that, not to make her act and be a character, suffering, crying, and so on. My whole effort was to make her look great, since this one was all about her looks, her performance, her singing. We chose the colour palette and costume very carefully, since she is very choosy about what she wears and how she looks. And, of course, she is a fantastic performer!'

Dutt is accustomed to working with big-league performers; he is closely associated with Salman Khan and his family, having directed the superstar in songs in films like *Ready* (2011), *Bodyguard* (2011), *Jai Ho* (2014) and others, and having been associate director on *Dabangg 2* (2012). He had met Asha before, many years ago, when he was working on an episode of a television show dedicated to R.D. Burman for which she was asked to present a song. 'She was so involved that instead of one, we did four tracks with her! I think that's what makes her what she is … she delivers so much that you have to give her more, especially in front of the camera.' He was roped in to make the videos for the album, and after '*Aaj jaane ki zid na karo*' worked well for everyone involved and the audience, he started on '*Tum jo mile*' – 'a nice, sweet love song. I conceptualised it and decided we would shoot in Maharashtra, in the hills, during the peak of the monsoon. Ashaji loved the idea, since she could get out of the city and enjoy the fresh air and green surroundings.'

The film crew stayed in a small guesthouse on Malshej Ghat, Dutt remembers, 'where the rooms leak and there are bees. I told her to come back there the next day, she would be more comfortable that way. But she insisted on staying.' And they bonded, with Asha taking a liking to the young director. 'When she likes someone, she will call them what she wants to. She insisted on calling me Dutta sa'ab. No matter how many times I told her that my name was Sumit Dutt, each time she would say, "*Theek hai*, Dutta sa'ab!" and refuse to use my real name.' 'We went to Malshej and it was raining ... crazy weather! So we stayed inside and we had long discussions on food. The local cooks were all so excited to serve her that they were arranging everything they could find, all exotic food that I had never seen before in my life, let alone eaten. Ashaji got very interested, asking what was available and asking for a particular kind of fish cooked a particular way, and *desi* chicken, and telling them how to cook it her way. They made so much for her and she enjoyed herself thoroughly! She had a fun time, and was on a high, really childlike. She shows what she feels.' She is a fantastic cook. She has cooked for me a couple of times, too.

The next morning it was still pouring, but the team had to move on to a new location. Traffic was slow, halting, and then stopped completely. Getting out to see what had caused the hold-up, Dutt got a bit of a surprise. 'There was water flowing off the mountain into the middle of the road: a waterfall! Locals and tourists, seemingly half-drunk, in their underwear, were dancing in the rain and singing in the 'waterfall'. Asha insisted, "Dutta sa'ab, we will shoot here." She said that she would go there and stand under the waterfall and the shoot would happen. I was amazed, but I was not sure because she was so well-known. What if they mobbed her? She demanded that I agree, that I give her a few minutes to do what she wanted to. So I had to.' Asha got out of the car holding a large yellow umbrella and walked to the middle of the crowd. She stood right under the waterfall and started singing. 'Obviously they knew who she was – she's Asha Bhosle, after all! They were so excited, and so well-behaved. And she, she was so happy meeting people, talking to them in Marathi, standing there under the water with them, singing, dancing, laughing. That is what her rockstar qualities are: she doesn't give a damn about what people think, but if she feels this is the moment, she lives that moment. That is the beauty and charisma she has.'

Dutt is still amazed at Asha's ease of interaction and her enthusiasm. 'No star today would have done that – come out of her car and mingled with complete strangers. She is a born performer. At that age (she was 76 years old then), with a problematic knee, she did it all. Even while we were climbing the hills together, she kept saying, "I've never done this in my life! The things you making me do!" She was happy, absolutely happy.' And the film that resulted showed this elan. 'It's a beautiful video, very romantic, set in the mountains. Fabulous!'

The singer's involvement went all the way. 'She wanted us to go to her house in Panchgani to shoot the video. I went to see the house and realised that it would not be easy, so decided we should not use it. She was completely involved with the entire production, asking us what we wanted and giving it to us if she possibly could. She at actually stopped a shoot and demanded a retake when she saw that her blouse was a little crumpled at the sleeve. If she wanted a certain kind of jewellery, she would bring out all her stuff and say she wanted to wear a particular piece and refuse to use anything else; nobody could change her mind.' Asha's son had just bought her a new car, a Honda Accord, and when she heard that Dutt and his team were looking for a plush automobile for the shoot, she insisted we use hers. 'I protested saying, "You do not know what a shoot will do to your swanky new car," but she would not listen. We messed it up pretty good, but she was patient and chilled out. She loved every moment.' But mixed into the cooperation were flashes of the Asha temperament too, usually only spoken of in whispers in gossip and journalistic circles. 'She would open up her cupboard and say, "Look inside, you can use something." There was no sense of privacy that this is my bedroom, my closet. She will give you all that you ask for if she opens up to you. But she is fussy about what she wears especially, saying why this, why not that, so you need to explain what the story is and what the background will be and why she must wear what you have chosen and not what she wants. Ashaji would need reassurance first that I knew my job, asking me, "*Aapko pata hai na,* Dutta sa'ab?", and after a while, when she realised I did know what I was doing, she would do what I wanted her to.'

She wanted something for the shoot too, something that she eventually managed to get for herself. Asha, an avid Hindi television soap opera lover, wanted to cast a particular boy and girl she had seen in serials. Dutt had no idea how to get the TV stars to act in the short film, but Asha managed to do the trick herself. 'She called the producer, Rajan Shahi of Director's Kut Productions, and insisted that she had to have his lead actor in her video. And because it was Ashaji, Rajan rearranged his entire storyline, made it possible for his actor to take time out from the show – and you know how crazy television schedules are – to do the shoot with Asha. If she decides something, Ashaji will go out there and get it; she will not wait for it to happen. It is a lesson she has learned from life.' Shahi's hugely popular soap, *Sapna Babul Ka … Bidaai* told the story of a father and his two daughters exploring the social impact of skin colour. Kinshuk Mahajan, the young male actor that Asha wanted, was one of the male leads of *Bidaai* and a fan favourite. 'When I got that call from the production office, I thought it was a friend of mine playing a prank on me,' Mahajan has said in an interview. 'I never thought that Ashaji herself would select me for a music video with her. It was a fantastic experience for me, shooting with a legend like her!' Could Dimple Jhangiani be his co-star in Dutt's video? Asha requested. That too was arranged.

'First someone called me on Ashaji's behalf,' Shahi recalls. That was Dutt. 'I called her and we spoke a couple of times. She was very passionate about *Bidaai*; she had so much to say. She told me that she liked the love story because it was very innocent, not loud and dramatic, but very relatable. She knew every track, every character so well, that really surprised me.' Shahi did not know Dimple at the time, but Kinshuk was 'at the pinnacle of his success' at the time. 'We had such mad shooting schedules! Ashaji said she never missed a single episode; she was such a huge fan. She told me what she liked and what she didn't, what she thought was right and what was not and why. And then she said that she was very fond of Kinshuk – his character, of course – and wanted him to be in her new video. In spite of the crazy schedule, I changed the entire storyline so that he would be free to shoot with her.'

Shahi learned that during the shoot, Asha would talk to Kinshuk about the show, suggesting changes in his character and telling him what she liked most about his role. Her interest was so delightful that when Shahi heard that the singer had missed a few episodes of his soap, 'I told my team to make DVDs of the entire series so that she could watch! The encouragement that came from her was very nice; I never thought that she could or would give me so many tips. She suggested some changes in the story between Kinshuk and Parul (his other co-star in *Bidaai*) – that the narrative should be more aspirational and not sad, more real, sweeter, that the romance should be very endearing. She asked me not to keep a lot of false and negative emotion and tearful scenes, but to make it more happy, more positive. I took these pointers seriously, since they came from someone with such huge experience and who is so sensitive.' Dimple Jhangiani did two serials for Shahi after he had watched Asha's video: 'I didn't know her then, but after I was shown the music video, we kept in touch and I cast Dimple in two new shows. So in a way Ashaji was instrumental in getting Dimple to work with us.' The director–producer has not been in touch with the singer, but 'She gave us a lot of good wishes and blessings, as well as a pep talk that motivated and encouraged all of us. That felt really good. She is a legend, after all, a veteran, so it gave us a really big boost when I found that she loved the show. Very rarely do people actually go out of their way to motivate and encourage others!'

But while she is super-involved and caring, there is a diva side to the singer that cannot be denied. She is, after all, Asha Bhosle! Even as Dutt is all praise for her, he admits that he did tread carefully. 'I deal with so many very difficult people and one has to be careful dealing with her too. She is like Salman Khan – she lives from the heart. These people are masters of their craft, destiny's children who have been given a special magnetism, which is why millions of people are so attracted to them. They are not ordinary people, but they live their lives for their work, their craft. People like Ashaji are into it 24/7 – they talk music, live music, sleep music – everything is about music. And they need a certain kind of comfort and understanding.' It is when ordinary people, as Dutt terms them, are not on the same page and cannot understand these extraordinary individuals that fireworks can erupt. 'They are in a kind of trance when they are working and when someone tries to break that flow, for no real reason, they react. If you are on the same page, in the same kind of flow, they are the easiest people to deal with. When they see that you are adding to their craft, to their labour of love, they are all yours.'

Asha may have had a great deal of fun on the monsoon shoot, but there was only so much that she was willing to give. Dutt comments, 'She is very sensitive, so you need to be over-careful with her. After two days of running around and doing crazy stuff, she decided that she had had enough, no matter that there were one or two shots left. So she left.' But what she had given her director was more than enough and he was grateful for that. 'Every artiste has that point and you need to let them be. They give you everything and then they switch off; you cannot force them to deliver more. They create their own rules, they are emperors, rulers, who have all the power. She is strong-headed – that is what made her what she is. Mentally, they are in a different space, they give so much extra, they are sourcing it from somewhere, their thinking process is a different place. You need to be on the same page, and then they are all yours.'

That is the case with Asha too, Dutt found when he worked with her and became familiar with her style of functioning. 'Most people must have had the experience of her being difficult or whatever you want to call it, but in my ken she has childlike qualities and you should give her what she wants in order to deal with her easily. But that is what makes her so great, so big a person. Whatever she is doing, she gets involved in every aspect.' Even something as small as catering to a visitor, Dutt discovered from dropping by the Bhosle apartment in South Mumbai. 'If you visit her, she will ask what you want to eat and whatever you say, she will head straight to the kitchen and start cooking!'

Life for and with Asha is never dull, Dutt found. There was almost always a buzz within and around her. 'There was a lot of stress that she carried, with her children and her family. But the moment she is in front of the camera, she is altogether a different person. And everything is about the need of the hour – she will do whatever is needed.' For the director, 'Her voice was not the element that we were capturing, it was her expressions, and that worked out perfectly. It was not an easy shoot, since it was outdoors during the monsoon, and her knees were giving her trouble, but she was never one to give up. She is a very hard nut to crack!' Dutt discovered, as many before him had, that Asha was a special person. 'A great combination of an artiste of that stature who is so perfect with her craft and a tough person who has lived life on her own terms – not an easy state. Many people can go with the flow and lose the taste of living life; she loves living life, no matter what it brings her. There is a lot that has happened to her that would have defeated a normal person. Maybe her craft is her strength – she is a superwoman, a perfect housewife, a perfect mother, a legend, very emotional, very concerned about everyone. She is what show business is all about: she knows how to present her craft, to excite people, control them, direct their emotions. Her connect with her audience is fabulous; she understands them, and can dance with people on the street… she knows what to give to whom. She is still so high on life, even after having played such a long innings. It is purely her art that has given her strength.'

Alongside all this, Dutt insists that Asha is a very simple

person. 'Till today she is not starry, as long as you do not mess with her. If you do, she will put you in your place. If someone tries to get familiar, over-friendly, slightly rough, she knows how to deal with them. Otherwise, she is the simplest, sweetest, most easy person to be with. She is what she is: a real, basic, person with no *nakhras*.' He considers himself 'very very lucky, because the kind of connect I managed to create with her, I don't think she has with anyone else.' And proof of this particular pudding comes from a photograph: 'There is a picture of me hugging her and she says that is the rarest picture anyone can get, since nobody comes that close to Asha Bhosle.'

5

The Singer

While Asha Bhosle is now shielded by her family and prefers not to be interviewed by anyone she has not known for a long time (her caretakers insist that she is easily tired and does not want to talk much about herself), she has never been reputed to be unfriendly or rude. She will greet most people, known or unknown, with her warm smile.

And if she talks, there will soon be a giggle, a joke, a memory shared. She rarely wants something to be 'off the record', but has developed a little of the tact and reticence of her sister, Lata Mangeshkar, who was the epitome of diplomacy. When she speaks of her sister, there is a sense of great respect, awe and perhaps a tint of resentment in Asha's voice, while her children evoke a deep sadness and enormous joy, and music, her songs, her career are all light and laughter. Every time you watch her on television, at an event or doing an interview, there is animation, spontaneity, a degree of obvious introspection and a giggle or two. She is candid, or sounds so, and draws her audience into her conversation without being deliberate about it. She has warmth, appeal, charisma and, of course, that girlish voice that continues to charm.

That the world is vulnerable to that charm is evident.

In November 2015, Asha Bhosle was listed as one of the BBC's 100 most inspirational women, chosen from a host of world leaders in the realm of politics, science and entertainment, this time in the company of veteran actor Kamini Kaushal and tennis star Sania Mirza.

Her tweeted response: 'In a recent interview I had said I would be very happy if my music and life inspired people positively. I guess it did. Thank you BBC.' In an interview with the television service's *Asian Network* reporter Shabnam Mahmood, she said in her tentative English, 'Inside I am like thirty. I can do anything – you tell me, I will do it.' About changing to suit the time, place and situation, she was clear that every song had a certain feel to it. 'If it is a sad song like '*Chain se*' (*Pran Jaye Par Vachan Na Jaye)*, composed by O.P. Nayyar, we think of something sad, but when you sing a happy song like '*Piya tu*' (*Caravan*), you can change your mood *phataphat* (quickly).'

Asha has had to reinvent herself and her style over and over through the seven decades or so that she has been working. 'Yes, I have to, otherwise I will remain where I was. If you choose to work with youngsters, you have to sing a '*Kambakth ishq*' (*Pyaar Tune Kya Kiya*) or a '*Le gayi le gayi*' (*Dil To Pagal Hai*, 1997). You just have to. I did not feel uncomfortable singing those kinds of songs – they are good songs, very nice tunes; I don't feel like it is bad music or bad wordings.' Things have changed somewhat today. 'Now there is no dialogue, no good acting, nothing. Now there's only dancing, not good music, only rhythm, rhythm, rhythm. I don't like it. At that time, when I sang '*Piya tu*', people said it was all bad lyrics. But now I feel that that was a bhajan, a devotional song! Nowadays, the words used in songs are very bad.' So does that influence the way people behave off-screen, often blaming films for their wrong actions? 'Bad people are bad people. When they see beautiful girls wearing very short dresses or bikinis, and dance, they naturally get affected, and behave vulgarly.'

She continues to sing 'because after so many years it has become a habit', she told journalist Subhash K. Jha in an interview. Some of her songs are classics, pure, deep and memorable. Others, she admits, are sheer nonsense. 'It is my job to sing, I am a commercial artiste,' she explained. 'I am on good terms with composers, so I sing the songs assigned to me. But when I feel that a song is not worthy of me, I refuse it. And music directors also have realised what is right for me.' There is a reason for her accepting assignments not worthy of her: 'I can't wait around for good songs to fall into my lap. The standard of film music continues to decline every day. Even then I pour my life into the composition! Now I am shifting to singing more classical songs. I've started singing the songs from the musical plays my father did, since they have a large market and should not get lost. Also, I want to sing one raga for two hours on stage …' A candid thought. Even perhaps a tactless one, or a deliberate revelation: 'I believe in the truth, in singing or in living; nowadays that does not count.

> *Maybe I'm old-fashioned, but previously we would work hard on a song to make it win appreciation. It was our sweat that made it happen. Today, awards are handed out like fruit from a tree – records become gold or platinum hits without even being heard!*

It took thousands of copies being sold for '*Dum maaro dum*' to be called the first silver disc. If platinum discs had existed in those days, I would be sitting on them!'

Once, in 1947, Asha was on a train e route to an audition; crowded alongside were dozens of families escaping the trauma of Partition, distraught and weeping, their lives destroyed by a line drawn arbitrarily across a map. But all she felt was her own battle, 'and the fact that when I got to the audition I would be told, "Don't call us, we'll call you".'

Her reported rivalry with Lata is media-contrived, she has always insisted. That same drive that kept her going and took her to the top so many years ago has not faded ... not discernibly, at least. As she once said, 'Ambition has no limits. It is human nature to want to go higher. If tomorrow I want to become Margaret Thatcher ...!' And it was ambition and determination that helped her vault over her rivals and circumstances. When the songs of *Naya Daur* grabbed attention, she started getting playback assignments for the heroine's voice rather than just the vamp's. That eventually led to Asha singing in *Teesri Manzil*, which in turn segued into her success with *Umrao Jaan*. 'I need lyrics and tunes that inspire me, and O.P. Nayyar, R.D. Burman and Khayyam projected my voice in new ways,' Asha said in an interview. 'Each had his own style and with each one I have been a student.'

Interestingly, by this stage in her life and career, the student can morph into a leader, a teacher, perhaps? She said a few years ago, 'Honestly, we have always been sincere in whatever we do. We have been superstars for so many years. I never ever compromised. I never treated anyone with disrespect and never allowed anyone to treat me that way either. Even today, if I feel that I am not being treated right, I will walk out without hesitating. So now, if I were to become a music director, I would not ever tolerate interference from singers – being asked to change this, change that. And what's music direction today? People stealing each other's work? I am fed up of this kind of a thing.'

She has memories of some of her colleagues, she told Dr Mandar Bichu, who has written extensively on Lata's work. 'I had a good friendship with Kamal Barot, who was an educated and well-read lady. But her voice was screechy. In her duets with didi, like '*Akeli mohe chhod na jaana*' (*Madari*, 1959), she used to sound so out of her Kamal Parrot!' Of Suman Kalyanpur, she says, 'She was a very proud woman. Once we had decided to hold a meeting of all playback singers and she was invited. Her husband said, "I will be accompanying her to the meeting as we are from a respectable family. I don't want this *filmi* atmosphere affecting her." I remember all of us singers being quite annoyed with the prudish attitude. With Kalyanji–Anandji's troupe, she had gone to Goa for some programmes. While returning from Goa, everyone in the bus was singing and enjoying but she was sitting separately, engrossed in some thoughts. So Anandji asked her what was the matter and she said, "Anandji Bhai, I was just remembering the omelette that Goa cook had prepared. It was so good!" It was a big joke. Afterwards the musicians would say, "Her brain is full of omelette!"'

The talk of any rivalry with real rivalry with Geeta Dutt was nipped abruptly in the bud during the recording of an S.D. Burman song, '*Janoon janoon re*' from *Insaan Jaag Utha* (1959). Burman wanted Geeta to add the sound of laughter to her voice for the number, but Geeta could not manage it, try as she did. Asha stepped in, sang the portion with an underlying giggle and made her mark with the composer and the audience.

Doing all this and much more, all at the same time, needs stamina. At ninety-plus, Asha still has the energy to tour, to perform, to create the magic she is known for. In 2014, she toured Europe, the Middle East and the United States, performing to packed houses and incessant calls for encores at each venue. And she tweeted from her hotel at 5.48 one morning, 'Good morning to early risers and to those still awake. In my younger days I often used to record all night long and sleep around this time'! True, she does get tired – as do would people half her age – and she has had issues with illness – tummy upsets, coughs and colds, fever, et al., etc., but her energy is astonishing, indefatigable. 'It is inside you,' she once told her an interviewer. 'You cannot buy it or take a tablet for it.'

This has been part of her magic ever since she was a small child. She was taught to keep busy, always, and she followed that dictum, by 'talking, singing, dancing all the time'. If there was nothing to do, she would 'sweep the floor or wash it with soap water. 'My mother would say, "You're a djinn – there is something supernatural about you!" And it will be that way till I die.'

She and her sister Lata are the only singers in the film industry who began their careers in what was British India. Asha has been witness to the days of pre-Independence, the freedom struggle. She remembers the dusty movie sets, people running around busily, lights, cameras, wires, the smell of makeup and the calls for silence as shooting commenced. 'And there was little me,' she recalled, 'falling asleep and being woken up every now and then to sing my part.' She remembered her first test. 'I was learning classical music from Navrang Nagpurkar and to take my music exam, a veteran musician, Shankarrao Sapre, came. I had just started the initial aalap and he told me to stop. I was wondering what was wrong when he said, "You don't need any exams. Come with me. I will compose a film song for you."'

The energy also feeds itself. If Asha is asked to sing

something that is fairly routine, she does not need too much effort or concentration, she cruises through it, not needing to exert her voice or her mind beyond the point of her usual standard of dedication and involvement. But if, for instance, it is a more complex composition, for which she needs to focus all her attention and perhaps even struggle a little to get it right, it inspires her to do better, to do more. She herself has cited the example of '*Maar dalega dard-e-jigar*' from *Pati Patni* (1966), in which Rahul Dev Burman brought in the rhythms of the Bossa Nova, something not heard before in Hindi movie musical scores. It was not a '*seedha saadha* (simple) tune with straight counting of the *matra*s that a performer with any vocal training could sing,' Asha once said. 'I had to keep careful count of the beat – it was so unusual.' And the song not only made all her senses sing with the challenge it posed, but also made her sit up and take notice of its composer. 'I came to see that even a seasoned singer like myself had to be alert while negotiating his tunes, which are not easy to sing even as they appeal to the ear.'

Pancham was pleased with her virtuosity, and gave her the '*Aaja aaja*' number from *Teesri Manzil* with its challenging hook line of '*Aaja a-a-a-aaja*', slight tremolo, difficult breath control and all. He said while talking about that song, 'Asha's ability to act and mimic in her singing is what puts her in a class of her own. She is so full of life when putting over a fun number that it's infectious.' Asha herself agreed with:

> *I tire of the same routine sooner than most people and look for some change of pace in my work. So I would go to Pancham's recordings full of anticipation! He was able to bring out every nuance of the lyrics, every shade of the mood when he tuned a song. His comprehension of that mood was instinctive.*

He could do it because he was a singer himself and could 'think out' the song as he made up the tune.' She soon became R.D. Burman's muse, the one for whom he composed some of his most memorable tunes. She was told by David Harrington of Kronos Quartet that he thought Pancham was 'Mozart', which 'makes me feel very good and also very sad, because he is no longer here to hear this. I felt the same when I saw the film *Amadeus*. I cried that day.'

For Asha, singing has never been just a job, but life itself, every assignment being much more than just a few hours in a studio. 'Each song is an emotional and a vocal experience for a singer, all at once.' The relationship between the singers recording for a single track is not impersonal; instead, both (or more) play characters conveying not just a story, but the feeling that flavours that narration and the experience of being part of it. 'There is a certain mood, a certain emotion going with the song, and you need to put that precious feeling into every take.' When she started out in the business, it was a long-winded process, one that she understood but was often amused by, especially when she thinks about the infinitely less arduous process it is today. She has said, 'First they composed music, then they played it for us and told us how they wanted the song to be sung. Then we read the words and worked out what feelings they wanted. And by the time I was in front of the mic, believing I was the actress, I could sing exactly what had been perceived.' An extension of that would be to compose music or become a music director, but Asha would rather not, as she told B.R. Ishara, maker of films like *Chetna*, *Charitra* and *Milap*, when he asked her to take on one of his movies. But she did compose for herself, for a music and video album called *Aap Ki Asha* (2001), with lyrics by Majrooh Sultanpuri, whose last work it was.

When it comes to knowing what working with Asha is like, ask singer–composer–actor Sonu Nigam. He had heard her often, but was truly impressed when, as a thirteen-year-old boy in Delhi, he listened to *Meraj-e-Ghazal*, an album that had Ghulam Ali collaborating with Asha. 'The whole orchestra world in Delhi was talking about it. I was expecting Ghulam Aliji to sing, since he had a fabulous voice, and that Ashaji would sing along. But when Ashaji's voice came in, I was flabbergasted. I thought, "Oh my God! How can someone sing like this?" She was giving Ghulam Ali ji such competition in his own field! I will not say who was better, but I'd say to just sing what Ghulam Ali ji could sing and do so with such assertion, such prowess, is something that elevated her in my eyes. I loved all the ghazals on that album, especially '*Kai dino ka suraag le kar*'.'

Nigam first met Asha in 1994 when the two singers were working on songs by Babul Bose. 'We were shooting a video for '*Oh mere sona, sona re sona*'. There were others singers there, including Shaan and Sukhwinder Singh. She came in, and I lay down in front of her in a *shashtang namaskar*, flat on the ground. While we were shooting, she saw how much I adored her and she started singing, '*Oh mere Sonu, Sonu re Sonu*' just to tease me. She was always very active and flamboyant.'

The singer was part of Asha's performance tours of the United States in 1996 and 2007 and spent as much time as he could with her. 'One of my favourite memories of her is when we toured the USA in June–July 1996. It was my second tour, and I had some experience, but since I was performing with Ashaji, I had gone with a lot of reverence. I got to spend time with her, travel with her, see her … I soaked her inside my system. Those were beautiful days.'

They had performed at a wedding together before that. 'Ashaji's throat was very bad – she had to sing '*Jhoote naina bole*' from *Lekin* (1990). She asked me to sing with her, since she was feeling unwell. I said I would sing as much as I knew. I stood with her on the stage, but the lady sang it herself – she did not need my support. That's how aggressive and strong-headed she is as a person. All respect to her – that is why she is what she is today; even at her age she is singing, performing, is active, with her sense of humour very much intact, she has the *jeene ki chah*, that drive to live, *zinda dil aurat hain*, (she is a free-spirited woman).'

He found out just how competitive and possessive Asha was during their 2007 tour together. 'I would do the song '*Dil mangta hai dil dil*' from *Mujhse Shaadi Karoge* (2004) and merge some lines of '*Kajra mohabbat wala*' (*Kismat*) into that, totally forgetting that it was Ashaji's and Shamshad Begum's song. During one performance I did just that, since it had been my habit over the last four years. It was totally inadvertent.' But Asha, sharp as she was known to be, was ready and waiting. 'The next show, she sang '*Kajra mohabbat wala*' before I could! She made it a point to make me realise that "Hello, this is my song, baby!" She is very vigilant and picky about things, which is good; she is not someone who will let it go.' There was a personal touch to their relationship too. Sonu managed to blend respect for the older singer with affection for the mother figure that she could be. 'She used to have a spike in her heel – a bone spur or something; my mother had it and would cry in pain and I would massage her foot. I saw the same thing happening to Asha ji, so one or two nights I massaged her heel – it was *guru ka sammaan*, respect for a senior. It was for me a beautiful moment, where a teacher is lying down and a student is pressing her feet.'

Nigam knew that Asha was versatile, but was astonished to find how technically perfect she was as a singer. 'No singer, male or female, can beat her. She can sing natya sangeet, lok sangeet, ghazals … when she sings those, even ghazal singers would feel humbled! Bhajans, qawwalis, whatever. She is perhaps the best singer India has ever heard, and that sets her apart from everybody else.' The image he had always had of Asha is 'a *jwalamukhi*, a volcano, more specifically a *tapaswini*, a female ascetic, with a volcano inside her. I see her as somebody who is restless because her older sister was Lata Mangeshkar and since that is the competition, she knows that nobody will allow her an entry into the same field. So she had to figure out, "How do I make myself distinctly different? How do I shine with her? How do I not get camouflaged by her glory? How do I set myself apart from her? How do I create my own genre?" That was her endeavour always, and with Lata ji around, she had to work even harder, since people do not generally want two members of the same family on the same platform. But Ashaji gets full marks for making her name in spite of everything, which is why I call her *tapaswini*.'

Adoration aside, Nigam considers Asha's music to be 'seamless, infinite. She will never get that eighteen-year-old Asha Bhosle back, the one she kept alive into her late fifties. I think that if she could have lived for a thousand years and kept her youth for seven hundred or more, she could have encompassed all genres, she could have done anything, could have sung anything … if she had the luxury of age on her side.' Singing with luminaries like Asha, Lata or Manna De, as Nigam has done, is not easy, he said, since 'They are gods for you, they are the people who have inspired you to be a singer. So to sing with them is more than an achievement, it is a very humbling experience, like karmic bliss.' Over the years, his interactions with Asha have decreased for some reason, Nigam rues that, but he still has a connect with her 'on a soul level. I am a similar person; I am not somebody who thinks too much before I speak. I am pretty clear about how I come across to the world, and she has been that way all her life. Maybe it's about how opposites attract and similar poles don't. She loves me and she knows I love her, but she doesn't know the level of love that I have for her.'

It is almost as if she can do anything, people say. As director Sumit Dutt insisted, 'She is a rockstar, a real rockstar. She is someone who lives from the heart – a legend, different in every way; she can talk to you about the biggest musicians, Indian and Western,' many of whom she knows personally and has worked with. 'But she is still the most ordinary person and can talk to you about how much lemons cost! She will tell you she won't shop in Cuffe Parade because *sabziwalas* there cheat her, so she goes to Dadar market and picks out her vegetables herself. That's what keeps her so real, so grounded, so genuine with people. Somewhere inside she still does not want to acknowledge that she is Asha Bhosle, not unless and until it is absolutely required. When she wants you to understand that she is Asha Bhosle, she will do it – she can switch from being an absolutely humble person, so ordinary and real, to being a star, if you mess with her. If you do not fit her behavioural guidelines, you can be in big trouble.' But whatever her nakhras and whims, her diva behaviour and her much-vaunted temper, she is still a great artiste 'because she gives one hundred per cent to whatever she does', Dutt insisted. 'I have a very friendly relationship with her – I am a director and she loves the camera. Whatever voice she has given to Helen ji, there is some left in her, and you can see that in the way she loves to dance, she loves to face the camera, she loves to look great, she is high on life itself! After all, that she has gone through, she is still the brightest person in the room wherever she goes.' And she is always singing.

> *Some of the music that R.D. Burman made with Asha is kept alive and upfront by music uber-fan Manohar Iyer. His eighteen-year-old organisation,* Keep Alive, *is focused on the revival and popularisation of vintage Hindi film music.*

Iyer is often called a 'musicologist' or 'walking encyclopaedia' of the genre, and holds regular shows to keep his passion alive and bring in new fans from the younger generation. He has written songs for singers like Alka Yagnik, Usha Uthup, Sonu Nigam, Shaan and others, soon moving to big screen work with composers such as Amar–Utpal, Jatin–Lalit and Anu Malik. With Keep Alive, he creates a kind of musical biography, telling stories, airing old recordings and conducting concerts with his group of singers and orchestra. A Lata Mangeshkar fan all through, he does acknowledge Asha's talent as he analyses that time in Hindi film music. 'In some families, people are blessed; they are born great, rather than having greatness thrust upon them. Asha Bhosle's father was a singer and composer and that talent has trickled down to his children. Maybe the next generation will not be as talented, but Lata Mangeshkar, Hridaynath Mangeshkar and Asha Bhosle certainly inherited it.' Iyer's fanboy side is clearly dominant: 'Can there be another Lata in our enormous population? What she sang in the first five or so years of her career was enough to make her a legend. But Asha had to work. Once you are second, you always remain second, no matter what.'

Iyer is proud of Keep Alive. 'Many people have followed me, but first credit goes to me. In the same way, Lata was destiny's child. If her father had not died when she was just thirteen, or if they had not been from a very ordinary family, or even if she had been a beauty, or a boy, she would not have found such greatness. Ma Saraswati blessed her.' With Asha, things were rather different. 'Sometimes life is a series of accidents. Ravindra Jain once said about the sisters, '*Ek mann se gaati hai, ek tann se gaati hai*' (one sings from the mind, one sings from the body). What he meant was that one is more considered, suave, refined, while the other is more colourful, exuberant, outgoing in whatever she sings and says and however she behaves. Inadvertently, that one will be more direct and seem more flippant and frivolous, which is reflected in her songs and singing style.'

Both had distinct voices, Iyer explained. 'If they were the same, the people who did would not have favoured them. Lata's was divine, crystal clear, sweet, which comes through even in a *kotha* (brothel) song like '*Raina beeti jaaye*' (*Amar Prem*). When Asha sings '*Sancha naam tera*' (*Julie*), it has a come-hither feel (even though it is a song sung for God), maybe because of the glide she adds or maybe even because she sang in her own style that she developed with the kind of songs she was given – that slight voice movement changes the mood of the song.' Asha could have copied Geeta Dutt, who was her direct competition then, Iyer suggested, but believes, 'She was definitely moulded by O.P. Nayyar. All this made her different from Lata.'

His store of anecdotes is endless, some garnered from personal experience, others from stories narrated to him by the music-makers he has been so closely associated with. Lata was more strait-laced, unwilling to take risks and compromise her image. 'In *Taxi Driver* (1954), Lata sang most of the songs that were composed by S.D. Burman with lyrics by Sahir Ludhianvi. There was only one that Asha sang: '*Jeene do aur jiyo*'; Lata refused to sing that one because it had lyrics that went '*chadti jawaani ke din hai*' (these are the days of blossoming youth), so the song went to Asha by default. But the definition of vulgarity and what is good changes with time, because about fifteen years later Lata sang '*Chadti jawaani meri chaal mastani*' from *Caravan*.' This is where Asha was able to cash in so admirably and get more work from the various composers and filmmakers who had always favoured her elder sister. 'In 1954–55, Lata was supposedly suffering from a sinus problem, so Naushad, who was a total Lata devotee, gave two songs to Asha for *Amar* (1954). Both are good songs: '*Ik baat kahun*' and '*Radha ke pyare*', and both are definitely in Lata's typical style. But her sister got to sing them instead.'

Asha sang whatever came her way, Iyer has kept track. 'In *Ruksana* (1955), Sajjad used Asha in many songs: '*Tumhe yaad karte hain Din raat*' and a few duets with Kishore Kumar including '*Tere jahaan se chal diye*' and '*Yeh chaar din bahaar ke*'. But it was a fact that the best songs always went to Lata, while Asha got the B-graders, the mythologicals and the stunt films.'

There must have been feelings of hurt, since Asha did make a few remarks that betrayed her sensitivity. 'Perhaps in jest, she said at an event honouring the late Madan Mohan that he had given Lata all his best songs, but one '*Jhumka gira re*' (*Mera Saaya*) was enough for her. There will obviously be hurt somewhere that she was relegated to second position most of the time and was not given the best songs.' But it was inevitable, Iyer felt. 'Even if you have a good song but sing it in a style that doesn't suit it, it doesn't work. "*Raat akeli hai*", for instance, from *Jewel Thief* (1967), composed by S.D. Burman, worked well because it suited her style and voice.

Some songs that she sang for Ravi did well they were hits, but they were perhaps not what the composer had aimed at, they had an unwanted pathos, but they worked with the public.

She had many of what I call *bazaaru* (vulgar) songs. She has a lot of popular songs to her credit, but not that many classy ones.' Asha sang Ravi's first film composition, '*Chandamama duur ke*' for *Vachan* (1955) and followed that up with bhajans for *Gharana* (1961 – '*Yeh zindagi ki uljhane*', '*Yeh duniya ussi ki*'), *Grihasti* (1963 – '*Jeevan jyot jale*'), *Kaajal* ('*Tora man darpan*') and *Phool Aur Patthar* (1966, '*Sun le pukaar aayi*'), giving her more serious, leading-lady numbers at a time when she had been relegated to doing more vampy, sexy-siren songs. And then there was the delightful and fast-paced '*C-A-T cat, cat mane billi*' from *Dilli Ka Thug* (1958), picturised on Kishore Kumar and Nutan.

Iyer's film song catalogue is a large and comprehensive one, with stories and memories filling his home and his head. He is a Lata Mangeshkar fan, but his knowledge of her sister's work is immense. 'Asha had an inherent sensuousness, sort of like Madhubala. She sang "*Aaiye meherbaan*" for the actress in *Howrah Bridge*; it was very seductive, but innocent and sweet. There was pure magic, pure romance in it. But she had to wait ten years to get that, her first solo hit. Her big songs in *Naya Daur* and other films were duets.'

The sisters' repertoire had parallels. Lata sang for *Pakeezah*, while Asha did playback for Rekha in *Umrao Jaan*, for which she won a National Award. 'In later years Lata's voice became shaky, while Asha has managed to retain the youthfulness in hers. Somewhere I feel maybe she never took her music or her career as seriously as she should have, apart from in her initial struggling days.' Iyer explained, 'She got only three composers to perpetuate her career: O.P. Nayyar undoubtedly; then because S.D. Burman fell out with Lata, Asha got him for five years and did films like *Nau Do Gyarah*, *Kala Pani* (1958), *Bambai Ka Babu* (1960) and *Lajwanti* (1958); then there was Ravi; and finally, R.D. Burman. With RD, the era changed and she got lucky. Kishore Kumar also fit in. They did many songs together.'

Luck played a bigger than usual role in the singer's life, Iyer said, with the minuses being outweighed by the pluses. 'Yash Chopra did not favour Asha at all. Even in *Dilwale Dulhania Le Jayenge* she got only one song: '*Zara sa jhoom loon main*'. There are comparatively very few songs that she sang that are sober and sensitive.' She sang for C. Ramachandra in *Navrang* (1959), where Sandhya brought every word to life with her acting and dancing, but that was because the composer fell out with Lata, so Asha was roped in to do the memorable '*Aadha hai chandrama*' with Mahendra Kapoor, the solo '*Aa dil se dil mila le*' and others. 'Each composer has a style and that was reflected in the notes they used; in turn, those had to fit the singer. Jaidev made the most of Asha's voice in extracting the maximum from her; even the intricacies and nuances of his music were suited to her. Unfortunately, very few of the songs they did together were hits. Today when she does concerts, she sings numbers that were hits, most of them light and popular.'

Music journalist Narendra Kusnur is also a Lata Mangeshkar fan who would rate one sister above the other, until he 'started recognising the good things about Asha's music'. For the past twenty years or more, he has been writing on music, following his passion even while in a job that was woefully non-musical in every way. Most recently a columnist for *The Hindu*, Mumbai, he writes a blog on music, and contributes to several newspapers, magazines and websites. 'I'm a fan of both sisters, but perhaps more of Lata, maybe because I've grown up on her music. I had of course heard Asha's songs, mostly the '*Dum maaro dum*' kind. The amazing thing about her is her consistency and versatility. And even now, she has not lost it – she still does songs for films and shows and more. I've also observed her non-film music quite a bit – most people know her only for her film songs.' During the time that Kusnur was working for a tabloid, Asha was trying her hand at some interesting music outside of the film world. 'In 1995 she released *Legacy* with Ali Akbar Khan – I was at that concert and it was my first interaction with her. She sang some classical compositions while he played the sarod. And then the Indi-pop phase started.' Alisha Chinai made it big, and earlier, Baba Sehgal had already grabbed attention – and Asha entered that arena with '*Janam samjha karo*'; she had already done the remix album *Rahul and I*. 'So apart from film songs, she was making inroads into new things too.'

The journalist first interviewed her some time in 1996. 'It was my birthday and I had thought to celebrate by going out of town, but I was told that she was available only that day. It was quite a memorable time. I kept following her – she did another album called *Asha*, then another which was ghazals, trying to redo the *Umrao Jaan* phase perhaps. Then she did an album with Kronos Quartet (*You've Stolen My Heart*), for which I was the project manager. We got a scratch copy, an unreleased version, not the final, so that we could start preparing for the release. They had a completely different marketing plan in the United States and I was asked to prepare one for India. Ashaji was getting ready to release a brand-new album which had her version of '*Aaj jaane ki zid na karo*' and we sat down together to discuss plans for the Kronos album. Her son Anand was very involved with the project, so she left it to us to sort out.' Since it was all being done at such short notice, the press conference was held at the Western India Automobile Association (WIAA) club on Malabar Hill. 'Anand initially objected, saying it should be in a five-star hotel, but nothing else was available then.' Sadly, the Kronos album did not do very well, since most people in India already knew the songs, and also the time for remixes had passed. There was one more thing – the Indian ear was not really tuned in to the Western music system, so the sounds of the instruments being used, like the viola and the cello, seemed strange. 'Also, Kronos was not well known here, so the album did not pick up very well in terms of sales. That was my last interaction with Ashaji.'

Kusnur said what is so special about the singer's voice is basically that it fits into all kinds of music. 'There are people who can sing only sad songs or just item numbers or whatever. Though she does not vary it too much, she can take on almost anything and fit into whatever she is asked to sing. There is a lot of melody in her tone, whatever she does sing. And there is that willingness to experiment, perhaps because of the R.D. Burman influence. He was into so many kinds of music, so she was also exposed to various influences and would experiment with her sound. I cannot imagine R.D.'s songs doing as well and being as varied if Asha had not sung them. And since they were together in their personal lives too, they were constantly working on new projects and creating new sounds. The consistency that he had in the '70s was with her – R.D. Burman changed the kinds of music in films and Asha was the perfect voice for him to do that with.' With Pancham, Asha stayed ahead of the competition; the rivals that she had started her career with had by then already faded. 'Geeta Dutt did more of Asha's style of songs long before Asha. Shamshad Begum had her own particular voice and did not suit every song. So Asha managed to stand out in spite of the competition, which actually could have been more intense if Geeta had not been ill.'

But the singer's strength lay not so much in her voice as

in the fact that, as Kusnur explained,

> *She was never straitjacketed; she could do classical and ghazals and pop and film music and whatever she was asked to do, always adjusting and adapting. She was a good performer, with good stagecraft – she still is.*

She knew some songs would work, like '*Dum maaro dum*' and '*Chura liya*', and then she would add some other styles and make a good mix. That holds true even today, to a great extent. 'Her voice has not shown signs of ageing, it is what it was, except for a difference in strength and a greater coarseness, but far less than most others. She has somehow managed to preserve her voice and has been able to keep herself going so long. Maybe it's because she followed the rule of "If you cannot sing in that pitch, high or low, don't". Also, she has got composers to create music for her.' The story goes that Asha told music directors what she could sing and what she would sing, and most would work with her on these lines. 'Now she's working with a lot of young people too, so she can dictate terms, but all along she has chosen the right song and is careful about how she experiments. She has always known what she can do and does it well.'

While Asha does her job well, better than most even in her nineties, she does admire and respect a few singers that she has worked with, known or just listened to. She described them as having 'God-given voices' and 'in a class by themselves' since they 'apply both their heart and their brain'. These include Mater Deenanath Mangeshkar ('My songs would be nothing had it not been for my father.'), her sister Lata Mangeshkar ('Whenever she sings, you will feel as if someone is singing in a temple.'), Mohammed Rafi ('His greatest ability was that he could sing at a high pitch and shift to a low pitch immediately.'), Manna De ('There was nobody like him when it came to classical songs.'), Kishore Kumar ('His only hobby was music.'), Mukesh ('He never imitated anyone, he was an original.'), and Hemant Kumar ('His voice was like the deep ocean.'). And as she collaborated with these musicians, she learned a lot, using all that experience in her own work. She told singer Sonu Nigam in a special interview for *Stardust* magazine, 'Kishore da used to tease me and also teach me. He was very innocent, but he was also moody. His mood could be predicted by what he was wearing. If he wore a *lungi* and entered, that meant he was in a bad mood. But on the days he wore pants and a shirt, the studio would get jubilant. Rafi *sa'ab* would always enter the studio with a perfumed handkerchief, and its fragrance mesmerised the studio just like his voice did. He was God-fearing. Mukesh*ji* was very cheerful and would practise a number of times. Hemant da directed as well as sang some great songs. They all were humble and didn't carry a superstar attitude on the sets. They all were older than me and it was a learning experience. They laughed at me and nicknamed me *Moti* (fatso). There was no jealousy among the men. However, you could sense jealousy amongst the women.'

Hrishikesh Kannan is a lifelong fan and someone who has associated with her personally and professionally, albeit at a respectful distance – popularly known as Hrishi K., Radio One producer and host. In a blog he wrote:

> What do you do when you are in the company of a legend? Are you tongue-tied? Or are you like yours truly? Wanting to live every moment twice, or hanging on to a single moment and concentrating on it really hard in the hope that you will keep it in your memory cells longer?

> Asha Bhosle came on to my show the other day. It was a live, unplugged performance with just an acoustic guitar and a keyboard for accompaniment. But then, would Ma Saraswati's avatar on this planet need anything more to supplement her voice?

As a friend of her grandson Chaitanya, better known as Chintu Bhosle, Hrishi K. was one of the 'privileged few to be invited to the hallowed portals of her residence', to be greeted by 'some swell aromas wafting through her kitchen as well as all her cookbooks strewn in her waiting area plus her gorgeous 77-year-old warm smile …' She called him Hrishikesh, 'my full name. She insisted then and still calls me that.' Only his mother and his wife had done so until then.

'She is aware, she is intuitive, she thinks from the heart. But that is always backed up with lots of hard work. I have done two standout sessions with her – in the first, she invited us to her house because she couldn't come to the studios and it was memorable.' The session thereafter was better, Hrishi K said. 'I spent an entire say with her doing an unplugged studio session – we recorded all her popular songs with just one acoustic guitar for accompaniment. She talked to us – conversations over a couple of hours with her voice stripped down bare…unlike with large orchestras and big musical arrangements where the singer is drowned out, she realised it was only her voice that would do the talking.' The unplugged session was special because he saw Asha as she would have been throughout her career.

What struck me was her sheer tenacity at getting a song right. She would rehearse every song at least three times before she did a take – she must have done these songs thousands of times in her life, but she insisted on rehearsing. And even the rehearsal was spectacular.

The nuances of her age are not audible to the naked ear. Of course, voice texture is bound to change with age, but with Asha, the sur, the tone, has never gone. She just gets into the whole groove, the rhythm of it. Unless she feels it is perfect, she doesn't go on. At the heart of singing impulsively, this is the person who has based her career on hard work.' Asha spent the whole day at the radio station doing songs that ranged from work with A.R. Rahman to Khayyam to R.D. Burman. 'Surprisingly, I have never faced her temperamental diva side. She is old-school – you have to give her that respect. I can never slap her on the back and say "Hey!" – which I can do with someone like Usha Uthup – or call her Aunty; I call her Ashatai. You know she is what she is, a legend, and you have to behave with her that way too. She gives you respect if you respect her.' And she respects hard work done, as Hrishi K. did before the interviews. She said to him, 'Lagta hai ke tum padke aaye ho, tum sunke aaye ho (Seems like you read up and listened before you came here).'

Music director Shamir Tandon also knows Asha's hard work and professionalism well. He first recorded '*Huzoor-e-ala*' from *Page 3* (2005) with her, and then 'I did a lot of shows with he, including one in Bangladesh, when she was 80.' He saw her perfect showmanship firsthand. 'She was emcee-ing her own show. She didn't have a co-singer, but Sudesh Bhosle was with her for the male voice – she carried the whole show on her own shoulders – at her age! She also played the tumba and the congo drums towards the end of the show. For a lady who was eighty and had a knee issue, it was great!' In Tandon's opinion, 'The goddess is a beast! She is wild, only getting younger every day. She's raring to do new things! Whenever I see her she is bubbling with new ideas, but still stuck with the roots she has had since she started. She is not demanding, asking to travel first class, stay in a suite in a seven-star hotel and such like; she eats everything, stays anywhere. She told my wife, you are North Indian, call me for a meal but don't make the usual fare like *paneer* (cottage cheese) and rajma (kidney beans), but do something different, maybe *karela* (bitter gourd) and *turai* (bottle gourd). She's in another space. I remember in Delhi we were doing a promotion and were staying in a five-star hotel, but she refused to eat anything for breakfast from there; instead, she wanted food from Chandni Chowk. The whole team went there to get parathas and chaat. But with a diet so varied, her vocals are fine – she always says, "As long as you do riyaaz, you will be fine."'

Tandon also saw a facet of the diva he still marvels at. 'She's always turned up before time for recordings. In fact, that can come as a big shock because you plan your day and suddenly you find her turning up early!' It happened to him one morning, when he was lingering at home and was shocked by a call from Asha asking why he was not at his studio, since she had already arrived. 'She is always enthusiastic and interested. She refuses only when she sees that the intent of something or someone is not correct.' Otherwise, 'no' is not a commonly used word in her vocabulary, Tandon found over the years. 'I have never seen her saying no to anyone about anything.' But the singer has a very sensitive side. 'If she feels someone is going to make an ass of her, she will be hurt. She never gets angry, but gets hurt very easily. On the whole she is pretty much a cool cat actually, youthful and exuberant, and can talk about anything under the sun.' And she is willing to work on as many takes as are needed to get a song right, he discovered, when she sent him three different versions of the song she sang, alone in a studio in the United States with no one from the film's crew for company.

There have been more takes that could be counted easily for the lady with the voice that has echoed with clarion intensity for so long. But she has often said that her career is about three stages, each describing a separate phase in her musical existence. First there was O.P. Nayyar, who 'exploited my quality as a bass singer'. Then 'Shankar–Jaikishan tested my singing ability only as it stood.' And finally, there was R.D. Burman, the only composer who managed to get Asha to, as she says, 'uncover my range as a singer. Till Pancham made me explore the inner depths of my own voice, from high *pancham* to low pancham, I did not even know that I could sing with such suppleness of throat!' Today she is still singing strong and true, a lot of which comes from her constant riyaaz – she sings while she exercises, while she cooks, while she travels in her car ... 'Can a *pehelwan* (body builder) stop exercising? If he did, his muscles would become flab, no? Same way, you have to wake up in the morning and fine-tune your vocal cords. I was and still am a professional singer. So it is my duty to do my job to the best of my ability. I like to work and take on something new and challenging all the time. I never say die!' That same attitude percolates into her everyday interactions too, as well as into the increasingly rare interviews and public appearances Asha participates in. 'My age is such that I do whatever I like, say whatever I like. Where is the time for it to catch up with me so that I can feel old? You are as old as you think, *hai na*?' she says with a smile.

That heart has kept her going through success and tragedy, highs and lows, sadness and great joy. All through, her music has been the fuel on which her engine runs, the energy that keeps her going no matter what life throws at her.

Asha is clear on how long she will keep singing. 'The day my voice tells me I can't sing, I'll stop. Until then, I'll keep going. Music is like my breathing,' she has said. 'The day it stops, my breath will stop too. There is so much to do and I'm afraid that there may not be enough time left to do it all. I hope I can keep singing in my next birth.'

6

Sisters Forever

Asha Bhosle and her older sister Lata Mangeshkar shared an interesting relationship. While at home they may have been siblings with four years between them and had a bond that was all about love, affection, respect, sibling rivalry and family revelry, at work it was an entirely different story. Lata was always known to be very correct, very diplomatic and very image-conscious; Asha, in contrast, has always been more blunt, more open, more giving. This reflected well in their singing styles too, with the older sister favouring the classical, and the younger, the mood-based. As actress Poonam Dhillon, who shares a special bond with Asha, said, 'Lataji's personality was not as gregarious and outgoing as Asha's. But they were a very close family, very bonded. Each had her own house, but they had bedrooms connected with each other's and they would go in and out without anyone outside knowing. They were very close, as is the entire family, every generation. They lived close by and met each other regularly.'

So is there really a difference that can be qualified? What makes Asha so unique, with an essence that is not Lata's?

It all started at home. Apparently, she was never thought to be particularly talented, achieving by hard work and diligence rather than inborn talent and any special spark. Her own brother, Hridaynath Mangeshkar, has said, 'She was not gifted like Lata didi. She had an ordinary voice, but she worked on it. And now she has carved her own niche. It has been a long struggle.' Incredible, that may sound, but Asha did always have a problem with confidence, especially where her sister was concerned. O.P. Nayyar, who took credit for the phenomenon that she became, said in an interview that his favourite singer and rumoured lady love had to work for years to create a voice and a style that was very different from Lata's, all so that she could carve her own niche and not have to face the comparison of being 'not as good'. But she has her staunch supporters too. Naushad, for one, believes that Asha has done more of significance than Lata has. More importantly, 'Time has not touched her voice – she can still please pop lovers with rap and remix, even while she has the ability to match the tunes of Ustad Ali Akbar Khan.' Her son Anand Bhosle is, like his mother, forthright in expressing his opinion. He told an interviewer, 'Unlike *mausi* (aunt Lata), she doesn't think with her mind, but with her heart. She didn't get what she deserved, neither from the family nor from the music world or officialdom.'

One notable instance where Lata was cast as the villain of the piece and Asha was the hapless heroine who lost out was when the two sisters were asked to perform for then Prime Minister Jawaharlal Nehru. It was during the Indo-Chinese war of 1962 and spirits were low. Kavi Pradeep, known for his patriotic songs and nationalistic sentiments, was moved by the casualties of the war to compose the poignant '*Ae mere watan ke logon zara aankh mein bhar lo paani/jo shaheed hue hai unki zara yaad karo qurbani*' (O countrymen of mine, shed a tear, remember the sacrifice of those who died fighting for your country). C. Ramachandra, known for tunes that could make listeners react instantly and emotionally, composed the music and was to rehearse with the singers. What most people do not know is that the song was meant to be a duet and Asha and Lata were to sing it together. But something went wrong and Asha refused, reportedly telling a persuasive but doomed to be disappointed Ramachandra, 'I very much want to come, but you know as well as I do that Lata didi will never permit me to do so.' Lata, on the other hand, always said that she wanted to sing this one with her sister. 'I suggested we format the song into a duet with me and my sister Asha (Bhosle). But Pradeepji wanted it to be a solo. Asha too opted out. I tried to convince her to change her mind, arguing that her name had even been printed in the newspapers as one of the singers,' she recalled. 'Composer–singer Hemant Kumar had orchestrated the whole project. I told Hemantda about Asha's decision. Hemantda also tried to convince Asha. But she would not agree. It was left to me to rehearse alone for the song.' What was the real story? Unless someone involved tells all, no one will ever know.

Asha's 'struggle', as many have called it, was rooted in a well-thought-out strategy to at least match her sister's career as a singer, if not beat her at her own game. She was perhaps always aware of the superiority Lata had, if not in talent, in age, those four years giving her an edge, the advantage of time. Many staunchly believe that Lata was more skilled in classical music, better trained and intensely practiced – it is likely that she was, since her father Deenanath Mangeshkar had spent more time with her as the firstborn. As Asha said, 'Classical *toh ghar mein chalta tha*.'

The family also watched a lot of English films. Those voices stayed with Asha, shaping her linguistic awareness and making her phonetically more sensitive; she could use English words without mispronouncing them too drastically, for instance. And since her sister's style and voice had 'cast such a spell on people that another voice in the same style would never stand a chance', she had to come up with something different. 'I felt I had to come up in a different *rang* (colour); I had to cultivate a Western style of singing – I had no choice there,' Asha said. She knew that:

> *Didi and I had to be different singers. Copying her would have meant the end of my career before it had even started. Nobody would have entertained a copy of didi.*

Most critics, fans and listeners agree that the main difference between the divas Lata Mangeshkar and Asha Bhosle is that they were, are and will always be, known for the kinds of songs they sang. On a broad canvas, Lata rarely took risks, sticking to what she was most comfortable with and essaying the music and lyrics that were 'safe'. These had no innuendos, no *masti*, no double meanings; more, they lacked the off-the-classical-scale experimentation that could have made them more fun and trendier. In other words, the timeless songs that Lata excelled in were often based on classical ragas, with lyrics that were sheer poetry. They were 'respectable', because they were sung for characters that had virtue, heroines who were willing to sacrifice all without compromise or bending of scruples and to love with a spiritual fervour, all of it lauded by the audiences that lapped up every soundbyte, be it dialogue or refrain.

Asha, on the other hand, was far less focused on 'goodness'; she sang for the sake of the character, changing her style and attitude, her octave and even her accent, to suit the woman who lip-synced onscreen. She was willing to play with languages and intonation, adding the occasional English word, Hindi colloquialisms and, once in a while, a polite *gaali* (swear word) or two, all without losing touch with the character, the film, its plot and the actor involved.

Shamir Tandon, who composed the music for Makrand Deshpande's offbeat *Sona Spa* (2013), had Asha sing '*Hum neend ka business karte hain*' with Sudesh Bhosle; it was a retro number that needed Asha to sing in the style of singer-comedienne Uma Devi, aka Tun Tun – 'It goes with Asha's personality, as she is naughty even now!' He knew her well, since he had already done the music for *Asha and Friends*, a compilation album on which the singer had actors Sanjay Dutt and Urmila Matondkar, cricketer Brett Lee and others for company. So when he talks about her, it is not just as a fan, but a some-time colleague, a director (of music) and someone who is obviously very fond of her. 'She was the first singer to use English words in Hindi songs, simple words like love or sorry. Those days songs were sung mostly in the classical style, with lyrics written in the Hindustani tradition.' His memories have amused affection flavouring them. 'She once had to sing a very high note. I said to her, "*Tai*, you used to touch the high key when you were young." And that was a challenge! She said, "I still can. I am a true Mangeshkar Maratha. I will do it." And she did!'

That much-vaunted rivalry probably began very early, when Lata was thirteen years old and Asha only nine. It was 1941, in Indore. Their father, Pandit Deenanath Mangeshkar, had just passed away after a heart attack and the two girls chose the only route they could manage to support the family: singing and dancing. Film producer and close family friend Vinayak

Damodar Karnataki became a mentor and the entire clan packed up and moved to Bombay. The plan was to use their talents in Marathi – the language they knew best – movies, singing playback for the female actors and the child stars. Lata made her debut in 1942, while Asha followed a year later, in 1943. That more or less set the tone; Asha was always one step behind her sister. The sisters would need to practise for months before actually recording a song, since technology was nascent and corrections and retakes were more than just difficult. They also had to absorb the character of the actor they were singing for, and reflect that in the voice they used. When they sang together, there was magic in the air. Their first duet was '*Yeh ruki ruki hawayein*' in *Daman* (1951), and they went on to do '*Man bhawan ke ghar aaye*' in *Chori Chori*, '*Sakhi ri sunn*' in *Miss Mary* (1957), '*Main chali main chali*' in *Padosan* and '*Mann kyun behka re behka*' in *Utsav* among many others. When asked in an interview, Asha said she enjoyed singing most with her sister, since 'there was always that challenge *ki kuchh karna hi hai*'.

One person who has examined the sibling story very closely is Sharjah-based paediatrician Dr Mandar V. Bichu, who wrote *Lata: Voice of the Golden Era* (*Popular Prakashan*, 2010), a coffee-table tome that includes some rare photographs of the singer with various musical greats she has worked with over the six decades that she reigned in the film world.

Lata's voice captured my imagination when I was about six years old. The song that did the magic was R.D. Burman's '*Aaja piya tohe pyar doon*' (*Baharon Ke Sapne*, 1967). Sweetness, tenderness, emotions … that voice made me realise that I was listening to something special! The fascination never went away. Later in my medical college years, I started to systematically archive her songs on cassettes and simultaneously delved into other singers' outputs from the Golden era of Hindi film music. I also devoured a lot of written material about that era and those artists. While doing this exercise, I realised that Lata was the predominant musical force of the proverbial golden era (1950–75) and she had played an immeasurable role in practically every major composer's, lyricist's, filmmaker's and actress's rise to artistic and commercial success. No other singer could challenge her in this particular aspect.

In 1996, Bichu wrote the Marathi *Gaaye Lata Gaaye Lata*[5], published by Pallavi Prakashan, attempting to explore the unique equation between Lata and all the major composers of Hindi film music. In 2011, the same theme found a much more researched and analysed expression in *Lata: Voice of the Golden Era*, which looks at the singer as India's top musical and sociocultural icon.

But in all his years of researching his passion, Bichu met Asha just once. 'It was in 2004. Her restaurant (Asha's) in Dubai wanted to create an archive of her songs and I helped them. The reward was a luncheon meet with the diva. They discussed almost everything that he could think of, but her bond with her sister Lata was paramount. Asha is quoted as saying, 'In the early days, after separation from the Mangeshkar family, I sang with didi in many songs – she used to sing for the good girl and I would sing for the bad girl! From my side, I never had any bitterness towards her, but my husband Mr Bhosle didn't like our interaction. Even didi was quite okay when we used to come together for recordings, she would suggest adjustments in my pitch if she felt it was too high for her. She was always cordial, but then she never publicly

---

[5]*Gaaye Lata Gaaye Lata*, by Dr Mandar V. Bichu, Pallavi Prakashan, First edition: 1 January 1996

displayed any emotions. Recently we were watching television together and our classical duet '*Meha aao re*' (*Sangeet Samrat Tansen*, 1962) was on. Didi said, "Such a lovely song!" I also like that song very much. In the movie, two sisters Tana and Riri sing that duet. Then I like '*Chhaap tilak*' from *Main Tulsi Tere Aangan Ki* (1978). It was adapted from Aamir Khusro's popular sufi song by Sukhwinder, who assisted Laxmikant at the time. In fact, Sukhwinder was responsible for many good Laxmikant–Pyarelal tunes like '*Koi shaheri babu*' (*Loafer*, 1973).' In Calcutta's Salt Lake stadium, Asha happily recalls, 'Didi and I did a show where I sang her songs and she sang mine.'

Bichu never directly discussed Asha with Lata at any time. But 'It is quite clear that both of them remain very loving, respectful and cordial in the public domain, but at the same time, it is hard to miss that there is a definite professional rivalry beneath the siblings' affection for each other. Lata complimented Asha as the most versatile singer in Indian popular music. She also accepted that she won't be able to sing some of her younger sister's songs, at least not in the way she (Asha) has sung them.' In the Marathi book *Phule Vechita* (a collection of articles by Lata since 1952, edited by Madhuvanti Sapre and Dinkar Gangal), Lata wrote how the family relations with Asha soured when the younger sister eloped to marry Ganpatrao Bhosle. 'Lata said that she had even beaten Asha at that time! During the early 1950s, there were many Lata–Asha duets, but the sisters would hardly interact, since Mr Bhosle did not approve of them talking with each other. It was when Asha became a mother that the family relations started to improve.'

Bichu analysed how Asha and Lata differed in their approach and personalities. 'Lata's almost immediate success and her top position made her a choosy singer who selected songs carefully on the basis of composer, tune and lyrics, becoming a barometer of class and quality. At the same time, she had the guts to pick almost any newcomer composer and "make" his career just by singing for him. Ask Laxmikant–Pyarelal, Kalyanji–Anandji, Ram Laxman and Uttam Singh! In fact, such was her confidence that she never shied away from locking horns with industry bigwigs like C. Ramchandra, S.D. Burman, Mohammed Rafi or Raj Kapoor on various issues and almost every time came out the winner. She was an uncrowned empress in a male chauvinistic Indian film industry.'

But all this also took its toll. Rumour mills never stopped churning out nasty stories about her, turning an already introverted Lata into a stoic loner. 'She became an iron-willed lady of a few words and even fewer friends.' Bichu saw Asha as a fighter. 'Her long-drawn battle for survival in the early years didn't leave much scope for choice. She sang whatever came her way, initially just to keep the home fires burning. But sadly, this lack of judgement was to become a norm for her entire career, even after she had attained the stature to pick and choose. She was an extrovert, ready to share her deepest pains and pleasures with almost any sympathiser.' It is this initial struggle that made her edgy about her own ability, Bichu believed. 'Throughout her career, to make her musical mark she always needed a proven maestro like O.P. Nayyar, S.D. Burman, R.D. Burman or Khayyam to stand by her.'

In general terms, Bichu found that 'If Lata was sugar, then Asha was spice; if Lata was finesse, then Asha was force! Lata's singing is a classic example of underplay of emotion and subtlety of expression, whereas Asha's is almost like a public performance or an unabashed exhibition of wealth. In Lata's songs the nuances smoothly blended within the main body of the song; in comparison, Asha shows off the nuances like expensive ornaments.' His bias showing strong and clear, Bichu believed that 'Lata's interpretation of any composer's tune is simply the best. Her success with practically every composer across the eras was because of her unique ability to read the composer's mind and render the tune as per his vision and take it beyond, adding that inimitable Lata touch. In contrast, Asha requires a composer who reigns in her enthusiasm to 'show off'. In order to sparkle and dazzle, she often overdoes the oomph factor or the musical calisthenics. That's why her main success is with a limited set of composers who exactly knew her strengths and curbed her weakness for playing to the gallery.'

The various influences that coloured the way the two artistes sang and projected their voices also varied, correspondingly. Lata has always said that Indian musicians have had the most impact and effect on her music and her performance. Her favourites have been K.L. Saigal and Noorjahan, both traditional, classic, of the old school that believed in raga rather than rap. Asha, on the other hand, showed some of that risk-taking acceptance and influences of Shirley Bassey, Umm Kulthum, Santana, Blood, Sweat and Tears and many more that her husband R.D. Burman introduced her to initially, and then her children and grandchildren played in the house. That opened her senses not just to other styles of music, but also to scales and octaves that were different from those used in Indian classical compositions. She once told an international magazine, '[Lata] Didi is a more conservative singer and I enjoy being experimental and working with all types of music.' They both had 'sweet voices' that were 'innocent' (as they were usually described), but the difference in their personalities was clearly reflected in the way they sang. Even though Lata did do an occasional 'sexy' song, it was an understated seductiveness, a gentle vamping of both notes and the actor onscreen and the audience in the theatres. Asha was more blatant, with a far greater flair for the dramatic. Lata tended to stay within the high notes, though she was master of everything she put her mind and voice to. Asha showed off greater full-throated vocal flexibility with elan, acing the lower octaves, perhaps seeing that as her way to cover territory that her sister did not already rule.

It is said that the relationship was strained at home and that showed during performances too. Asha and Lata rarely communicated while on stage, even turning away from each other when they sang together. But that was not because of any animosity, Asha has always insisted. 'Didi has always held the song paper in her right hand, I in my left. So, as we looked at our papers, we would be looking away from, rather than at each other. And there would almost always be an *alaap* in any duet we put over together!' But the bond was strong, so strong that 'Even without being able to look at her to get the cue for the starting, I instinctively knew that if she lifted her hand and her head went back a little, she would start, so I too would synchronise, and our timing would work out perfectly.'

Perhaps that came from Asha's conditioning by Bhosle, for whom Lata once said to radio veteran Ameen Sayani, 'He used to instruct her not to talk to me during duets.' Rumour once had it that Lata was scathingly critical about her sister's relationship with O.P. Nayyar, saying something that upset Asha enough to make the rift between the two visible. Close family friend Gautam Rajadhyaksha said, 'It was not open hostility – their family bonding was stronger than their personal sentiments.'

One person who helped Asha make her name in the Lata-dominated musical world was O.P. Nayyar, the composer with whom she is said to have shared much more than just a professional relationship.

He professed that 'I was successful without Lata's voice. No doubt Lata's voice has a spiritual quality, but it's just that her thin, thread-like voice wasn't suitable for my rich, robust, romantic compositions. Shamshad Begum, Geeta Dutt and Asha Bhosle were my kind of singers.' But Nayyar clarified that while he made some of his best music with and for Asha, he still considered Lata to be the better singer of the two, though he see-sawed in his opinions, perhaps with changing emotions for the person rather than the voice. 'Both are wonderful singers. The flexibility and *murkiyaan* of Asha's voice, the control on her breathing, laughter and sighs, the romanticism in her voice, is indeed nature's gift. These specialities of her voice have embellished and made memorable even some of the relatively weaker compositions of mine. Lata's voice is very melodious and sweet. My personal opinion is that if a voice like Lata's is born once every hundred years, a voice like Asha's is born once in every thousand years.' Later, when he and Asha were no longer on speaking terms, she refusing to give him credit for any change in her career, Nayyar mentioned the irony of R.D. Burman – whom Asha was married to then – giving his best compositions to Lata to sing. This Asha has also talked of, saying that it was a sore point between her and her husband. But perhaps the true irony is time itself.

In the first decade of the 2000s, the age difference became clearly visible and audible. While Lata sang rarely, if ever, in public, her voice on recordings began to sound less firm and clear than it was in her heyday, when she hit the very high notes – for about nine years (1956–65) using what experts call her 'chest voice'. Of course, this could have been because of Lata's chronic sinusitis problem, especially when she was younger. Asha managed to stay strong in the higher ranges for longer (twenty-four years, 1957–81), but she 'cheated', in purist terms, by using her 'head voice', allowing the sound to resonate in her nasal sinuses rather than her chest cavity. Even in *Dil To Pagal Hai*, while Lata tended to quaver a bit in songs like '*Pyar kar*' and '*Koi ladki hai*', Asha belted out '*Le gayi le gayi*' with her well-known level of power and stability. In '*Tere liye*' from *Veer Zaara* (2004), the vocals are definitely far shakier than anyone would have expected of Lata. Asha too is not as sure and firm as she was in her prime, showing a more gentle and careful use of her voice even today as she performs live all over the world for enthusiastic fans.

Kumar Sanu, who has songs with both sisters, insists, 'Of course there was rivalry between the sisters! There had to be. It is healthy.' The singer, formally named Kedarnath Bhattacharya, knows quite a bit about competition in the music business. After all, he has been one of the most popular and prolific playback artistes in Hindi cinema, once even recording an astounding twenty-eight songs in one day! Sanu started with a number for the Bangladeshi film *Tin Konna* (1986), directed by Shibli Sadik, and launched his career in Hindi films with Jagjit Singh's composition for *Aandhiyan* the next year. His respect and admiration of both Asha Bhosle and Lata Mangeshkar shows: 'Ashaji is like God to us. Lata didi, too.' To him, the differences between the two sisters was obvious. 'Competition pushes you to do better every time. If one sang a song one way, the other got pushed to sing her song even better.' Asha was very competitive, he found, she wanted to be the best. 'And so, she has never stopped pushing herself to be better than anyone else. Even now, she puts her heart and soul into whatever she does, whatever she sings.'

Comparisons are inevitable, but Sanu insists that nobody should compare the two women, the two singers. 'Lata had a voice that you can call a *bansuri*, a flute. Asha's is like a violin with an edge to it. Lata's voice had a sweetness, an elegance. Asha's was more expressive, more *bindaas*, more uninhibited.' The performance styles of the two sisters, too, differed: 'Asha would come to performances in her grand saris, flashy jewellery, her hair loose.' In contrast, when Lata sang, 'She would have her *pallu* draped tightly over her shoulders, she would be all covered up.' And they were like that as people too. 'Lata was more introverted, quieter, did not talk much, so her singing was also like that – restrained and elegant, very sweet, not loud or overtly sexy. Asha, on the other hand, is *moohphat*, open, frank, often tactless, like I am. We both say what we want to say, without holding back.' And that same spirit shone through in her music, making her the star in the *dhinchak*, spangle-sexy numbers that she sang so many of – the perfect cabaret voice, the lady with the wicked in her tone.

Amazingly, Asha and Sanu have sung many songs together, but none at the same time, he says. 'By the time I came into the music industry, technology had changed so much that many tracks could be recorded separately and then mixed,' so that it all sounded like a harmonious collaboration. So when the two had a song 'together', Sanu would record first 'because I was very fast, so when she arrived she would tell the music director, "Let Sanu sa'ab finish, he goes so fast; I will wait." I think the longest I have ever taken in the studio for one song is one hour.' Kumar Sanu also has the perfect explanation for the hours of practice that both Asha and Lata would put into getting one song just right. 'In those days, when Ashaji and Lataji started, they would record with huge orchestras, maybe of a hundred people. If there was one mistake by anyone, they would have to start all over again.' That tedious process cost money, apart from time and energy, so it made sense to get it spot-on in as few tries as was possible. Today, of course, things are much easier, with editing software and sound correction programmes that can make any singer, good or bad, sound great. Sanu reminisces, 'My first song with Ashaji was in *Khiladi* (1982) – '*Dekha teri mast nigahon mein*'. The last has been the title song of *Utthaan* (2006).'

Asha Bhosle started her film career as an actor in 1945. She was twelve years old. Her father Deenanath Mangeshkar had died three years earlier, in 1942, and her sister Lata, who was four years older than her, was already set to make a living as a singer. The film in which Asha made her debut into the world of cinema was called *Badi Maa* and starred Kathak queen Sitara Devi and Girish, with the voice of Noorjehan being the most prominent. Datta Korgaonkar aka Datta K. composed the music for this film. The sixteen-year-old Lata sang playback for her sister ('*Mata tere charnon mein*') and more or less set the tone for the future: the elder would always come first, ahead of the younger. Six years later, Datta recorded '*Yeh ruki ruki hawayein*', a song from *Daman* (1951); it featured both sisters in a duet. In 1948, Asha made her first vocal appearance in Hindi films with '*Saawan aaya*' with Geeta Roy (later Dutt) and Zohrabai in Hansraj Bahl's *Chunariya*; her sister sang solo in '*Dil-e-nashaad ko jeene ki hasrat ho gayi tum se*'. The story goes that Bahl initially rejected Lata ... but then realised how the audiences loved her and so, had her sing for the film.

That seemed become the story henceforth. *Andaz* (1949) with '*Koi mere dil mein*' and '*Tod diya dil mera*', and *Barsaat* (1949) with '*Jiya beqarar hai*' and '*Hawa mein udta jaye*' made Lata invincible. And with Raj Kapoor's support, patronage and – it is said – adoration, especially with '*Ghar aaya mera pardesi*' from *Awara* (1951) and '*Jaago mohan pyare*' from *Jagte Raho* (1956), she was the top voice in the movie business for some years. But *Sangam* in 1964 brought with it some unfortunate problems. The film, starring Raj Kapoor and his rumoured beloved then, Vyjayanthimala, was a superb frame for Lata's vocals: '*Har dil jo pyar karega*' (with Mukesh and Mahendra Kapoor), '*O mere sanam*' (Mukesh), '*Yeh mera prem patra*' (Mohammed Rafi) and the ever-popular '*Main kya karoon Ram*'. But the matter of royalty payments put a spoke in the R.K.-Lata wheel. Lata insisted on a 2.5 per cent royalty. She also refused to work with Mohammed Rafi again after a minor argument escalated. And, as a big star and with perhaps under the arrogance of her position at the time, she did not think it was necessary for her to go through long hours of rehearsals and bonding that Raj Kapoor and Shankar–Jaikishan wanted for the music of *Mera Naam Joker*. She argued with Kapoor about '*Ang lag jaa baalama*', a sensuous number that Shailendra had written for Padmini, the star of the film. She refused to be a part of it, saying that it was too blatant, even vulgar. That is when Asha stepped in. Her voice fit, since it was perfect for that kind of sexy song. But even though Kapoor had the young and talented Asha and his stalwart support Mukesh, he had lost the drive he usually had for making the music of his films, which eventually contributed in making his films super successes. This was one of the reasons *Mera Naam Joker* failed. Some say that it was because the music was too obviously sexy, which made audiences uncomfortable, putting them off the movie, which also was rather too 'out there' for mass viewing.

> *Music directors did their bit to keep the sisters apart. They worked almost in different realms, with people who had strong loyalties. Those who favoured Lata – and there were many – refused to consider Asha a potential replacement.*

Like Sajjad Husain, who made music for *Rukhsana* (1955);

Lata Mangeshkar sang '*Tera dard dil mein basa liya*' and then fell ill with the chronic sinus infection that plagued her and could not do more. So Asha took over and it is rumoured that Husain lost interest, letting the younger sister sing as she pleased without direction from him. 'You call Asha Bhosle a singer? After you have heard Lata, how can you bear to hear anyone else? I can't,' he apparently said. But Asha made her mark in the film with solos '*Tumhe hum yaad karate hain*' and '*Din raat zafaye karte hain*' and duets with Kishore Kumar. Naushad too roped in Asha when Lata's sinus trouble flared up during the recordings for *Amar* (Madhubala, Dilip Kumar) to sing '*Ek baat kahoon mere piya*' and '*Radha ke pyare*'. She did a good job, but Naushad insisted that 'Asha did not have that special something that Lata did.' Later, when coaxed by well-known journalist Raju Bharatan, the composer admitted, '*Asha ki awaaz mein se aaj tak bazarupan nahin gaya*' (the mass market quality in Asha's voice has still not gone).

But O.P. Nayyar managed to tap the various nuances of the singer's vocal ability and made her a star, her elder sister's status at the top of the musical heap notwithstanding. He understood that Asha needed longer notes to show off her skill and the elasticity of her vocal chords, and that she was a true alto, steadier in the lower octaves and able to sing very low without losing hold. He also knew that Asha could lose her vocal poise very easily if she knew that Lata had just recorded something fabulous, and needed to be shown that she had a voice that was special, individual, and could evolve a singing style that was unique. Nayyar managed to bolster his pet singer's confidence, especially when it came to her sister, and tap into the latent emotion in her voice. He once said that while destiny may have made Lata great, that same destiny made Asha no less great. All Asha really needed to flower, he insisted, was to work with a composer who truly believed in *her* and not in her sister Lata. After all, if she could be at par with Geeta Roy (later Dutt) – which she did with '*Aaiye meherbaan*' against Geeta's '*Mera naam hai chin chin chu*' in *Howrah Bridge* – she could beat Lata at the vocal stakes. When told this, Lata was scathing – 'O.P. Nayyar is not even worth four annas in our house,' she apparently exclaimed.[6]

But there were others who supported one sister over the other. Their own brother Hridaynath Mangeshkar chose Asha to sing his first Hindi song for *Prarthana* (1969): '*O baanwari jayegi tu kaise piya dware*'. It had no sexy vibe, no sensuousness, no modern beat, but it was perfectly suited to Asha's voice and she sang it perfectly. The film had three songs in it – two sung by Asha, one by Lata.

Khayyam had his own point to prove. Perhaps it was a battle for supremacy against Madan Mohan in which the Asha–Lata divide came into play, or perhaps it was a deliberate attempt to prove the sisters' equality, but when Khayyam composed the music for *Umrao Jaan* and had Asha sing now-classics like *'Dil kya cheez hai', 'In aankhon ki masti', 'Yeh kya jagah hai doston', 'Jab bhi milti hai'* and *'Justju jis ki thi'*, he showed that there was parity. Khayyam could get Asha to match Lata's mastery over the ghazal by asking her to lower her voice an octave, creating award-winning music. He also reportedly convinced her to sing for the period movie by saying that if Lata could do it in *Pakeezah*, which had music by Ghulam Mohammed and Naushad Ali, Asha could easily carry it in *Umrao Jaan*. The National Award that the music director got for the film not only made the ghazal newly popular, but also showed that

---

[6] *Asha Bhosle: A Musical Biography*, by Raju Bharatan, Hay House LLC, 2016.

it was not only Lata who could sing it to the satisfaction of listeners. And it managed to get Asha a certain special status on the success ladder – in the music numbers game, Lata's songs were at positions one through five, while Asha's numbers occupied slots six through ten, with a boost from *Umrao Jaan.*

The rivalry between the Mangeshkar sisters was perhaps rooted in Asha's elopement with ration inspector Ganpatrao Bhosle, who was reportedly Lata's secretary as well. Asha was about fifteen and Lata had just started establishing her own career as a singer, bringing in money to support the family. Obviously, she had to carry the entire burden, unable to depend on her sister for any help. The strain between the sisters was exacerbated by the marital stress Asha was undergoing.

> *Once Asha was married, her husband did not want her to have anything to do with us. She wasn't allowed to see us or write to us. This was the situation for years.*

Lata told author Nasreen Munni Kabeer in an interview for a book on her. 'Bhosle used to take Asha to various music directors and make her audition for them. He believed that she would earn him lots of money and wanted to control her.' When the marriage broke up, Asha set up her own home as soon as she could, with her three children. She has staunchly denied that any issues she faced in her relationship with her sister resulted from her marriage. 'Didi didn't react at all. To date, she has not spoken on this relationship with me.' It could also have been that an acerbic comment Lata made about O.P. Nayyar and his relationship with her sister caused the bond to be stretched. That, too, has never been substantiated.

Asha's son Anand Bhosle saw the relationship between his mother and his aunt grow, evolve, change. He has said in an interview, 'As sisters, they were closest to each other. Mom was four years younger than Lataji and was a cute chubby child whom Lataji would treat like a doll, carrying her around all the time. Once she fell down the stairs when she was holding Mom and you can still see the scar on her forehead from that! They were inseparable – they would go to school together and when the teacher said that two students could not study if only one fee was paid, Lataji refused to go to school again – she always teased my mother saying that she is uneducated because of Mom! Whenever some singer who happened to have an academic degree was praised by a music director, Mom would bluntly tell him that the singer may be educated, but she could never be Lata Mangeshkar – that is how protective Mom was of Lataji.' With the protection came the honouring too. As Anand said, 'I used to often think of my mother singing '*Bahon mein chale aa*' from *Anamika*, instead of Lataji. Actually, Mom has sung it on her tours, but she always says before singing the song that she is simply honouring her sister's talent.' Music writer Ken Hunt had his perspective: 'Lataji seemed like a very different artiste from a distance. From a distance, because I've never spoken to her. As to whose voice suited which experimental approach the better, it would have to be done on a song-by-song basis. To give two examples from the 1950s: I don't want to imagine her doing her sister's '*Eena meena deeka*' (*Aasha*, 1957). Or the other way round – Ashaji doing '*Chandni raatein pyar ki baatein*' in *Jaal* (1952). They were both dissimilar, era-defining songs. In her time, Lataji did experimental songs and she took risks. Still, let's be honest, which of her experimental songs spring to mind ahead of Ashaji's?'

Her forays into newer music may set her above her sister, but there have been some bitter words said about the relationship, mainly by Asha. She once told a television interviewer that

'Didi could have helped me, but she didn't. With her help I could probably have succeeded earlier than I did.' She knew that there was already a huge star in the family, so 'others have had to suffer in spite of being talented'. The downside? 'One had to face constant comparisons.' Asha felt at one stage that the film industry was not giving her what she felt she deserved. She got step-motherly treatment, she has said, and never got the best songs to sing. But she did not blame her sister, not publicly, at least. 'The fact is that after hearing didi's voice, composers could think of no other. I used to feel bad about this. My children had to be brought up decently and be well-settled. I have achieved that. I have no further ambitions. And by God's grace, whatever songs I got became hits.' Music producer–entrepreneur Atul Churamani has observed that Asha wanted her sister's approval for every song that she sang, and looked up to her. Interestingly, 'I know that in her car she has music of Lataji and Ghulam Ali, the only two artistes she listens to.'

Most of the stress and striving for acceptance and approval is not real, some feel. According to composer Shamir Tandon, who has worked with both Lata (*Satrangee Parachute*, *Jail*, *Page 3*) and Asha (*Page 3*, *Corporate*, *Ragini MMS*, etc), the rivalry is media-imposed. The sisters never competed against each other, he believes. 'Ashatai took a different route from didi; her style was different, her way of approaching things was different.' The penchant for portraying Lata as the villain does not sit well with him. 'To say that didi had been overbearing on Ashatai is preposterous!' He does a potted analysis, coming up with the theory that the contrast between the sisters is a matter of personality rather than style of music or ability. Asha is friendly, open, laughs easily, while Lata was more reserved, more aware of her public image, more tactful. 'Their singing was an extension of who and what they are.' Tandon has a notion that does sound logical – Lata earned a God-like status that cannot be shaken, whereas Asha is more human, flawed, someone who is not above criticism and does not take herself too seriously. That is why, he figures, critics have always said that she is better in lighter, boisterous, more sexy songs. For Asha, all this and much more is like the proverbial water slicked off the back of a duck. 'It is like sitting at Chowpatty one evening and enjoying the tamasha,' she has said.

From the perspective of having known both sisters for a while and having a special affection and respect for them, Tandon explained that 'I am very close to the family and I do not think there will ever be another like Asha or Lata. In terms of basic personality, even though people say they were different, they were both pretty much the same – the best human beings, pretty upfront about what they feel. Between the two, I have never seen any animosity; I've only seen love that the two sisters have for each other. Ashaji has always spoken very highly of Lata didi, and whenever I have sat with them for hours – as I have often – she would say, "Didi has sung this song so beautifully", "Didi does that so well", etc. There was this programme on Lataji where fifteen singers – Alka Yagnik, Sunidhi Chauhan, Mahalakshmi Iyer, Shreya Ghoshal and others – paid her a tribute. Ashaji heard them all and said, "They all sing so beautifully, they all idolise and worship didi, but unfortunately, not one of them *is* didi. My didi is my didi, she is very different, there will never be another." She always said that Lata was something else. "We are very proud of her. Didi is number one, I can never be number one."' Professionalism is what the sisters have based their careers on, Tandon recognised, 'They both come prepared with the song, they carry food, they are warm and make you comfortable, they discuss the song with you at length before they start. I have never experienced a single rude or mean moment, or an unfamiliar or unexpected situation that would have been better not experienced. I've never had an iota of a negative thing to say about either. I've never seen any rivalry, whatever the public perception may be.'

Tandon is an admirer of Asha, seeing her as a 'very positive person. In spite of everything that she has been through, I have never seen her cry, except when her daughter passed away, the way she did. Someone who has seen so many ups and downs … she still is so positive and exudes that quality.' The work never stops no matter what she is doing. 'I've seen her do riyaaz – while she is cooking, with the tanpura playing in the background and the food sizzling on the stove. She is still a student, even now. She once told me that Kishori Amonkar was singing something very difficult and she demanded to learn it!' In his opinion, 'She can play another innings of eighty years!'

The secret of Asha's success, Tandon said, was that 'She's always been the innovate-or-perish kind. She has always sounded different from her contemporaries, trying something new and adding something special – a smile, an English word, etc. She can run an empire with her management skills, her innovation, her execution, etc. She is an animal of another nature, one that cannot be categorised, a rare species. There cannot be another like her ever again. To make a mark for yourself when your sister is numero uno just by differentiating your product and your vocality, and the way you are singing, attacking a song, expressing yourself!'

Tandon admired the way Asha had no qualms singing for a vamp or anyone else, with the *bon mot* of 'no risk, no gain, so she has taken such risks and succeeded, made a mark for herself. That is her.'

Whatever his thoughts on the two singers, Tandon is convinced that 'It is inappropriate and incorrect to compare legends. Anyone who ever says the two sisters should be compared is a fool. When it comes to being versatile, Lataji did it in her way; Ashaji has taken risks and they have paid off for her.' Along the way, vocally speaking, 'Of course there is an immense amount of learning, some weight, experience, depth, where to put and how to put in nuances. One thing Ashaji has always said is that there is a gargantuan difference between singing and playback singing. Everyone sings and has learned from great teachers. When they sing with a mic, they do a beautiful job, as with reality show singers. Playback singing is an art too – you need to create a character with your voice. You are not singing a song that has been sung by someone before, but something that becomes yours as it becomes the character in the film. It's true that when a playback singer sings for different actors, you can tell who they are singing for. They read scripts, understand the film, the character, the actor, the situation. She is versatility personified, that is undeniable. She must have been the playback singer with the largest range, from low notes to high ones, always sung with equal ease. I don't think many singers have that range. At no point does she sound shrill or flat. She can also slip octaves from the Western to the Indian styles and she is one of the first to embrace the Western styles.' But all the while, 'I have only seen similarities between them'.

Journalist, filmmaker, public relations expert and much more, S. Ramachandran has an unusual view of the relationship between Asha and her elder sister Lata Mangeshkar. 'You know the Shiva–Parvati legend where the parents told their children, whoever goes around the world first gets the *laddu*? Ganesha chose the easy path, going around his parents, while Karthikeya chose the tough option. That kind of sums up how the two sisters go about their tasks. Over the years, the kind of singing that she has done, you could always tell the difference between Lata Mangeshkar and Asha Bhosle. There is a lot of music both have made. Asha is always trying to do something different. She has never been happy singing the same thing and taking the money back home. It's been a need to be seen differently, to do something more than what she has done before. She did an international collaboration primarily because she wanted to go beyond the realm of what she had done before. A lot of offers have come in from various people to do these projects. What Priyanka Chopra is doing now, Ashatai did long ago. With her, I think it's also the personal tragedies that colour her songs and give them that special emotion, that feeling, instead of a classical correctness that Lata made her forte. There is a huge difference between the two. Lataji was more been there, done that, ready to go. She was four years older, with a far less colourful life than her sister's. She was far more discreet, with no drama.'

Clarification is vital here, since both sisters have denied anything more than normal family dynamics. There was a connecting door between their apartments and they were constantly in and out of each other's homes. Lata was a good dancer, fun person, a totally different woman at home, Asha always said.

> *Of course there was competition between them, both accept, and each always wanted to outdo the other. But it was a healthy competition, all about who could sing better, rather than who could pull the other one down.*

'I always wanted to sing better than didi, but never wanted to bring her down in order to reach her level,' Asha said. 'There is no fun competing against a weaker opponent – that's why I don't enjoy singing these days.' Personally, there may have been stress caused by Asha's very early marriage to Ganpatrao Bhosle. But once she left that relationship, things were more or less back to normal. Then came a new challenge when O.P. Nayyar entered the circle. Lata was never happy with that bond between her sister and the music director. And when the relationship – whatever it may have been – ended, she was happy. And this, in spite of the fact that after being fostered, nurtured and developed by Nayyar, Asha was almost at par with her older sister. As Lata said in an interview, 'We're sisters and we have always been that. I'm very proud of Asha – she can sing every type of song. Thank God she didn't adopt my style of singing, or else we would have become competition for one another! She went on her own path and she has become a very good singer.'

Asha has always maintained that her favourite duet partner has been and will be Lata, 'Because there was always a challenge within that I have to do something special,' she told journalist Shekhar Gupta in an interview. Even today, when there is a comparison made between them, 'That comparison is unavoidable because we are sisters. And since I am the younger one, people will tend to compare my singing with hers. Had I been from outside the family, these things could have been avoided.' On another occasion, she told a story that could be a portrait of their working styles. 'Once I was singing a song with didi under the music direction of Shankar–Jaikishan. The song was '*Kar gaya re*' (*Basant Bahar*, 1956). The song was based on the Indian classical raga Bhairavi, so we did a lot of rehearsals. On the day of recording, I was ready, but didi was still practising. The same evening, I had another recording with a big music director, so I was getting impatient. I waited for a few hours, but didi had still not come into the recording studio, and I lost my temper and yelled at her, "Didi, hurry up! I cannot wait any longer!" She just smiled at me and said, "It is always better to practise thoroughly before recording to avoid errors." That answer left a deep impact on me and all my anger fizzled out. My respect for didi grew manifold after that.'

While with Bhosle and Nayyar things were negative, the story with S.D. Burman was somewhat different. Lata did not sing for the music director for fourteen years because someone she knew had played mischief. SDB refused to have Lata sing his compositions, and Lata refused to sing for him. Asha took over, and cut a swathe through the established echelons of Hindi film music. And then one day, out of the blue, as Lata said, S.D. Burman called her to sing '*Mora gora ang lai le*' and '*Jogi jab se tu aaya mere dware*' for *Bandini* (1963) and the fight was over and done with. It was Sachin da's son Rahul who managed the rapprochement, Lata was told. So when her sister Asha and Pancham got into a relationship that ended in marriage, how could Lata possibly have any kind of objection?

'Comparing Asha Bhosle and Lata Mangeshkar is meaningless. It is just like comparing two flowers!' Satish Chopra, retired banker and writer of *Forgotten Masters of Hindi Cinema*[7] is not so much a fan of musicians as of music itself. His book includes informative essays on K.L. Saigal, Pankaj Mullick, Anil Biswas, Khemchand Prakash, Husnlal Bhagatram, Kidar Sharma, Naushad, Sajjad Hussain, Shyam Sunder, Roshan and Shailendra, composers familiar to the music-loving public through the voices of Asha and Lata. And he has rare photographs too,

---

[7]*Forgotten Masters of Hindi Cinema*, by Satish Chopra (2015); Prakash Books, New Delhi

including of Lata cooking with Anil Biswas and the singer posing with C. Ramachandra, Madan Mohan, Hemant Kumar, Ghulam Mohammed and others. His aim, he has said, was to 'keep the memories of these greats, who provided me immense solace and left an indelible imprint, alive and intact … I wanted to share this feeling with others.' The book was born out of thirty-five years of gathering details and facts and meeting living relatives, friends and families of the artistes, intensive research and a love for music. 'Asha Bhosle was and is a versatile and talented singer, most importantly because she has a very large range of songs of all moods, in a number of ragas. Her ability is obvious in the classical numbers she has done, as composed by Ustad Ali Akbar Khan. And at times she was even better than all her contemporaries, the other female singers of that time, including Lata Mangeshkar.' For Chopra, 'Asha was certainly at her best with her mentor O.P. Nayyar. Her singing in a film like *Howrah Bridge* – just listen to '*Aaiye meherbaan*'! And in *Naya Daur* in particular, she was simply superb – '*Maang ke saath tumhara*', for instance, was beautiful!' The author also spoke of other classically tuned numbers that for him are unforgettable: '*Ab ke baras*' from *Bandini*, and '*Kuchh din pehle*', '*Koi aaya*' and '*Gaa mere mann*' from *Lajwanti*, all composed by S.D. Burman; Naushad's '*Radha ke pyare*' from *Amar*; '*Dharti se door gore baadalon ke paar*' from *Sangdil* (1952), by Sajjad Hussain; '*Tora man darpan*' by Ravi from *Kajal* (1965); '*Nigahen milane ko ji chahta hai*' from *Dil Hi To Hai* (1963); and C. Ramachandra's *Navrang* classic, '*Tu chhupi hai kahan*'.

The maternal role that the elder sister took on when she was still very young and carrying baby Asha around wherever she went became second nature to Lata till the very end. In fact, when Asha was getting ready to make her acting debut as an adult in the thought-provoking and touching *Mai* (2013), she needed a pep talk from didi. Lata assured her sister that she would do a good job, since acting was in her blood – after all, her father, Deenanath Mangeshkar, had been an outstanding stage artiste. But the sense of strict discipline and an ever-present awareness of what is right and proper is tempered with an indulgence she had for a sibling she once mothered, 'Asha is my younger sister. She is four years younger to me and has always hassled me – but I always forgive her. I have to.' And as that younger sister's fond response, 'Only a mother forgives!'

Radiant in ivory and gold

The Mangeshkar sisters (from left to right): Lata, Meena, Asha and Usha

Asha with her sister Usha and brother Hridaynath Mangeshkar

With son Anand

Three sisters: Usha, Lata and Meena

With Sachin Tendulkar

With actor Padmini Kolhapure

Cross-border bonds - Asha with Pakistani playback singer and composer Abida Parveen (on Asha's right), and Bangladeshi playback singer and composer Runa Laila

(From left to right): Gautam Rajadhyaksha, Asha Bhosle and Mickey Contractor

With Aamir Khan

Ready for a shoot

Wearing her favourite pearls and diamonds

Various Moods of the Diva

colors

City

7

Her Music Directors

In a career of over sixty-five years, there are bound to be ups and downs aplenty. And in a world as mercurial and whimsical as the Hindi film industry is, each bump in a long, winding and often lonely road becomes hugely significant, often even changing the course being charted by an individual. There will be drama, spiced with healthy dashes of love, death, heartbreak, betrayal, elation, ecstasy and everything else that could go into the recipe for a super-successful television soap opera. Asha Bhosle's working life has had all these ingredients and much more. Some episodes have been carefully edited, moments deliberately forgotten and vignettes deleted, while others remain, times that are cherished and celebrated with the world.

The work of music director O.P. Nayyar fits neatly into this synopsis. Many have speculated that Asha shared a romantic relationship with Nayyar, and his own words have added fuel to that particular fire on a number of occasions. In an interview done years ago the composer said, 'Now that I am seventy-six, I can say that the most important person in my life was Asha Bhosle. She was the best person I ever met.' Was he speaking only from the point of view of the music the two talented people made together? Or did he imply a far more personal aspect of the bond between them? Whatever the reality of that situation may be, there is no denying that without Nayyar, Asha would never have become the star she has been for so many decades – at least not in the way she did. Nayyar once famously declared that he did not find Lata Mangeshkar's voice suitable, saying that 'her thin voice did not suit my style,' hastily adding when he refused to accept the Lata Mangeshkar Award from the government of Madhya Pradesh that 'I swear I have nothing against Lata Mangeshkar. But sorry to say, my inner soul does not permit me to accept honours in the name of living artistes.' He was successful without Lata, who was then at the top of her musical game, and insisted in an interview with *Filmfare* that 'I have no doubts that Lata is a great artiste. I have never had any problems with her. And that's the truth.'

The partnership began in 1952. Nayyar met Asha when the music of the P.L. Santoshi film *Chham Chhama Chham*, starring Kishore Kumar, Mohana and Pran, was being recorded. Nayyar recalled, 'I thought she sang very well and I told her that.' Asha sang '*Yeh zindagi hai jeene ke liye*', '*Aa pardesi baalam*' and '*Achha wo tum thhe*' as solos, and a number of other songs with Kishore Kumar and one with Jagmohan. Nayyar was obviously happy with her voice and rendition and called her back for *Mangu* (1954), for which she sang '*Bol pardesiya ye tune*', '*Dol mere man pyar se*' and '*Mann more ga*'. 'She made my songs come alive – as did Geeta Dutt and Shamshad Begum. I moulded Asha's voice and gave her style and respectability. I polished her voice, realising that its potential was immense. Till then, composers had considered her fit only for cabaret numbers. I fought with filmmakers for her.' But he did not take credit for Asha's success. 'She is truly a very gifted singer. I could not have done much if she didn't have the talent. And her voice was made for my tunes. It was great to harness that raw sensuality that oozed from her throat.' But he has contradicted himself too, saying that 'I do not claim at all to have made Ashaji what she is today. I only served as a mere instrument to mend her style of singing. When I recorded her song for the first time, she was already a good singer.'

There was joy in every note that seemed to reflect the closeness between music director and artiste. *CID* (1956), a thriller starring Dev Anand, Shakila and Johnny Walker followed, where Asha shared the studio with Shamshad Begum and Mohammed Rafi to record '*Leke pehla pehla pyar*'. The other songs were sung by Geeta Dutt and Shamshad Begum, and every track in the film is popular even today. But it was *Naya Daur* the following year that really pushed Asha onto the centrestage. Nayyar recalls, 'When B.R. Chopra signed me for *Naya Daur*, he insisted that I should take Lata Mangeshkar. I stood my ground and told him that it was either Asha and me or Lata Mangeshkar. He decided on Asha and me.' And with her sweet young tones in '*Maang ke saath tumhara*', '*Reshmi salwar kurta jali ka*', '*Saathi haath badhana*' and '*Udein jab jab zulfein teri*', with Mohammed Rafi and Shamshad Begum for company, the young sister of Lata Mangeshkar was creating her own ground for a hugely successful future and a potential personal partnership. By the end of 1959, buzz had it that Asha and Nayyar were emotionally, perhaps even romantically, involved. Nayyar is reported to have said, 'Since 1959, she was emotionally and professionally involved with me. Asha objected to my working with other singers and made me promise that I wouldn't work with anybody but her. And since I was involved with her, I agreed. I deeply regret the fact that I neglected Geeta, but there were certain songs that only Asha could have sung to my satisfaction.'

It was obviously a happy time for Asha. There was elation

in her voice – a fresh, fizzy note that had not really been heard before in Hindi films. It could have been the singer's youth that inspired Nayyar, or the high of success that created such upbeat songs, or even a bond that the two shared, but the light, peppy, almost-sexy output from the music recording studio rang the bells that heralded a bright future for the music they created together. *Howrah Bridge*'s drawling and seductive *'Aaiye meherbaan'* was easily outdone by the sensuously languid '*Yeh hain reshmi zulfon ka andhera'* from *Mere Sanam*. Asha Parekh crooned '*Jaaiye aap kahaan'* to Biswajit in Bhosle's voice in the same film. The voice turned languorous and inviting in '*Aao huzoor tumko'* (*Kismat*), as a tipsy Babita did her best to charm the same hero. Hit songs from *Tumsa Nahin Dekha* (1957), *Ek Musafir Ek Hasina* (1962) and *Kashmir Ki Kali* (1964) kept the momentum of the partnership going. Nayyar has said that he fell in love with her, which led him to slowly stop working with Geeta Dutt and Shamshad Begum. There was a huge change in the kind of songs that the 'hit pair' of Asha and Nayyar brought to the big screen – they were modern, contemporary, playful, sensual, with a delightful give and take between the hero and the heroine, with both on an equal footing in the relationship, whatever it may be. Nayyar has said that Asha was the love of his life: 'They say that when a woman loves, she loves with her soul. And when she hates someone, she becomes *Chandi*, the warrior form of Shakti. That was true of Asha too – when she sang for me, she would put her heart and soul into it.'

And then the stars stepped in. According to Nayyar in an interview many years later, 'I know astrology very well. I knew that one day I had to part with her. I also knew that I was reaching the end of my career. Something also happened that upset me, so I left her.' He believed that if 'I didn't leave then, I would be kicked out. And there were also personal differences between us. I realised that one should never get involved with a career-oriented woman; you will always be only her second love. She will throw you out before she lets go of her career.' Nayyar remembered that 'We split on 5 August 1972. It was then that Asha left that beautiful scar on me.' The memories are fond. 'She is a good mother, a great artiste and a wonderful human being. It's the mean world that taught her how to be cunning. She wasn't like that when I first met her.' Fate may have separated the composer and his muse, but '*Chain se hum ko kabhi*' from *Pran Jaye Par Vachan Na Jaye* brought them both awards a few years later. The song is often said to describe the relationship between the two – poignant, passionate and filled with pain. It became hugely popular and lauded, winning the most prestigious award of the movie industry at the time. But Asha did not attend the Filmfare awards ceremony. 'She probably felt I deserved it, not she – and she was very bitter about it (the break-up),' Nayyar mused. He received the black lady statuette in the glittering awards ceremony; gossip has it that he threw it into a garbage heap on his way home that night.

He was perhaps at the lowest he had been; the film was not successful and the song was edited out of it. His career was almost over. His family had not forgiven him for being involved with Asha while he was still married. When he took on Krishna Kalle, 'Asha could not bear it. That was the last I saw of her. But she has not been an ungrateful person.' The offers petered out, the songs did not work, the singers failed. Nayyar was resigned to what would happen. 'It was destined. The girls were not to be blamed. I worked on Asha for fifteen years, whereas these others were with me at most for one or two films. Given time, I am sure I could have worked wonders with them too. But what would have been the point? I knew my bad period had begun, so I left the industry.'

But there is another story that made the rounds. Buzz had it that one day Asha saw Nayyar slap her adolescent daughter. That made her she walk out of his life forever. The 'marriage' that those two had participated in, ceremony and all, may have been invalid, legally speaking, but at that point it was at an end, even from the point of view of a professional partnership. There was nothing left except history and Asha never acknowledged that beyond a very cursory mention of having worked with the musician. She avoids the very thought of him, it seems, as she has said that 'Whichever composer gave me work, it was because my voice was suited to his music at that point. No *one* musician did me any favours by asking me to sing for him.' She accepts that *Naya Daur* was the launchpad for her super-successful career as a playback singer, but gives the credit for that first big break to B.R. Chopra, the producer, never acknowledging the role that the music director played in her popularity after that film.

Nayyar had his version. When asked to describe Asha as a person and a singer, he was enthusiastic, 'As a woman, she was superb. She was a great mother to her children. She was so innocent and straightforward, though of course with experience, she became shrewd and clever in dealing with the world. She was not like that when I first met her. They say that when a woman loves, she loves with her soul. As a singer, she understood the feelings, emotions and sadness in my music and gave me what I wanted – she sang all my songs with her heart and soul. All said and done, she has not been an ungrateful person. But she never kept in touch with me. And though the Mangeshkar sisters were great artistes, they never had any schooling or breeding. So they have suffered from complexes.'

Though Nayyar never worked with Lata, he always respected her voice and talent, as he said, 'People came to me with offers where they wanted her to sing. I refused. I am the only successful music director to have never had a song sung by Lata.'

As important in the career of the songstress who is often easily identified as just 'Asha' was Khayyam. Her partnership with the music director began with his first film, *Biwi* (1948), for which she sang '*Birha ki raat mose*'. *Phir Subah Hogi* (1958) had Asha singing '*Phir na kijiye meri gustakh nigah ka gila*' with Mukesh, and *Dard* (1981) is remembered for '*Qubool kijiye*' and '*Pyaar ka dard hai meetha*' in Asha's tones. But it was *Umrao Jaan* that truly showed the singer's classical ability, as she was asked to sing in a lower scale than the one she normally used. '*In aankhon ki masti*' and '*Dil cheez kya hai*' are still favourites at film events today. Lata would perhaps have been the natural choice for the playback voice of Rekha in the film; Khayyam has his explanation: Rekha had a fairly low-pitched speaking voice and Lata's higher tonality would have created a dissonance between the speaking and the singing voices for the heroine. Additionally, Lata had made a memorable mark with her songs for *Pakeezah*, based on a similar storyline as *Umrao Jaan* – about the life of a courtesan. The music director made a wise choice, and garnered a National Award for his work on the movie.

Khayyam gives the pride of place to '*Suhana hai mausam salona mera balam*' from *Footpath* (1953). It is, he claims, Asha Bhosle's first ever cabaret number. But the music director has a gripe about the song: 'I gave Asha her first cabaret number for *Footpath*, but does anyone talk of that? Only O.P. Nayyar and R.D. Burman are given credit for making her sing these kinds of songs – that really hurts!' In the fifty-nine years of his career, Khayyam composed 624 songs for films and other projects. Asha sang a phenomenal 111 of these, according to the book *Khayyam: The Man, His Music*, an anthology of the music director's work put together painstakingly by Vishwas Nerurkar and Bishwanath Chatterjee in 2006. The book was released by Asha, who talked about their first encounter – it happened in Borivali, and Khayyam thought she was the maid come to clean his house!

Remember '*C-A-T cat, cat maane billi*'? That cutely funny number from *Dilli Ka Thug* was composed by Ravi and sung by Asha and Kishore Kumar. They also did '*Yeh raatein yeh mausam*' together for the same film and these songs made them popular across time. No wonder then that music composer Ravi always insisted that Asha was one of his favourite singers. The collaboration between composer and singer began with the hugely popular lullaby '*Chandamama door ke*' from *Vachan*.

Then came the string of successful bhajans in *Gharana*, *Grihasti*, *Kajal* and *Phool Aur Patthar*'s emotionally powerful '*Sun le pukaar*'. This was in such contrast to Asha's image at the time of a voice best suited to B-grade titillating that to many, even those connected with music in the film world, it came as a surprise that she could sing numbers imbued with spiritual longing, paeans to the divine. Mellifluous tracks for movies like *Chaudhvin Ka Chand* (1960), *China Town* (1962), *Gumrah* (1963), *Waqt* (1965), *Bahu Beti* (1965), *Humraaz* (1967), *Aadmi Aur Insaan* (1969) and *Dhund* (1973) cemented the musical partnership.

Asha Bhosle, like many singers, did not restrict herself to singing in Hindi or Marathi, her mother tongue. She branched out into south Indian languages and composers working in southern cinema too. One of her favourites was Ilayaraja, with whom her collaboration began in the early 1980s.

It started with *Sadma*, (1983) the Hindi version of '*Moondram Pirai*' and the sultry *'O babua yeh mahua'*. Asha said, 'I have always enjoyed singing for Ilayaraja for his unusual rhythm pattern. I did not realise this would turn into such a sensual song – it is picturised on Kamal Haasan and Silk Smitha. It is just *wow*!' She slid into Tamil for *'Shenbagame'* from the 1987 film *Enga Ooru Paatukaaran*. The 2000 theme song for '*Hey Ram*', *'Nee partha parvai'*, translated into *'Janmon ki jwala'* in the Hindi version, had Hariharan providing the male voice. She sang *'Mazhai megham'* for *Sakkarai Panthal* (1988), *'Adikaalai neram'* for *Naan Sonnathe Sattam* (1988) and '*Oh butterfly*' (*Meera*, 1992) among others, for the composer.

One person who always wanted to work with Asha was Hariprasad Chaurasia, who worked in collaboration with Shiv Kumar Sharma – the duo was known as Shiv–Hari. Chaurasia was born into a family of wrestlers in Allahabad. He lost his mother when he was just five and his interest in music would have earned him a beating from his father Srilal, a well-known wrestler who had a hot temper and an agenda chalked out for his son. So the young Hariprasad led a dual life – training to be a wrestler to make his father happy and learning how to sing to make himself happy. He soon found that his voice did not have the range needed for classical vocal music, so he switched to the flute, 'an instrument you can sing through'. The truth had to come out one day. The teenage Chaurasia was offered a job as flutist with All India Radio in Cuttack, Orissa, and had to tell his father what it was all about. 'To become a musician, I had to leave home,' he said. Soon Bombay beckoned. In 1962, he moved to the city, where the film world found him. O.P. Nayyar, S.D. Burman, Salil Choudhury, Roshan, Madan Mohan – they all wanted him. It was exciting, and a process of growing up for him.

'I was brought up in the film industry,' he said. 'Long before Shiv–Hari, I was a musician playing different kinds of songs, all day and all night, all the time in the studio with my flute, my toothbrush in my pocket and a handkerchief. I would just wash my face and start playing the flute.'

Bombay was an expensive city, Chaurasia found. 'My pay was nothing. Just going from one place to another and having a cup of tea and a snack used up all my money. It was kind of a punishment, getting the same payment and living in a metropolitan city. But I was here and I had to do something to live. The film industry seemed the place to be. Soon I was playing for Lata Mangeshkar and Asha Bhosle and so many new singers. They would come to the studio and we would work, sometimes for three or four days at a stretch. We worked as a family. I was associated with everybody, not just the Mangeshkar family, but also Hemant Kumar, Manna De, Mohammed Rafi, the great singer Shri Ramachandra, Noor Jahan...there were many others. I was running from one studio to another – I refused to let go of a single rupee! Sometimes I would play three recordings at one time, there would be three flute boxes around me.' He started composing music in 1972–73, after gaining much experience with some of the great music directors. 'They were like different gharanas of music. If you entered the studio, you would find a different kind of sound, depending on who was composing. Each had a different stamp.' And he did some private work too, including albums with Lata in Marathi, 'There would be myself, the tanpura and Lataji. We recorded the *Dnyaneshwari*, the *Gita*, Meera bhajans...so many lovely songs!'

It was then that he met Asha Bhosle. 'She was really wonderful! What a character, what freedom of singing, what a voice! Lata was a little reserved, but Asha was open, free...

My goodness! I have never heard or seen this sort of thing. Anybody could ask her to do anything and she would sing better than them.' He discovered that Asha could sing any kind of song: 'classical, light, ghazal, modern, jazz, anything. *Ishwari shakti*, that is what Ashaji has that nobody else does. The kind of songs she sang needed courage, a special talent, and she had that. And to convince people that you can sing whatever they ask you to … what fabulous ghazals she has sung for Ghulam Ali – *Wah!* Could anyone else sing like that?! Some people can sing in one particular style; she could sing in any style and she sings like that even now. She can do anything; she is such a bold lady. When she is recording, she owns the studio, the music, the tune, the audience – everything is hers. Her songs, her voice, her rendition, her style, are unmistakeable. Nobody can mistake her for anyone else. She has a specialness. People have copied her, but she is unique. I am a great fan. I love her singing.' His admiration rings clarion. 'She was childlike, yes, but whatever she felt was shown, open, and obvious. The songs she sang for O.P. Nayyar were special. They worked so well together. The bond between them was fabulous, the love and affection shows.'

Sadly, Chaurasia never composed for Asha. 'She would even get angry with me for that. Ashaji did not do that many non-film songs, and none with me. There will never be anyone like her – but then there will never be anyone like anyone else, be it you, me or anyone else! She has suffered, yes, but she is just what she is, whatever God made her.' He did create songs that she eventually sang, in *'Yeh kaafile yaadon ke'* and *'Faasle hain bahut'* from *Faasle* (1985), *'Tera karam hi tera vijay hai'* and '*Rakhna athanni sambhal ke*' from *Vijay* (1988) and *'Parbat se kaali ghata'* in *Chandni* (1989).

A few years earlier, life had started getting exciting for

Asha. It was 1957. One of the most harmonious – literally speaking – partnerships of the day had fallen apart. The prince of Tripura, Sachin Dev Burman, had broken off all ties with his once-favourite singer, Lata Mangeshkar. The story goes that he wanted changes made to a song that had been recorded and she was too busy to do so. It was a time when Lata was incredibly busy and did not have a moment to spare to re-record '*Pag thumak chalat balkhaye*' for *Sitaron Se Aage* (released in 1958), as S.D. Burman wanted. He called her, over and over, but she could not fix a date for the job. After all, this was the time that Lata was hugely in demand, completing work in hand, singing for almost every film being made, doing concerts, foreign tours and more. But for every music director, his compositions are obviously of primary importance, and Sachin *karta*, as he was often called, was no exception. He firmly believed that the singer should give his request priority, especially since he had given her some of her best songs to sing. But like anyone with an artistic temperament, he reacted to not getting his way with drama and attitude – he cut Lata off.

Then, he got the best revenge that could be dreamed – S.D. Burman signed on Lata's sister, her reported rival, Asha Bhosle. She had made her foray into the film world, but her elder sister always won any assignments that were worth taking on. Lata's star was shining brilliantly and nobody else was considered for a song unless the reigning diva was not available. So when S.D. Burman invited Asha on board his very successful train to the big time, she jumped on to it. It was indeed a big breakthrough for her. In those two years – 1957 and 1958 – she turned her image around completely, moving far away from the shadow cast by her sister and into a new limelight. She was no longer 'Lata Mangeshkar's younger sister who also sings'. She was Asha Bhosle, the singer who soon became a significant part of Indian film history. As Sachin-*da* said, 'Lata's sister is a top-class artiste. She has a youthful vigour in her voice.' And he managed to tap that.

The songs she sang for S.D. Burman were popular, even if the films did not always do well. *Chalti Ka Naam Gaadi* (1958), *Kala Pani, Insaan Jaag Utha* (1959), *Sujata* (1959), *Bambai Ka Babu* (1960), *Kala Bazaar* (1960), *Manzil* (1979) – there were so many and almost all of them had a unique flair that had become so exclusively Asha's. SDB taught her how to add a little *adaa*, or attitude, flavouring the lyrics with a mood-setting giggle, a sigh, a husky 'oh' and more. The results were fabulously appealing, and Asha uses those touches even when she sings on stage today. The flirty *'Haal kaisa hai janaab* ka' (*Chalti Ka Naam Gaadi*) that Asha sang with Kishore Kumar is still heard today, as is her delightful coaxing as Madhubala's voice in '*Achcha ji main haari chalo maan jao na'* as Mohammad Rafi cavilled with all Dev Anand's most charming gestures in *Kala Pani*. Equally popular was her vocal partnership with Geeta Dutt in *'Jaanu jaanu ri'* from *Insaan Jaag Utha* and *'Dekhne mein bhola hain'* with its folksy Punjabi lilt and teasing tone from the Dev Anand-Suchitra Sen starrer *Bambai Ka Babu*.

But it is '*Tum jiyo hazaaron saal'* from *Sujata* that is perhaps most interesting, with its backstory and current status. Asha sang it in the final version, but it was credited for years to Geeta Dutt; in actual fact, Geeta did sing the original, but that was re-recorded by Asha and included in the film. Recordings cited Geeta as the singer for many years and Asha did not correct that – not wanting to scrap over credit, it is said, because that seemed to her to be undignified. Rahul Dev Burman, who was SDB's assistant at the time, issued a clarification, and record companies made the correction. And twenty-seven years later, Asha admitted that it was her voice. The song is often used as the Hindi '*Happy Birthday*' track even today!

Burman did something that nobody expected, especially his singers. He reversed roles. It happened when, after five years, Lata came back into the fold. It was Sachin's son Rahul Dev Burman's idea – he wanted 'Lata didi' to sing his first song as an independent music director, and his father had to agree. Lata came back to SDB with the raga-based '*Jogi jabse tu aaya*' and '*Mora gora ang laye le*' from *Bandini*. But Asha was not abandoned. She sang '*O panchhi pyare*' and '*Ab ke baras bhej bhaiyya*'. And listeners were stunned when they realised that a switch had happened – Lata had sung the light and frothy numbers, while Asha had to her credit those that had gravitas, sadness, depth. But her forte was seduction, mischief, a sense of madness almost, that she showed off to great effect in '*Raat akeli hai*' from *Jewel Thief* – the sudden rise in volume and pitch in the line '*Jo bhi chaahe kahiye*' was a surprise that Burman threw in and gave Asha careful instructions to add in. And it worked, especially with the sinuous moves of Tanuja to spice it up visually.

The relationship between Asha Bhosle and S.D. Burman took a new turn when she married his son Rahul in 1980. While Sachin may have given his favourite Lata his best work after the singer and composer reunited, Rahul composed some of the most memorable contemporary works especially for his new partner in life and in song, Asha.

The bond was strong, and while some say that there was never a formalised marriage between the two, Asha has made it clear that she was indeed wedded to Rahul. And it was made in heaven she believed, saying that 'R.D. Burman has come into my life like a balm. Ours is not like a marriage of sixteen-year-olds, it is a communion of minds.' That is not to say that there were no problems. There were. And they carried into Asha's future too. Rumour has it that she sequestered her aged mother-in-law Meera Deb Burman – also an accomplished singer, lyricist, poet and dancer – in an old age home for the rehabilitation of paraplegics in Navi Mumbai. Sachin's wife was looked after by nurses at the facility for about seven months, but was moved back to her son's home in September 2005. Her condition fast deteriorated further and she passed away in November that year at the age of eighty-four. Asha announced it, but kept the details private.

For some years before this, the singer had taken a backseat, allowing the newer generation to bask in the limelight. Voices that were stronger and far more modern – even considering Asha's adaptability and youthful tone – were being given precedence by the filmmakers who saw Bhosle as the past rather than the future they sought. 'There was a certain amount of hesitation' to approach her, she recalled in an interview. And those who knew her and her husband R.D. Burman – like Ramesh Behl, for one, who made films like *Anamika* (1973), *Kasme Vaade* (1978) and *Indrajeet* (1991) – had 'either passed away or had scattered in different directions', she said regretfully. But what really pushed Asha out of the spotlight was, she felt, 'I've never mixed with the film industry; I've never gone to parties or tried to strike up friendships for professional gain, from the beginning. I have never sent bouquets of flowers and tiffins of food to film people. I have never indulged in fake *wah-wahi* (praise).' Instead, 'I devoted my time to bringing up my children and looking after the house, content in my own little world. I thank my lucky stars that I have been able to maintain my dignity and integrity. And when my songs are appreciated by the public and the critics, that is one more feather in my cap.'

That cap was refurbished dramatically by a brand-new talent that burst into the world of Hindi films: A.R. Rahman. He is often called the 'Mozart of Madras' and is still best remembered for his Oscar-winning work for Danny Boyle's hugely celebrated *Slumdog Millionaire*, more recently making a splash internationally with the virtual reality film, *Le Musk* (2024), which he produced, directed and wrote. But he was first heard in non-southern circles with compositions for Ram Gopal Varma's *Rangeela* (1994), starring a newly sexy Urmila Matondkar and ageing heartthrob Jackie Shroff. Rahman created music for the film that 'terrified' its director, who said, 'The songs were so awesome, I felt I wouldn't be able to do visual justice to them.

'He composed '*Hai Rama*' and '*Tanha tanha*' in Goa and the title track, '*Ho ja rangeela re*' in my flat in Mumbai. For '*Hai Rama*' I gave him the brief to create a sound like '*Kaate nahin kat-te*' from *Mr India*, but his composition sounded like a bhajan. I told him so and Rahman, who has no arrogance, immediately redid the tune. His music always comes from the heart.' And the composer's choice was Asha, about whom he said, 'She has got a voice with a face. She is still sixteen at heart!'

It was that same film that brought Asha, then sixty-two years old, back into the musical reckoning. She sang '*Tanha tanha*' and '*Ho ja rangeela re*' for Rahman, new compositions with a new style. Like her sister Lata Mangeshkar, Asha had decided years earlier to stop accepting or even vying for awards for playback singing, and music directors were starting to shy away from her. But a special honour was decided on by *Filmfare* magazine for her work in *Rangeela*. For '*Tanha tanha*', she received the Filmfare Special Jury Award in 1996. She said of Rahman's work, 'He understands the youth of today – he has brought about a freshness, a new sound to film music. He is always experimenting, doing something different, which is very inspiring for a playback singer.' And the rewards poured in, more as fan reactions than trophies, but that is what was important. She recalls, 'Some months after *Rangeela* released, I was in San Francisco where I had gone to cut a record, *Legacy*, with the great Ali Akbar Khan sahib. And I started getting numerous phone calls telling me that my songs in *Rangeela* had become extremely popular. '*Tanha tanha*' was topping the charts! I felt like what my mother had said was coming true. It's because of what my mother and my father made me believe in – honesty and straight talk – that I am still here after all these years. Imagine, I have won the Filmfare Special Award at the age of sixty-two!' And with that recognition came more offers of work, some from the same people who had avoided her a short while earlier.

But *Rangeela* was only the start of a happy collaboration between Asha and Rahman. The two spoke in English, since 'He doesn't know Hindi fluently. When I was singing I would ask him, "How is it? Alright?" and he would quietly say, "Yes, it sounds alright." And after *Rangeela* I have sung many of Rahman bhai's scores – for *Tara Rum Pum Pum* and for Mani Ratnam's Tamil film.' And there was music not related to films too that they planned to work together on. 'When he gets time off from his assignments, I think his project (a non-film album) will become a reality. I have a feeling that it will be a ground-breaking album!' In 1999 came *Thakshak*, in which talented actor Tabu did what could be called an item number. '*Rang de*' was fast-paced and complex, a challenge for any singer. Asha said, 'It was a difficult song that A.R. Rahman made me sing. I felt breathless, as the lyrics and the tune coiled and overlapped.'

The two went on to do a number of songs together. '*Radha*

kaise na jale', with its gentle old-world charm, had Gracy Singh dancing as Aamir Khan watched, in the award-winning *Lagaan* (2001) directed by Ashutosh Gowarikar. With Asha's voice setting the musical scene, Urmila Matondkar bopped along to '*O bhanware*' (*Daud*, 1997). '*Kahin aag lage lag jave*' (*Taal*, 1999) featured Aishwarya Rai, as did '*Vennila vennila*' from Aishwarya's first film, the Mani Ratnam directed *Iruvar* (1997, Tamil). The sultry '*Dhuan dhuan*' from M.F. Husain's *Meenaxi: A Tale of Three Cities* (2004) had his then-muse Madhuri Dixit in the lead role. In spite of the challenges that Rahman threw at Asha and the complex and unusual flavour of his compositions, she maintained that 'He is very talented; he is open-minded and lets me improvise, but I still think that R.D. Burman was in a different league.' The affection the composer and singer have for each other showed loud and clear a few years ago, when she turned seventy-seven. Asha tweeted, 'Many thanks to A.R. Rahman for greeting me on my birthday with seventy-plus red roses. Innovative style, like his music. Thanks.'

But years before Rahman, Asha found a close friend in composer Jaidev, who was once S.D. Burman's assistant. She considered him special, since he had always stood by her, personally and professionally, even though her sister Lata was his favourite singer. Almost all his songs were based in purely classical ragas. And with Jaidev, Asha pushed her vocal skills further than she herself perhaps believed she could. He insisted on perfection even in the most intricate of *harkat*s and *murki*s, and the *sapaat taan*s had to be timed just so. The music the two of them made together was memorable, even if the films the songs were set in were not successful.

There was the thumri in raga Pilu, '*Hum sang naina kaahe ko lagaye*' from *Joru Ka Bhai* (1955) and the unforgettable '*Raat ke pichhle pehron main*' from *Anjali* (1956), based on the rare raga Chandranandan that was invented by Jaidev's guru Ustad Ali Akbar Khan, and the popular raga Malkauns. *Mujhe Jeene Do* (1963) had '*Nadi naare na jao Shyam*', based on Bilawal, flirty and folksy, while the more pathos-laden and pleading '*Jaa ri pawaniya*' from *Do Boond Paani* (1972) with its roots in Maand was a musical contrast. '*Ek to yeh bharpur jawaani*' from *Reshma Aur Shera* (1972) has erotic undertones, with a solid rooting in rhythm and ragas (Shivaranjani, Khamaj and Kalavati), while the Meera bhajan in *Des*, '*Piya ko milan kaise hoye ri*' (*Andolan*, 1975) is more staid, evocative, prayerful. The duo created magic with about seventeen songs. They also made a music album together, with non-devotional songs and ghazal compiled into *An Unforgettable Treat*. When Jaidev passed away in 1987, Asha released a collection of songs he had composed for her but were never widely heard, called *Suranjali*.

Time passes fast. In the film industry in particular, what is flying off the shelves today is well past its sell-by date tomorrow, be it people, stories or songs. Musicians walk the same well-trodden path. History has proof – so many composers, arrangers, singers have come in with the proverbial bang and then faded into time, often ending their days dependent on family, or unknown and destitute. There have been others who have managed to create a legacy for their children, grandchildren and other relatives. Sardar Malik was one of them.

Known more for being music director–composer–singer Anu Malik's father, Sardar Malik was born in 1925 and trained as a dancer by Uday Shankar at Almora and in music by Ustad Allauddin Khan. His voice and singing style got him work as a singer and a composer, but he was rooted in reality – he knew that with voices like Mohammed Rafi and Mukesh ruling at the time, he would never find the prominence he could earn in another branch of the profession, so opted for music direction instead.

The 1950s was the time of change. In Bombay, he worked in films like *Renuka* (1947) and *Stage* (1951), which did not do particularly good business. But in 1953 he, along with Ghulam Mohammad, was part of *Laila Majnu*, remembered for songs like '*Dekh li ay ishq teri meherbani*' and '*Baharon ki duniya pukare tu aaja*'. And what made these more special was the voice that sang them: Asha Bhosle, with Talat Mahmood. She had sung '*Dil machalne laga*', '*Kisi ke ghar mein to ghee ka chirag*', '*Jagmagati Diwali ki raat*' and '*Jisko na lagi ho chot kabhi*' for *Stage*, and her voice was perfectly controlled and flexible at the time. The early 1950s were ruled by Lata Mangeshkar and Geeta Dutt, so a new and talented singer had to fight her share of battles to win attention. Though with Malik's compositions, Asha managed to hold her own. *Thokar* (1953) made Malik a name to be reckoned with in Hindi film music, especially with songs like '*Jhilmil sitare chanda ke dware*', '*Hawa gungunaye fiza muskuraye*' and '*Yeh kaisi raat aayi hain*' sung by Asha.

The two – music director and singer – managed to capture audiences and loyalties with their work in that decade: '*Tum salamat raho hazaar baras*' from *Aulad* (1954), '*Ho gaye gentleman balam mere*' from *Taxi 555* (1958) and '*Kisi se aankh ladi badi mushkil hai*' in *Maa Ke Ansoo* (1959). And then came *Saranga* (1961), the film that is still considered one of the best in the history of Indian cinema and the definitive best of Sardar Malik's works. It had Lata given more prominence, but Asha's '*Kin ghadiyon mein preet lagayi*' made its mark. Malik never hit the big time or had the top-rung movies in his repertoire, but he gave everything he did his best, it is said. His last film was *Gynaniji* in 1977, which had four songs, each including an ensemble of singers, Asha being a part – she sang in '*Ek pyaar ne yaara dekho*', '*Aayi rut ab pyaar ki*', '*Aao sunao dus guruon ki*' and '*Mai hoon aashiq tere geet ka*'. Malik passed away in January 2006, but left behind a legacy: his children, Anwar (Anu), Abu and Daboo. While Abu manages stage events and Daboo acts, directs and composes music for films, it is Anu who is best known.

At just over sixteen years old, Anu Malik started his career as a music composer in 1977. His father Sardar Malik was unwell and needed to take time off. But *Hunterwali 77* (1978) could not wait – there were songs to be completed so that it could be released. Actor–producer Mohan Choti asked Anu to step in, with '*Zulmon sitam par itrane wale*'. It was not the young lad's first shot at composition, but his work in *Maano Ya Na Maano* a couple of years earlier was never seen, since the film was not completed, hence remained unreleased. Though *Hunterwali 77* was not a success, Anu's first song was with Asha Bhosle. And that, he has always said, was an auspicious beginning. Recognition came with *'Aasman pe likh doon naam tera'* from *Ek Jaan Hain Hum* (1984), and while ups and downs have shadowed his career, he is today one of the well-established names in the film music business. Real success followed after the release of *Phir Teri Kahani Yaad Aayee* (1993), a made-for-television film by Mahesh Bhatt.

Anu Malik's style cannot be clearly defined. He is versatile, and while rhythm is central to every composition, each one is distinct and often features high on the music charts. He has worked extensively with most contemporary vocalists, including Asha Bhosle, who has sung in his first complete film *Sohni Mahiwal* (1984): '*Rab tumhe maaf kare*', *'Bol do mithe bol'*, *'Mujhe dulhe ka sehra'* and others. *'Kitaabein bahut si'* from *Baazigar* (1993), just four lines in *'Jab dil mile'* in *Yaadein* (2001) and '*Yeh lamhaa filhaal*' from Meghna Gulzar's first film *Filhaal* (2001) are especially memorable. And more recently, the singer and the composer have worked together for a common cause – no, not a film, but a reality show, *Indian Idol*, where both were on the judging panel. While he was strict and severe, she was the softer arbitrator, encouraging and maternal. As Ashaji said, 'Anuji makes participants nervous with his harsh comments, but they should not feel bad about it, and take his advice in a positive way.'

Anu is all praise for his co-judge and star vocalist. He said, 'There can never be another Lata Mangeshkar, Asha Bhosle, Kishore Kumar or Mohammed Rafi – they are in a different league. Nobody can be like them. Nobody can reach their level. I cannot explain the phenomenon of these legendary people!' And when he received the Asha Bhosle Award in 2010, he was moved to tears on the stage. The honour was established in August 1996 to provide upcoming young artistes with a platform to nurture their talent. The first award was given to Asha's sister Lata, following which Khayyam, music director Ravindra Jain, music master Bappi Lahiri and Pyarelal of the composer duo Laxmikant–Pyarelal received it. The positive vibe between Anu and Asha was proved once again when the music director finished the work in *Ghatak* (1996) and *Gang* (2000) that R.D. Burman's sudden passing had left incomplete. Asha sang in both films: '*Aaki naaki*' in *Ghatak* and '*Chhod ke na jaana*', her husband's composition, in *Gang*.

Even as Asha was trying to find her own niche and steady partnerships to take her playback singing career to the heights that her sister had achieved, she did manage to grab assignments that Lata was not given, or sometimes, had even refused.

Whether it was a political game or the fact that she was actually as good – and in some genres better – than her senior has never been commented on, except perhaps by Naushad. When he was asked about what made one sister better than the other, he said, 'Asha lacks a certain something that Lata and Lata alone has.' But sometime after that he admitted that he had been unfair to the younger sibling. 'Maybe I said it because I then had a closed ear for Asha,' he agreed. The two worked together on a number of songs, including '*Diwali aayi ghar-ghar deep*' in *Leader* (1964), '*Tum ishq ki mehfil ho*' from *Saaz Aur Awaaz* (1966), '*Saawan aaye na aaye*' from *Dil Diya Dard Liya* (1966) and '*Aaj sakhi ri more piya ghar*' from *Ram Aur Shyam* (1967).

Another partnership that was infrequent but successful was that between Asha and the composer duo Shankar–Jaikishan. The music directors Shankar Singh Raghuvanshi and Jaikishan Dayabhai Panchal bonded while scouting for work and though they split acrimoniously many years later, they produced seminal work that changed the tone of Hindi film music. Backed and encouraged by actor–director–producer Raj Kapoor, they had the reputation of having broken new ground in composition, using their solid background of Indian classical music overlaid with Western rhythm patterns and orchestration. In fact, they were perhaps the first to do away with the orchestra sections as a filler in a song; instead, the complex harmonies became part of the song itself, expressing and enhancing emotion and pushing the story to the next level. Each film they worked on had at least one classical or semi-classical raga-based number. As Raj Kapoor said, 'Innovation is the life's breath of art, and in the field of movie-making and movie music, Shankar–Jaikishan can be proud of a record of innovation which began nearly twenty years ago.'

Like so many others, the composer duo played favourites with Lata Mangeshkar. She was the preferred voice for most of their compositions, but the two did memorable work with Asha Bhosle. '*Parde mein rehne do*' in *Shikar* (1968) won Asha her second Filmfare award, but her stab at the yodel in *'Zindagi ek safar hai suhana'* from *Andaz* (1971) was a bit of a damp squib compared to Kishore Kumar's version of the same song. Again, Lata's loss was Asha's gain when Raj Kapoor decided that he would not have anything to do with the older sibling and the songs of *Mera Naam Joker* (1970) dropped right into the younger sister's lap. *'Ang lag jaa balma'* proved that Kapoor had chosen the right sister for the song. She also sang '*Zuby zuby zalembu*' for *Evening in Paris* (1967), '*Aaj raat hai jawaan dil mera na tod*' for *Bhai Bhai* (1970), '*Jao na satao rasiya*' for *Roop Ki Rani Choron Ka Raja* (1961) and many others that worked her magic on Shankar–Jaikishan's musical scores. Asha told Dr Mandar Bichu, chronicler of Lata's work in *Lata: Voice of the Golden Era* and other publications, that 'We could make out who had really composed the tune. Out of the two, the person who would teach the tune to the singer was the composer. The other would then just supervise the recording. Jaikishan used mainly minor notes, whereas Shankar preferred high notes. Like Lata's '*Main piya teri*' (*Basant Bahar*, 1956) was a typical Jaikishan tune, whereas '*O basanti pawan paagal*' from *Jis Desh Mein Ganga Behti Hai* (1960) was a classic Shankar composition. Most of my songs like '*Sooni sooni saans ki sitar pe*' from *Laal Patthar* (1971) were Shankar's tunes.'

Asha also worked with Madan Mohan, whose last few works were among those heard in the 2004 Yash Chopra film *Veer Zaara*. This movie featured Lata Mangeshkar rather than Asha. The composer came from a family with deep interests in music – he is said to have inherited his talent from his mother, a poet, and his grandfather. When his father made the move to Bombay, young Madan made friends with 'filmi' folk – Raj Kapoor, Nargis and Suraiya among them. A stint in the army gave him a sense of discipline, organisation, punctuality, endurance, courtesy and physical fitness, all of which came in handy when he finally decided on music as a career. He had a secret desire to be an actor, but destiny had other plans. His second film, *Adaa* (1951) had eight songs and seven singers, but Asha's voice played a small part in making the music popular as she sang '*Sab kuchh karna is duniya mein pyaar na karna bhool ke*' with S.D. Batish.

She was also known for a fairly substantial serving of songs by Madan Mohan, including *'Thodi der ke liye mere ho jao'* from *Akeli Mat Jaiyo* (1963), '*Banda parwar raat ke andhere mein*' in *Pooja Ke Phool* (1964), the hugely popular '*Jhumka gira re*' from *Mera Saaya*, '*Chale ladkhada ke*' in *Parwana* (1971), '*Chalo aao jaam uthaye*' from *Inspector Eagle* (1979) and '*Ek mutthi mein dil ek mutthi mein pyaar*' from *Sharafat Chhod Di Maine* (1976). Madan Mohan's composition for *Senapati* (1961), '*Dil dayi dayi oh na layi layi*' was one of the few songs that featured the sisters Lata and Asha singing together! For special fans, a more recent offering is a mujra, '*Aaj ki sham pehlu mein tu*', reportedly recorded by Asha to a tune by Madan Mohan, who passed away on 14 July 1975, for a film called *Rehnuma* in the 1970s, but there is no confirmation of the existence of this project that was never finished. It was released on 25 June 2011, the day the composer would have turned eighty-seven. The poetry is by Naqsh Lyallpuri and sounds perfect for a dance sequence. Could it have been danced by Hema Malini or Neetu Singh? Or even Zeenat Aman or the ravishing Helen? We will never know.

The bias for Lata Mangeshkar was shown quite often and clearly by many composers. One such was Salil Chowdhury, who wrote music for Bengali, Hindi and Malayalam films. He passed away on 5 September 1977, aged seventy-three, but left behind a vast repertoire of work. He was a professed Communist whose beliefs were reflected in his early work, songs that were, as his granddaughter Aurina Chatterjee has said, 'raw, angry, shamelessly political … anti-colonial, anti-zamindari, anti-war. Bapi's idealistic ideas for a newly independent India, his poetic cries for justice were framed in complicated, meandering melodies, supported by beautifully feisty harmonies.' A kind of music that would perfectly suit the zingy, spirited, high-energy character of Asha's voice, anyone would agree. But Salil-*da*, as he was called, had his favourite: 'Practically all my songs have been sung by Lata. I've rarely felt the need to turn to someone else. Lata is a trained singer and so versatile. She can sing anything from classical to even frothy songs. Lata is a phenomenon. She is one of a kind.'

Chowdhury evolved into a composer who could project that anger and fire. He was a poet and playwright who could play the flute, piano and esraj, and worked in various languages, even winning a prize at the Cannes International Film festival as music director of *Do Bigha Zameen* (1953). He worked on Bengali and Hindi films for twenty years and then decided to explore southwards, starting with the Malayalam *Chemmeen* in 1965, and did over twenty-five others in the language. He also composed music for Marathi, Tamil, Telugu, Kannada, Gujarati, Oriya and Assamese movies, blending East and West in his work, thinking of himself as Mozart reborn. As he said, 'I want to create a style that can transcend borders, a genre that is emphatic and polished, but never predictable.' The only problem was, he could not decide what he really wanted to do. 'I do not know what to opt for – poetry, story-writing, orchestration or composing for films. I just try to be creative with what fits the moment and my temperament.'

Creativity ruled when Chowdhury and Asha collaborated, especially for Hindi films. In *Chand Aur Suraj* (1965) Asha's

'*Bagh mein kali khili*' and '*Main aur unki preet purani*' made an impact even though Lata sang two strong songs. In *Jaagte Raho* (1956), while '*Jaago Mohan pyare*' in Lata's voice was a standout, Asha's '*Thandi thandi saavan ki phuhar*' is still remembered. And of course, there is that now-classic upbeat number with K.J. Yesudas, '*Janeman janeman tere do nayan*' from *Chhoti Si Baat* (1975) that made a small film a big success. She also sang for him in a number of other films: '*Jab tumne mohabbat cheen li*' in *Amanat* (1955), '*Baat koi matlab ki hai zaroor*' from *Apradhi Kaun* (1957), the provocative '*Meri beri ke ber mat todo*' from *Anokhi Raat* (1968), '*Chandni ki paalki mein baithkar*' from Shammi Kapoor's debut film *Jeevan Jyoti* (1976), '*Jaane kaisa jaadu yeh chal gaya*' in *Aakhri Badla* (1989) and many more.

Perhaps as challenging is the music created by Sandeep Chowta, who has a different sensibility when it comes to music. Influenced heavily by his training and interest in jazz, along with Western classical music, international film soundtracks, Carnatic music, '70s rock and Hindi film music, he incorporates all this and more into his compositions. As the self-confessed Spyro Gyra follower said, 'I listen to just about anything and use various influences in my sound. I'm a big fan of S.D. Burman and R.D. Burman, as well as of jazz artistes like Pat Metheny, Jay Beckenstein and Chick Corea. Since I was with a fusion-rock band called Pulse – with percussionist Sivamani, bassist Keith Peters and guitarist Allwyn Fernandes – I do a lot of that stuff too.' Chowta was born in Ghana and brought up in Nigeria, but visited Mumbai regularly. His maternal uncle worked in a studio and the youngster started with learning how to play a guitar. When Pulse broke up, he worked on the music of *Ninne Pelladatha* (1996), a Telugu film starring Nagarjuna and Tabu that did very well at the box office. And Bollywood, as the Hindi film world is known, decided to tap his talent. He has worked with Asha Bhosle on a number of songs including '*Kambakth ishq*' from *Pyaar Tune Kya Kiya*, '*Khallas*' from Ram Gopal Varma's *Company* (2002), '*Hum tum*' from *Sandwich* (2006) and '*Na Govinda na Shahrukh*' in *Mast* (1999).

While Jatin–Lalit have composed music for Hindi films for many years now, not many have been sung by Asha Bhosle. The career of the brothers together started with '*Yaara Dildara*' (1991) and the oft-remixed '*Bin tere sanam*'. *Khiladi* (1992) with '*Kya khabar thi jaana*' that Asha sang, and *Jo Jeeta Wohi Sikander* (1992) and its now-iconic '*Pehla nasha*' made them known in the film world. The two work separately now. Jointly, the composers became top sellers with the music of Yash Raj Films' *Dilwale Dulhaniya Le Jayenge* (1995) in which Asha sang '*Zara sa jhoom loon main*', and the songs they composed for Karan Johar's *Kabhi Khushi Kabhi Gham* (2001). With Asha they have a few songs to their credit, including '*Dil nashi hai*' from *Vaade Iraade* (1994), '*Ek ladki mili khoobsurat lagi*' from *Gangster* (1994), '*Kyun aanchal hamara*' from *Daava* (1997), the innovative '*Ajnabi mujhko itna bata*' from *Pyar To Hona Hi Tha* (1998) and '*Jung ho ya pyar*' from *Kranti* (2002), among others.

There were more collaborations. With Bappi Lahiri, '*Inteha ho gayi intezar ki*' (Kishore Kumar was the male voice) from *Sharaabi* (1984) was a seductive and superb standout. With Usha Khanna, the relationship was much closer; Asha called the composer her 'daughter', and sang a number of songs, including '*Jab apne ho*' from the 1983 film *Souten*. *Do Shikari* (1979), the film that was best known for showcasing Rekha's first kiss onscreen, included Asha's song for composer Chitragupta: '*Honth ye mere aag se nahi kam*', perfectly suited to the situation. With Roshanlal Nagrath, better known as Roshan, she sang songs like '*Tera dil kahaan hai sab kuchh yahaan hai*' in *Chandni*

Chowk (1954), '*Nigahen milane ko jee chahta hai*' in *Dil Hi To Hai* and '*Kahe tarsaye jiyara*' in *Chitralekha* (1963) with her sister Usha Mangeshkar.

Added to the long list was Kalyanji Virji Shah and his brother Anandji, the composer duo who managed to change the world of Hindi film music. Kalyanji started off with *Samrat Chandragupta* (1959) and was joined by his sibling in *Satta Bazar* (1959) and *Madari*. But it was *Chalia* (1961) that made them famous, especially with '*Dam dam diga diga*', sung by Mukesh. They were known for their spirituality and charity work and gave many a young singer a break. And they managed to charm Western audiences too, with their compositions from the 1970s being used by musicians such as Black Eyed Peas, DJ Dan the Automator and others and their '*Pal bhar ke liye koi humein pyar kar le*' (*Johny Mera Naam*, 1970) used in an episode of The Simpsons. Kalyanji passed away in August 2000 and Anandji continues his work today. The brothers tapped into the vast directory of singers in their realm, and did many a well-known number with Asha Bhosle. Some of these are '*Bichhde hue milenge*' in *Post Box 999* (1958), '*Tu jahan bhi chalega*' from *Chameli Ki Shaadi* (1986), '*Tum salamat raho*' from *Ghungroo* (1983), '*Main hoon tere saamne*' in *Nastik* (1983), '*O saathi re tere bina*' from *Muqaddar Ke Sikandar* (1978), the inimitable '*Yeh mera dil*' from *Don* and the feisty '*Chakku chhuriyan tej kara lo*', Jaya Bhadhuri's introduction to Amitabh Bachchan in *Zanjeer* (1973). But the bond between the composing duo and the singers was far stronger than merely professional – they became friends. They visited each other's homes, ate meals together and stood by each other in times of crisis. Like the time when Kishore Kumar, who was supposed to sing at a Kalyanji–Anandji concert in Bombay, suddenly fell ill. Asha, R.D. Burman and Lata called individually to offer help. Pancham and Asha took over the concert, reprising major hits like '*Khaike paan Banaras wala*', all without accepting any kind of payment. Anandji has said, 'There was a misunderstanding with a producer, and Asha did not sing for us for a long time. But then things were sorted out and she was with us right till the time we stopped composing for films.' She was even given a change of image with the duo's poignant '*O saathi re tere bina bhi kya jeena*' from *Muqaddar Ka Sikander*. And the proof of the musical pairing being successful is the iconic number that Asha sings in every concert: '*Yeh mera dil*'.

There are a number of younger composers that Asha has sung for who have made memorable music. Pritam and Jeet Ganguly's '*Sharara sharara*' from *Mere Yaar Ki Shaadi Hai* (2002) marked a sort of comeback after a hiatus for Asha, becoming a popular number that is played at celebrations even today. Shailendra Barve harnessed her voice for '*Hum neend ka bijnis karte hain*', a retro-style track Asha sang with Sudesh Bhonsle. '*Chanda ki bindiya*' from her acting debut, *Mai*, was composed by Manoj Tapadia, while the non-film '*Kabhi to nazar milao*' (2005) was the creation of Adnan Sami, a musician discovered by Asha and Pancham in London when he was ten years old.

If there was something new and exciting to be sung, Asha's would almost always be the voice singing it – like '*Huzoor-e-ala*', which she sang for composer and corporate consultant Shamir Tandon for *Page 3* (2003), a National Award winner directed by Madhur Bhandarkar. Interestingly, Lata was also part of the soundtrack with '*Kitne ajeeb rishte hain yahaan pe*', a far more classical and quieter number. Tandon also composed music for the director's *Corporate* (2006) and *Traffic Signal* (2007). For Tandon, 'Asha Bhosle and the Mangeshkar family are demi-gods, because I started my career with them. I was completely unknown; I had never scored music for a film. *Page 3* was my first film, with a then not very big director called Madhur Bhandarkar. I sang a song to him called '*Huzoor-e-ala*'. He liked it and said, "Let's record." I said, "If it's Ashaji, we will; if it's not, we'll drop it and do another song." She was in San Francisco at the time.' The sticking point was that the song had to be finished quickly since the film was scheduled for release, but Asha was halfway around the world and would stay there for a while. 'I wrote a mail to her son Anand, saying "I am new, doing a small film, have no money, will she do it?". He said he would let me know.' And Asha showed interest. 'She said from there that "If the song is good, I will do it. If not, I will not." Tandon sent Asha the song recorded in his own voice and waited for an answer. Luckily for him, 'She loved the song and said to wait for two months for her to come back, when she would sing it. I said I needed it to be sung tomorrow. She said, "Take a flight and come." I said that I could not afford it, but I had an idea.' It was something new, almost guaranteed to tempt Asha to try it. 'In 2002, the Internet was still evolving, not the way it was today. I sent her some files, booked a studio in San Francisco, asked her to go there and we got on a Skype kind of situation. I told her to shut her eyes, imagine it was for Helen and sing.'

For Asha, this was a novel experience. Tandon was excited as well as amused. 'She told me that it was the first time in her life that she was singing a song in a studio when the music director, his assistants, the lyric writer, the musicians, director and producer of the film – nobody was present. She said, "I'm singing to a wall and a white-skinned foreign engineer, in America!" She sang it and sent three options, saying she was not sure which I would like. I used the first, because that is how I had conceived it… But *three*! That was professionalism,'

Tandon marvelled. 'When she came back two months later, she called me, saying, "Pappubhai, who are you? Show me your face! I sang for you, so I need to see you." I went over – I was shivering, but she made me very comfortable. She told me that if I had been present at the recording, it would have been so much better. "But I hope you are satisfied." Asha Bhosle asking me if I was satisfied with her vocals! That is modesty personified! Then she of course made me coffee and we spoke. That was the beginning of one of the most beautiful relationships of my life. I went ahead to do much more work with her. This was also a film where Lata Mangeshkar sang in the same film with her sister after many years, even though they did not sing together. She told me a very interesting story. I asked her, "Tai, what made you agree to sing this song?" She could have flatly refused, which she did at first, and then I had to convince her to do it. She said, "For the Mangeshkar family, if the song is good, we will lend our voices to it. It is not whether a composer is big or small, new or old, it is all about the song." She also said that "One of the reasons I sang your song is that Pancham once told me that if I don't shape up to technology, I will have to ship out. I will become obsolete. For me this was exciting use of technology. She said that her husband had said that she should evolve with the times. She knew this was new technology and she would embrace it to stay fresh and involved. That was a revelation for me as well.'

And then there was Rahul Dev Burman.

8

Asha and R.D. Burman

It was 1956. Asha Bhosle was twenty-three years old. Rahul Dev Burman was seventeen. She was an experienced singer for films by then. He was the son of music director Sachin Dev Burman. She was a mother of two; he was a teenager who had just dropped out of high school to make music. 'That day I was recording the songs of *Armaan* (1953) and someone gave me this copybook and said, "Autograph, please." I was tense because of the song and Sachin-*da* rescued the poor fellow and introduced him to me: "My son, Pancham." That was our first meeting. He was five years younger than me – tall, pale and thin, with thick spectacles.' Asha was appalled that the lad was not in school. 'Taking a chance, I scolded him in front of his father Sachin Dev Burman: "No studying! And he has come to the studio!" From then on I always rebuked Pancham on seeing him in the studio.' When Rahul came to train Asha a few days after they had met, she was not happy. She told him that he should have finished his graduation. 'And he sulked for the rest of the day!' She was not pleased to have the youngster working with her. 'I was enraged, and almost wept. I said to

Sachin dada, 'Why this boy? You teach me, please!' 'I saw that Pancham was smiling ...' His father told Asha that his son had been studying for his matriculation, but had dropped out and had started working. When she asked why, S.D. Burman said, "He failed," Asha remembered with a smile.

It was ten years later in 1966, that they worked together in *Teesri Manzil*, a film known for its new, sexy, sound. It was music that changed how Hindi cinema was seen – or heard – and brought a fun, risqué Western element into a world that was obviously far more raga-based at the time. R.D. Burman used funk, garage rock, jazz, pop, disco, rock and cabaret, apart from the conventional classic tones of ghazals and pure ragas. Asha used the power of her voice, its ability to morph from being set within a framework of traditional scales to finding liberation in emotion, especially of the naughty, sassy, cheeky, very saucy kind. She could power through hard, raunchy numbers like '*Piya tu ab to aaja*' in *Caravan* and tone it right down for the subtleties of '*Mera kuchh samaan*' from *Ijaazat* (1987) for which she won a National Award. She added her bit too, in songs like '*Haaye bichhua das gayo re*' from *Jheel Ke Uss Paar* (1973), where the opening lines were created by herself, Asha says. While many of his tunes 'really tested me, Pancham would reassure me by saying, "You are the best when it comes to *sur* and *laya*." His tune for '*Daiya yeh main kahaan aa phansi*' for *Caravan* was very difficult. After that song was released, one night I got a call from Sitara Devi: "I am Sitara, the dancer. You are really a great singer. How well you have sung such a difficult song like '*Daiya yeh main kahaan*'!" Compliments like these boosted my confidence.'

The road from co-workers to romance was a long and winding one. R.D. Burman (27 June 1939–4 January 1994) was the only son of S.D. Burman of the Tripura royal family and his poet–lyricist–singer wife Meera Dasgupta. Born in Calcutta, he was called Tublu by his mother's mother, but was soon nicknamed Pancham. Some say that it is because when he cried, it was in the fifth note 'Pa' in the Indian musical scale; another story goes as to how when the baby cried, it's voice oscillated between five notes in the Indian classical system, hence the name, 'panch' meaning 'five' in Bengali; Another lore tells of actor Ashok Kumar hearing the infant babble 'Pa, pa, pa …' as little children of that age do, and so he named the child Pancham.

At just nine years old, the youngster composed '*Aye meri topi palat ke aa*', a song that his father S.D. Burman used in *Funtoosh* (1956). The music for '*Sar jo tera chakraye*' followed, used by his proud father in *Pyaasa* (1957). Formal training in Bombay – where the family had moved to – followed, in sarod from Ustad Ali Akbar Khan and the tabla from Pandit Samta Prasad, with composer Salil Chowdhury acting mentor to the young man. Rahul became his father's assistant and played the harmonica with the orchestra that S.D. Burman used so well – he did it memorably in '*Hai apna dil to aawara*' from *Solva Saal* (1958). It is said that many of S.D. Burman's tunes were actually composed by Pancham, from '*Sar jo tera chakraye*' (*Pyaasa*, 1957) to '*Hothon mein aisi baat*' (*Jewel Thief*, 1967). Asha remembered, 'Sometimes as Sachin-da's assistant, he would start teaching me the tune, which was actually conceived by him (RD). But not knowing that, I often wanted Sachin-da to teach me the tune. Dada would then find some excuse to say, "Asha, you learn it from him now. I will take over later on."'

Pancham started being formally credited for his work as a 'Music Assistant'. *Chalti Ka Naam Gaadi*, *Tere Ghar Ke Saamne* (1963), *Bandini*, *Guide* (1965) and *Teen Devian* (1965) rank among the films he did with his father. He signed a contract in 1959 to be the music director of *Raaz*, being made by Guru Dutt's assistant Niranjan, but two compositions down – one sung by Asha, the other by Shamshad Begum – the project was shelved. Then in 1961, *Chhote Nawab* released. It was originally offered to Sachin-da by the reigning funny man Mehmood, who was producing it, but S.D. Burman cited lack of time for the film, and R.D. Burman was signed up. The story goes that Pancham was playing the tabla in a corner of the room that Mehmood and his father were meeting in. Impressed, the comedian signed Pancham on to create the music for his film. *Chhote Nawab* starred Mehmood and Ameeta, with Lata Mangeshkar's voice being the highlight of the songs. *Bhoot Bangla* (1965), its soundtrack also composed by the newbie RD, also had him in a cameo role, with Mehmood, Tanuja and Nazir Hussain as the lead actors.

Between the 1960s and the 1990s, R.D. Burman composed the music for about 331 movies, even singing for some of the songs he had composed. While his favourite singers were Asha and Kishore Kumar, he did tap into the talents of many others who suited his style. Success followed very soon. *Teesri Manzil* is still known for its peppy, fun music, with Asha's voice clarion clear in '*O mere sona re*', '*Aaja aaja mein hoon pyaar tera*', '*O haseena zulfon wali jaane jahan*' and '*Dekhiye sahiban wo kaun thi*', all duets with Mohammed Rafi. Director Nasir Hussain liked the music enough to sign Pancham on to do eight more films. And then there was the roll-on-the-floor-funny *Padosan*, with delightful music to match, in typically madcap R.D. Burman mode. Asha and Lata sang together on '*Main chali main chali*', but were outranked by Kishore's inimitable wit in '*Ek chatur naar karke singaar*' and '*Meri pyaari Bindu*'.

Even as he flew solo into the world of movie music, Pancham worked with his father on films like *Jewel Thief*, in which Asha crooned '*Raat akeli hai*', and *Prem Pujari* (1970). As S.D. Burman battled illness, his son took over the workload. Pancham was given the tag of associate composer for *Aradhana*, in which Kishore Kumar has captivated listeners – to this day – with '*Mere sapnon ki rani*' and '*Roop tera mastana*'. Asha sang '*Gun guna rahe hai bhanware*' with Mohammed Rafi for this film; her sister was given the bigger musical share. S.D. Burman too sang one song in *Aradhana*: '*Safal hogi teri aradhana*'. Asha remembers, 'In those days, Burman da (SDB) would offer me a song and I would ask him what the tune was like. He would ask me to learn it from Pancham. This happened again and again. I would naturally get upset, because Pancham was not the music director of the film, whichever film it was. And then, much later, I found out that the tunes had actually been composed by Pancham – he never took credit for them.'

It was the 1970s that belonged to RDB and Asha. As journalist–director S. Ramachandran said, 'R.D. Burman made Asha see much more. He found a voice that he could experiment with, since he experimented all the time. It was all about an artist finding his muse. He used to make her work very hard. RD and Asha together were RDX, with the X-factor.'

It was also the era of the vamp – Bindu, Aruna Irani and Helen. Pancham's music suited the wicked woman perfectly, while Asha's voice captured all of her naughty, sexy, sultry charm. So '*Mera naam hai Shabnam*' from *Kati Patang* (1970), '*Dum maaro dum*' from *Haré Rama Haré Krishna* (1971) and '*Piya tu*' from *Caravan*, to name just a few, had listeners shimmying along. But as the 1980s approached, the sun that was RDB started fading. The age of disco dawned and there were others, like the flamboyant Bappi Lahiri, who could do it faster and better. Class did win over chaos, albeit in a niche film that did not ring the cash-counters at the box office too loudly. *Ijaazat* released in 1987 and is still thought of as one of Pancham's best work. Asha Bhosle was his muse, his voice; she sang all four of the beautifully composed tunes, with poetry by the inimitable Gulzar. All was well again.

Filmmaker-writer Brahmanand Singh, who collected hours of footage of interviews collated as *Knowing Pancham* and made the film *Pancham Unmixed*, spent hours with RDB and Asha. 'I had always heard how RD was a genius and amazing and so on, but nobody had taken on the effort to understand his music for people like us. The need to know was like a fire inside me. I thought maybe Gulzar sa'ab would make a personal, beautiful film, or maybe Asha Bhosle would commission someone to make a film. So when that didn't happen, I thought I would do it. I had a very easy way to make a film with Asha and Gulzar in it and still make a decent, sensitive film. But I thought let me do it the tougher way – by talking to everyone who had worked with him and remembered him. Sadly, a lot of these people were gone. There were people still around but who might not be there a few years later. I built my narrative from that – people who knew him and had worked with him, and one lot from the current generation whom I respect.' An interesting project, it was a costly way of buying a ticket for a film Singh wanted to see, he laughed. Once it got made, the film did amazingly well. Singh found that 'RD had a wonderful exposure to Western music, but was rooted in the Indian raga system at the same time. Also, he had this driving need to experiment, with a complete disdain for what everyone else thought. What corrupted his music were the doubts he started having. Ashaji always said that he was not a singer, though the songs sung by him are memorable.' Singh spent time with Asha and Pancham together, trying to capture the essence of the composer. In that time, he learned a little about her too. 'Whether Ashaji was trained or not was never the question – her training was whatever she heard from Lata and her father. Deenanath Mangeshkar was a genius. His compositions were great.

> *Asha was trained in that sense. I think she had a natural ability to pick notes and add a flourish to them, embellishing the song with her richness of expression, which no amount of training can give you. That distinguishes her from Lata.*

Experience comes from life, they say. Asha would add that mischief, that raunchiness, that sexiness – everything that she never really had in real life – to her music.' And while O.P. Nayyar gave her that much-needed push with his provocative songs, it was Pancham who really made her what she is known for: her ability to sing anything.

But two years later, things changed. R.D. Burman had a heart attack in 1988, followed by a bypass surgery the following year in London. Much of what he wrote during this year was never released, but he did compose the music for two films by Vidhu Vinod Chopra: *Parinda* (1989) stood out for '*Tumse mil ke aisa laga*' sung by Asha Bhosle and Suresh Wadkar; and *1942: A Love Story* (1994) the music of which was beautiful, and fetched Pancham a Filmfare award. Unfortunately, he died before the film released.

Apart from his film work, he worked on devotional and pop songs too, besides private albums. A standout is '*Dil Padosi Hai*', which combines the mights of RDB, Gulzar and Asha – it was released on the singer's birthday on 8 September in 1987. The story goes that he was suddenly inspired to create an entire album of songs one afternoon while at Asha's house.

He called it '*bekaar ka kaam*' (pointless work), but when it came together – Gulzar's poetry set to Pancham's music sung in Asha's voice – it was magic. The original double LP had fourteen songs, each critically reviewed as being fresh and hummable, often cited by Asha as being one of her best works ever.

In a happy turnaround, many of R.D. Burman's songs have often been re-created, remixed and repurposed for albums released more recently. '*You've stolen my heart*' by the Kronos Quartet has Pancham's music sung by Asha. The pair also did a song with Boy George: '*Bow down mister*', a catchy take on the classic '*Hare Rama Hare Krishna*'. And she is the ideal person to take his legacy on into the future. From their first meeting in 1956 to their marriage in 1980, to his death in 1994, she was the voice of many of his most well-known compositions.

Asha was R.D. Burman's second wife. In 1966, he married Rita Patel, a fan who had bet her friends that she would go on a date to a movie with the musician. Odd as it may seem now, Asha was at the wedding. Unfortunately, the wager could not keep the relationship alive and the two divorced in 1971. Perhaps the best outcome of that fairly brief marriage was '*Musafir hoon yaaron*' in Kishore Kumar's voice, a lovely song from *Parichay* (1972) that was, as the story goes, composed in a hotel room where Pancham was staying after his split with Rita. There were other beautiful compositions that went relatively unheard because the films they were a part of failed – the Asha-Kishore number '*Aao aao jaan-e-jahaan*' from *Gomti Ke Kinare* (1972) and '*Chori chori solah singaar*' from *Manoranjan* (1974), also sung by Asha, among them.

Lata Mangeshkar's memories of the composer dated back to his childhood. 'I had seen him running around in his half-pants when I'd record songs for his father Sachin Dev Burman. Pancham was immensely talented. He could compose in any style. And he knew exactly which song to give to which singer. If he gave my sister Asha '*Piya tu ab toh aaja*' (*Caravan*), he gave me '*Raina beeti jaaye*' (*Amar Prem*). He also gave me '*Meri awaaz hi pehchaan hai*' (*Kinara*, 1977), the signature tune of my career.'

Pancham may have composed some of Lata Mangeshkar's best-known songs, but his relationship with Asha Bhosle was special. Professional when it came to music, but personal otherwise, the bond between the two was one that had to be lived to be understood. They met in 1956 – she was a mother of two young children, battered by the failure of a runaway marriage, and he was a teenager who had dropped out of school to make music. Asha has said, 'I remember the day we met very clearly. I was recording a song for *Armaan* (1953) and Pancham, who must have been in his final year in school, dropped in at the recording studio. Sachin da introduced me saying "Meet Asha, *yeh bahut badi singer hai*." I was already married then, had children and looked matronly, while he was thin and gawky. He left school and started assisting his father. I remember telling him that he should have finished his studies. Many years later he told me that I had upset him by saying that. He believed that if he had continued with his studies, he would never have become a music director.' While she found success with Madan Mohan, who had a very Indian style, and O.P. Nayyar, with his 'new' ideas, Asha believes the one who changed her life was R.D. Burman. '*Unhone sab badal ke rakh diya* (he changed everything), and I feel there hasn't been a single great music director after him. He brought in new rhythms, and initially even us singers found it difficult to figure out how to sing certain compositions. He has left a great legacy and people are making a living out of it.'

They were noticed as a successful duo with *Teesri Manzil*,

in which he composed the music and she sang four songs, all with Mohammed Rafi. That set the tone for many such projects, all brilliantly showcasing the *masti* in Asha's voice and giving the vamp or bad girl the best frame for her seductive-simmering act. But they also worked on more classical and devotional songs together in Hindi and Bengali, and the occasional English number. The two were known for their modern, youthful, peppy, occasionally raunchy songs, from '*Piya tu ab to aaja*' from *Caravan* to '*Duniya mein logon ko*' from *Apna Desh* (1972) and '*Jaane do na*' from *Saagar* (1985) with its sensuous rhythm and pure seduction that Asha imbued it with. Of course, the unforgettable songs from *Ijaazat* were subtle, delicate, intense, bringing in awards and a whole new audience that could never have imagined that the couple known for cabaret numbers – the 'item numbers' of that time – could produce such beautifully nuanced sounds. RD experimented with psychedelia in '*Phir se aaiyyo badra bidesi*' in *Namkeen*, which had lyrics by Gulzar and was sung by Asha. And then there were the Bengali songs that Asha sang under R.D. Burman's direction, like '*Mohuyae jomechhe aaj mou go*', '*Chokhe chokhe kotha bolo*', and more.

As they made music, love bloomed. She called him 'Bubs'. And she often fought with him, insisting that he gave the best of his work to her sister, especially the songs that were about romance, love, togetherness, longing. But he had an answer that could satisfy any woman with a peeve – if she refused to sing the kind of music that he conjured for her voice, the numbers with high notes, a quick tempo, gimmickry and a certain madness, he would never again compose them. 'Pancham loved rhythmic songs. Jazz and Latin American were his favourites. My professional relationship with him was just like the one I had with other music directors. But somewhere in my heart

I expected him to be partial towards me. He would not give me the kind of songs he gave Lata didi, but gave me the more *hatke* (unconventional) ones. According to him, only I could do justice to those songs; he knew exactly what suited my voice. He said, "Asha, only you understand *sur*, you can never go off-key even if you try to." So I had to give in.' She gave in personally too. 'He was after me for years to get married. After much persuasion, he convinced me that he'd fallen in love with my voice, it fascinated him. So I finally said OK.'

Asha recalled at an event, 'He once had a bet with Nasir Hussain that I could sing '*Piya tu ab to aaja*' from *Caravan* – he won! Pancham insisted that he would not have composed songs like '*Piya tu*' and '*Dum maaro dum*' if I had not been there to sing them.' Her initial association with her future husband came with games of table tennis in between rehearsals and recordings. 'His first independent composition that I sang was '*Maar dalega dard e jigar*' for *Pati Patni*. That was the beginning. We worked on many films and I came to know him better.' And he was her teacher too. 'He introduced me to jazz music. He would listen to Santana, Blood Sweat and Tears and the Rolling Stones.' Pancham used all this and more in his own work. 'He was one of the first music directors to blend foreign and Indian styles and started the use of the double bass here. His music had *aag* (fire) in it; his rhythms were challenging.'

An interview on 3 January 2016 with journalist–filmmaker Khalid Mohammed in *Quint* had Asha speaking about her late husband: 'Obviously I miss Pancham very, very much. He was my best friend. He was a great comedian; he'd keep me in splits.' The memories are legion. 'Once he scared the daylights out of me by wearing an Afro wig in the dark. He'd mimic everyone, including me.' And there was the romantic side: 'For years, he'd send me flowers anonymously. One day, the roses were delivered in the presence of Majrooh (Sultanpuri) sa'ab and Pancham. I said, "Throw them away. Some fool keeps wasting his roses on me." Pancham's face fell. That's when Majrooh sa'ab laughed, "It's this fool who's been sending you the roses!"'

She married the fool in 1980. Pancham was by then a full-fledged music composer. 'When Pancham proposed marriage to me, he told me, 'It was I who used to send you the roses'. I was astonished – there was so much going on inside his mind! At that time my condition was not such that I was crazy about the proposal. I didn't ever think of Pancham from that angle. The realisation that I loved him dawned on me very slowly. It took shape gradually ... and we got married.' It was not a passionately physical relationship, by all accounts; they lived in their own homes most of the time. 'Keeping my house neat and clean was one of my manias, but Pancham did not like it. He would say, "Asha *aayi mane safai*!" And one morning – it was my birthday – a flower bouquet from him came to me; it was beautiful, but when I looked closer, it had two brooms carefully tied to it! In spite of being angry, I could not help laughing ...' This was true healing for a woman who had been through a traumatic marriage. 'R.D. Burman came into my life like a balm. Ours was not a marriage of sixteen-year-olds, it was a communion of minds. Our conjugal life was not like other natural couples, our love was not confined to our bodies. A strange maturity surrounded us along with a deep understanding. We didn't need any special worldly comforts or money – we had enough. My children too didn't ever raise any unpleasant questions; Pancham also loved them very much.'

In some ways, it was a platonic relationship, a partnership of common interests – music, food, friends. 'We lived more like friends, as partners in our musical journey, than as husband

and wife. He had two passions in life – music, of course, and cooking; he liked chillies very much. Since I am also a good cook, we would often have competitions at home. He cooked to relax himself after thinking about music, composing tunes and experimenting with sounds.' But while he was an ace musician, as a husband – or even just a normal human being – he was not as skilled. 'He was so steeped in music that he forgot to live his life as a husband, son or whatever role society assigned to him. He would be, for instance, happy to sleep on the floor, but his music system had to be properly maintained. He didn't really care what he ate, because he ate, lived and slept music. You could not have found a more gentle or caring husband, as long as you left him in peace with his music!' And true harmony came, as in music, when nature was allowed to take its own course. 'Life with Pancham was absolutely serene once I realised that I should not try and control this wonderful talent by fitting it into a role that society gave it.' A close friend of R.D. Burman's, Sachin Bhowmick, had a different story that he wrote in his book, *Start Sound Camera Action...*: 'One thing that is clear from RD's interviews and those of his close associates is that RD was in love with Asha. Maybe it was not reciprocated. I asked him once, "Why did you marry Asha?" He winked at me and said, "I'm not married to Asha, I'm married to her voice."

It was a quiet wedding, she recalled. 'We didn't want to make a *hungama* of our marriage. At our age, the groom couldn't possibly have come to the wedding on a horse with a lot of *band baaja.* We couldn't have hosted a big reception at the Taj Mahal hotel. Pancham and I were no coy young couple. So we had a very quiet ceremony, an Arya Samaj wedding, and also a civil registry marriage. Our close friends were there – my sister too.' But Asha kept her name, her new husband believing that 'my name Asha Bhosle was very lucky for me. He pointed out that Geeta Roy's career had nose-dived after she had changed her name to Geeta Dutt.'

Asha's career continued on its course, the two newlyweds actually living in separate homes. There was romance of a very special kind. 'We would go on a long drive whenever we got the chance. How fantastic were those days! Only Pancham and me, with resounding music, cigarette in hand, a drink on the dashboard, and Pancham beating his rhythms on the ceiling of the car. It was as if we were lost. We would stop the car in any quiet, lovely spot, and listen to the songs one after the other: Santana's '*Listen to the pouring rain*' or '*Guantanamera*'.' The marriage was never in any danger, as some whispered. When she was confronted with the suggestion that there were problems between her and R.D. Burman, the singer was vehement: 'What rubbish! I wasn't a new bride who had to go into a new house and touch her mother-in-law's feet! Before we got married I told Pancham that I would look after both homes. He knew I was devoted to my children Anand, Hemant and Varsha. And they knew him – they called him Pancham uncle.' Of course, it was not all joy and roses. After all, 'All marriages have their own specific problems. The second time, I was more alert. And this time we both had our independence and yet were bonded. He wanted me to have my own identity and I tried not to be the typical nagging wife.' The love could never be questioned. 'He was crazily in love with me,' Asha has said. 'But he was more a friend than a husband; we lived together as friends. He grew up alone, with most of his childhood with his grandmother in Calcutta. So he didn't understand the routines involved in a marriage – he didn't understand why one had to get up at a certain time or eat at a specific hour.'

And the gentle soul that Pancham was, he accepted Asha for herself. When the dramatic and outspoken singer once said, 'From now on I'll change myself,' he responded with 'No, never change – I married you only because you are like this. If you change, the fun of our marriage will be spoiled!' And when she thought of a cosmetic change, a new hairdo, he reacted with characteristic wry humour. 'Yes, cut your hair, cut it up to your ears. And then wear jeans – you'll look superb.' Asha was puzzled for a while, then realised 'the poke of the humour. Pancham could not tolerate short hair!' While he seemed not to, he noticed everything. 'Just after we married I would take extra time to get dressed. Pancham made no comments about me or my clothes, but one day I asked "How am I looking?" He replied, "The bindi does not match your sari." I became very angry. "That means you watch every woman in such a minute way?" That day we had a big fight and after that he never said anything directly to me. But he wasn't the jealous type. He knew that I had made some mistakes. He understood that no human being is perfect. And he never liked hurting anyone. He was also very sentimental – he cried when his old car went into a ditch. When his dog Tipsy died, he wept for days!'

Success must have brought in big money, but Pancham did not believe that to be too important. 'When he saw me wearing a diamond ring, he asked me what the name of the stone was. And when I told him it was a diamond, he wanted to know if a diamond really looked like that – that was Pancham!' Asha laughs. He was extravagant, but never for himself, though he did spend money on equipment to make music. He did, however, go somewhat overboard when it came to his friends, Asha remembered. 'We didn't have any shortage of money. But from beginning to end I would be angry and often rebuke Pancham when he would squander money on his friends. Spending it on himself would be a justification.' And buying things for his wife? It was rare, but always special. He did give her a precious gift, one that she always has with her, especially during her performances – 'My lucky charm is a Ganesha locket that RD gave me. Once when I forgot to wear it, my daughter-in-law did not let me perform!'

Pancham's habits distressed his wife. 'I didn't approve of his drinking. He had diabetes, so I tried to control his diet too. But he was not a two-year-old – I could not hold him down in my lap and spoon-feed him! When I was out at concerts or recordings, he would go back to his old habits – stay awake late into the night listening to music or go out to a party.' On occasion, she would go with him, 'but I found myself drinking cups of chai throughout the night – I couldn't do that for long, because it would have affected my voice. Plus, I had to be fresh for recordings the next day, so I stopped going out with him late at night.' It was perhaps that lifestyle that eventually saw the end of a talented musician. Sachin Bhowmick wrote: 'A few days before his death, Pancham told me in confidence that their married life had come to an end. At that agonising period and age when a companion is absolutely needed, Pancham was all alone…'

The passing away of her second husband was a huge blow to the singer. 'Nothing could have prepared me for the death of RD. It's known that my first marriage was not a happy one; yet, I pulled myself together and I survived. Everything seemed to be flowing smoothly … then Pancham died.' The family, as it had done before, closed ranks, protecting her. This time it was her three children who stood by her, supportive and loving. But the world had much to say, including the insinuation that RD and Asha had not been married legally.

Asha said, 'If my children had not been around, I might not have got married again. But for their sake I wanted to stop tongues wagging. If we had not got married, people would have said, "She has no shame, going around with him like that!" But they talked anyway. From the moment Pancham died, I was stabbed in the back. My marriage had become a household topic, turned into a scandal. Circumstances after his death forced me to display my marriage certificate.'

Asha remembered that dreadful night. After a recording for a New Year's television special, Asha recalled, 'I went to Pancham's house in Khar around midnight but he was annoyed and told me he was going out. And when I asked him, he said he was going to Khandala with friends. I went home to Prabhu Kunj (Pedder Road). When I got a call that he wasn't feeling well, I rushed to him immediately. My son drove like mad – we got there in about fifteen minutes. Nandu (Anand) and I rushed him to hospital.' It was a tragic situation. No oxygen tank could be located for hours and clinics in the area shut the doors when requested to help. 'He kept saying, "*Bahut dard hai* … it's hurting!" And he was trying to call out my name, "Aa … aa …" but could not. We tried everything, but it was no use. I will always cherish the time I had with him – I wish it could have been longer; I wish we had been together forever. He was a gentle soul who lived his life to the fullest. I don't think he had any unfulfilled desires. I think he died a contented man.

'He once said, "Both of us will move to a bungalow in Khandala that we will build. We will take rest independently and listen to songs for the rest of our lives." How quickly the rest of our life together has been exhausted. Pancham has so much to give to this world. I feel he will come back again as a wonder-boy music director, and finish the creation of compositions that are not yet completed.'

Once the composer had passed on, the rituals needed to be completed. Asha has said, 'When he died, we had a religious ceremony of offering food to the crows and for that I kept a plateful of lunch comprising of his favourite *mirchi bhajiya* and other food on the terrace. The tree became fully crowded with crows, but not one came to eat for more than two hours. Someone even suggested we keep a peg of whisky there, but still there were no crows. Then I said, 'Pancham, I will take good care of your sick mother and also make sure to keep your music alive.' Immediately the crows accepted the offering!' Apocryphal or not, the story sounds typically eccentric.

Once R.D. Burman was gone, the talk began. Asha was painted the villain of this story and was accused of marrying Pancham for his money. She was indignant when she heard this. 'I am not money mad! If I were so, I would not have married Mr Bhosle, who made ₹100 a month! I give money, I do not take it.' It may have been a partnership made in musical heaven, but it was sadly brief, not the happily ever after that Asha longed for. But in that time, from initial friendship to that last moment before Pancham passed away, the duo made some of the most memorable and significant songs happen. And with that repertoire, R.D. Burman and Asha Bhosle will always be together, forever.

9

Let My Melody Merge With Yours

'I cannot live without music,' she said.

And music in India would never have been what it is without Asha Bhosle. She has been singing since she was only eleven, with now over thirteen thousand songs to her credit! But there comes a time when enough is more than enough, she decided a few years ago, when she chose to back away from her playback career. 'People retire at fifty, but I'm still singing. I've sung so much, so many songs with great singers, great music directors – thirteen thousand songs is not an easy feat. Now I'm tired.'

She will sing for a film only if it is 'something very special', like a song composed by Rakesh Adiga for Aryan Pratap's *Sarangi* (2016), which starred Pallavi Nayak and Mathews Manu. 'I liked the melody of this one. And it helped that it was not an item number,' she said of her choice. As always, she was ready for the challenge, singing in Kannada, which she didn't speak. And it fit into her ethos of leaving no genre unsung – 'you pick any song and you can say that Asha has sung one like this'.

But while she may have defocused from the world that has given her such a long and illustrious roster of film work, it does not mean that she has stopped singing in public. 'As a person and as a singer, I like doing something new all the time. I will keep doing that for as long as I can,' she said, 'I like it when I sing in English or Spanish or any other language – I feel good.'

Her work has taken her down roads that few travel – with not just film music, but into the realms of pop, ghazals, bhajans, traditional Indian classical, folk, qawwalis, Rabindra sangeet and much more. She has sung in over eighteen languages, including Hindi, Urdu, Marathi, Assamese, Bengali, Oriya, Nepali, Gujarati, Punjabi, Telugu, Tamil, Malayalam, English, Russian, Czech and Malay. And she has done all this all around the world, peripatetically globetrotting, spreading the music and her special brand of joie de vivre. In the 1980s and 1990s she was everywhere, from Canada to Dubai, from the United States to Great Britain and beyond. Asha covered thirteen cities in the US in a whistle-stop concert tour that lasted twenty days, singing with fever, a cough, weakness, even an attack of colitis. In 2002, she sang in London for a fundraiser concert with Sudesh Bhosle; in 2007 she travelled across the US, Canada and the West Indies on *The Incredibles* tour, accompanied by Sonu Nigam, Kunal Ganjawala and Kailash Kher; and in 2014 she toured the Netherlands, France and Belgium with the Grammy-winning Dutch Metropole Orchestra.

In September 2023, to celebrate her ninetieth birthday, she sang for over three hours on a stage in a packed-out arena in Dubai. She is perhaps the only one of her generation to do so much.

'Most of my colleagues have been working only in Indian music, not thinking about the world beyond what they know. But I always did and still do.' The truth is, Asha has said, 'I have a naturally outgoing nature and a great love for experimentation!'

Like she did when her son Anand told her that she would be composing for, interacting and singing with the British club-dance group, The West India Company, led by Stephen Luscombe from Blancmange. The music the band made blended electronic beats with Indian instruments and added desi voices to spark up the British music scene, albeit briefly. Asha would be one of them. She would also have to do live interviews on the radio and on television, all in England, hence all in English. Her daughter Varsha recalled how her mother woke every morning at 4, come rain or shine, plugged into her cassette player and studied spoken English for hours at a stretch. It worked. She sang '*Ave Maria*' with the group. The song, which had chants to the Mother of God and Lord Ganesha, was a straight-out dance track that made it to the Top 20 line-up. Asha was feted on radio and television, in newspapers and magazines, even giving interviews to the press in English that was fluent, idiomatic and natural. As she said at the time, 'After you have sung in Tamil, singing in English, Russian or Malayalam is so easy!'

As easy for her seems to be the capacity to live so many different roles with her music. Ken Hunt, who wrote for *The Rough Guide to the Music of India*[8], attributed her success to her ability to 'change the colour of her voice. She is convincing as the ingénue, the matron or the old lady looking back wistfully'. And there was enjoyment of every moment of each song and

---

[8] *The Rough Guide to the Music of India.* (2002). Published in London: World Music Network, p2002. Description: 1 sound disc: digital, stereo.; 4 3/4 in. Format: CD; Additional Credits: Hunt, Ken.

its making, along with the partnerships that made it happen. But there was one thing that really impressed Asha while doing collaborations with foreign musicians, enough for her to comment on it. 'International artistes are very professional – they are interested in your work, not in what you had for breakfast!' Most of all, Asha had a blast working with musicians from other parts of the world. 'It was fun and very easy.' But there were cultural differences, some amusing. 'When I met some of these very successful artistes, they were wearing rags. I thought they were very poor and needed financial help. Then my son Anand told me that it was fashion and these people were very rich!' And to someone accustomed to the reverence of the Mumbai film crowd, the casual working style in the West was a little difficult to adapt to. 'At a recording one day, someone said to me, "C'mon baby!" and I retorted saying I wasn't a baby ... they could call me Aunty, though. They didn't. So I asked them to call me Asha!'

But perhaps this experimentation was more because of Asha's own spirit than due to the need to boost herself over the hurdles of competition from home. 'I like challenges. I believe in moving with the times and enjoying myself,' she said. 'I had fun working with people like Boy George, Ornette Coleman and Michael Stipe. When I first met Boy George in London, I thought he was a pretty girl! Then we met at the Taboo Club and he hugged me and said he was a great fan of mine. When he came to India, I took him around Mumbai.' Working with the oh-so-dramatic pop singer was a bit daunting for Asha at first. 'I was a bit uncomfortable initially, but realised it was the same as working with any musician.' And she soon became fond of him and remembered with a smile that 'He would take an hour to do his makeup. And he did his eyebrows so well, he'd put any woman to shame!'

Boy George, who was born George Alan O'Dowd, is known as much for his exquisite maquillage as for his unique genre of music: blue-eyed soul, influenced by rhythm and blues and reggae, with a touch of glam later in his solo career. In the 1980s, he was the lead singer of Culture Club, topping the charts with songs like '*Do you really want to hurt me*', '*Karma chameleon*' and '*Church of the poison mind*'. '*Do they know it's Christmas*', made for food aid to Ethiopia, featured him as lead vocalist. Then, against a backdrop of drugs, weight gain and more, Boy George got involved with the Hare Krishna movement, from which time '*Bow down mister*' was born. The song became a UK Top 30 hit in 1991. The singer remembers, 'I met Asha through Stephen Luscombe (of Blancmange), when he flew me and a bunch of ragbag performers to Bombay to work on his West India Company musical project. I knew of Stephen through Blancmange, his 1980s pop group, and said yes to being part of his Indian extravaganza. I cannot remember everyone who was there … Pandit Dinesh, India's Godfather of percussion, Stephen Luscombe, of course, designers Mike Nicholls and Rachel Auburn, rapper MC Kinky, a singer called Hope and a group of Indian musicians. I remember recording a version of Abba's '*I believe in angels*' with Asha and a song about the elephant god Ganesh, which I still vaguely remember. I think it was a spiritual folk classic.'

Boy George does not know 'if very much happened with that project. I guess somewhere Stephen has those recordings, but after that trip I heard no more of it. I did however meet Asha and I vowed to record something with her, because I was so taken with her amazing voice.' That 'something' became a funky, fun track called '*Bow down mister*' that has a video that brings to the fore elements of psychedelia and more movement and colour than the eye can comfortably deal with. And even as the popstar sends out his message with his always meaningful lyrics, Asha's voice comes in clarion-clear in the *alaap*. Boy George recalls how it came together:

'During a trip to India I had written a song called '*Bow down Mister*', which was about my first trip to India and my association with the Hare Krishna movement. I was able to get a bunch of devotees to sing on the track in London, which I felt gave it a real authenticity! I reached out to Asha to find out whether she would sing on it with me and to know when she might be in the UK. I believe I talked to her son and eventually we got together in London.' It was a free-wheeling and happy recording. 'I asked Asha to literally freestyle over the song. She sang a verse with excerpts from the Bhagavad Gita and it was perfect and magical. I remember she was confused by the pop shield in front of the microphone and said something like "What is this thing?" – we left that at the very start of the song.' While Asha admired the eyebrows that Boy George had groomed so immaculately, he was a fan of her voice. 'Asha has the voice of a sixteen-year-old girl and of course, her sister Lata Mangeshkar is also amazing. It was such a fabulous musical connection we had then and the song remains a favourite in my shows. Of course, I have never shared an actual stage with Asha and can only imagine how fantastic that would be...!'

The story behind the 'song about the elephant God Ganesh, which I still vaguely remember', as Boy George put it, is one that is coloured by a happy haze of smoke from various sources and the freedom that came from being in a lovely beach house at the edge of the sea in India's commercial capital, far from the madding crowd of everyday Bombay. An *India Today* report from September 1990 describes it well:

> Within sits Boy George, the androgynous Liberace of the

> pop world, next to Stephen Luscombe who's going berserk on his synthesiser creating a new song with percussionist Pandit Dinesh. Nearby, Sultan Khan has just completed a soulful bandish on the sarangi in Raag Kedar, while Asha Bhosle and Jamaican jazz singer Hope Augustus make mental notes about the right pitch to strike. What's emerging from this cacophonous brigade is a new fusion album, tentatively titled *Ek Nervous Breakdown*, which aims to transform the Indian pop scene. But it's been a lot of hard work. Pandit Dinesh and Stephen Luscombe of the West India Company have put together an unlikely combination of musicians to create an album they're confident will be a chartbuster[9].

One aim of the exercise for Luscombe and his partner Peter Culshaw was to take Asha into a new realm and, incidentally, shoot her career into the stratosphere. The work started in May 1990, with songs being written, tunes being worked on, the editing, mixing and synthesising consuming everyone who was part of it. Luscombe was brought up with the strains of Hindi film music playing in the nearby suburban district of Southall, while Culshaw succumbed to Indian enchantment via music from the Dagar brothers, the dhrupad style of Dagarvani. Boy George was a Krishna bhakt and chanted Buddhist mantras, which added a spiritual quality to his collaboration with Asha, all the trappings of Westernism and personal eccentricities notwithstanding. As the lady said at the time, she found him 'enthusiastic, receptive. It was easy to persuade him to work on an album together.'

---

[9]https://www.indiatoday.in/magazine/society-and-the-arts/story/19900915-boy-george-brigade-hopes-to-create-fresh-fusion-music-812987-1990-09-14

But even as she sang alaaps for '*Bow down Mister*' (1990) with the former Culture Club lead singer, Asha essayed a Sanskrit verse with the erstwhile REM lead singer in '*The way you dream*' from the film *1 Giant Leap* (2002); the song was used on the soundtrack of the movie *Bulletproof Monk* (2003). According to Asha, 'Film music is good, but private albums give you an outlet for your own creativity. The songs are everlasting and the albums keep selling for years.' She has found some degree of international success with these songs too, adding to her repertoire working with Nelly Furtado via a remix version of '*I'm free like a bird*' in *Nelly vs Asha* in 2001, the boy band Code Red ('*We can make it if we try*', 1997) and others like Robbie Williams, Brett Lee, Kronos Quartet and more. Her ambition? 'I want to work with Quincy Jones. Pancham thought he was a god, so I can fulfil one of his wishes too!'

Perhaps her best international exposure across the UK and the USA came with '*Brimful of Asha*', a song by British East–West fusion band Cornershop that released in 1997. It was remixed by Richard Cook and Fatboy Slim soon after, both versions doing very well. The song is pure pop, loaded with meaning, sung by Tijinder Singh, who is of Punjabi origin but grew up in England. It described the Hindi film industry and, to some extent, the rivalry between Asha Bhosle (called '*saadi rani*' in the song) and her sister Lata Mangeshkar, with play on the word *asha*, meaning hope. The song speaks of the dream that a film gives to its audience, the hope that viewers find in the stories unfolding on the big screen and the escape from the harsh realities of life that they hear in the lyrics. '*Brimful of Asha*' made a kind of musical history – Asha's son Anand Bhosle heard it in San Francisco and told her about it. And when she was going through Immigration at Heathrow Airport in London and was asked about her profession of 'singer' cited in her passport, she told the official that she was the Asha of the song. 'He was so excited that he left his desk and called his friends to meet me!' It may have got the singer through airport checks faster, but more than that, it showed her what people she had never met thought of her. '*Brimful of Asha*' reached Number 60 on the UK Singles Chart in 1997, but after remixing and better marketing, it shot up to Number 1 in the UK and 16 on the US Billboard Modern Rock Tracks countdown. It even inspired an eponymous cocktail.

And there was plenty more. In 2005 Sarah Brightman – of *Phantom of the Opera* fame and ex-wife of Andrew Lloyd Webber – used a bit of '*Dil cheez kya hai*' from *Umrao Jaan* as the start of '*You take my breath away*' on the album *Harem*. In the same year, Black Eyed Peas added a touch of masala to their song '*Don't phunk with my heart*' by incorporating vignettes of Asha's '*Ae naujawan sab kuchh yahaan*' from *Apradh* (1972) and '*Yeh mera dil*' from *Don*. It was 2006 when Asha sang on '*You're the one for me*', a musical adventure for Brett Lee, better known as a cricketer; while the reviews of the song were not all positive, it did make it to the second position on the pop charts. The same year had her going cross-border. She sang '*Dil ke taar baje*' for the Pakistani film *Mein Ek Din Laut Ke Aaoonga* with pop star Jawad Ahmed. It worked, and both Indians and Pakistani audiences gave the song a thumbs up. None of these, Asha always said, were planned. 'They all just happened. Also, my son Anand has introduced me to musicians from the US, Spain, China and other countries who want to work with me. I am always ready to experiment with new ideas.'

But it was her collaboration with the string foursome Kronos Quartet, set up in 1985, that made the most noise. It all began in the 1990s, when David Harrington of the group heard '*Aaj ki raat*' from *Anamika* (1973). He was apparently so enchanted by Asha's singing and the song itself that he used in in the album *Kronos Caravan*. As Asha's son Anand mentioned in an interview, 'About fifteen years ago, David Harrington, the founder of the group, started listening to Hindi music. Every time he liked a song, he would find that it was composed by R.D. Burman and sung by Asha. He said he considers Pancham to be the greatest composer from India, on par with many Western classical greats.' In fact, what Harrington said was, 'I think R.D. Burman is one of the greatest composers of the twentieth century. As an orchestrator I would put him in the same sentence as Stravinsky and Debussy. As a melodicist, I would put him with Schubert or George Gershwin.' As for Asha, 'As a vocalist she has the largest vocabulary of vocal techniques I have heard.' The feeling he has for the singer is not just awe or respect. As he said it, 'The first time I met Ashaji, she had diamonds on and was dressed in the most beautiful sari I have ever seen and she looked very regal. Then I looked down and saw that the Queen of Bollywood was wearing tennis shoes. I thought, "I love this woman!"'

In 2005 the group put together *You've Stolen My Heart: Songs from R.D. Burman's Bollywood*. By that time RDB had died, but Asha agreed to be part of the project since it was a way that she could take Pancham's music to a global audience, something he had always wanted to do. The album features favourites with their translations re-sung by Asha, and included '*Chura liya hai tumne jo dil ko*' (You've Stolen My Heart), '*Dum maaro dum*' (Take another toke), '*Mera kuchh saamaan*' (Some of my things) and '*Ekta deshlai kathi jwala*' (Light a match) from one of the prayer albums made by RD and Asha. The singer called Kronos Quartet 'a very serious group of musicians', but showed off her ability to work hard and sing by recording three or four songs in one day, all at the age of seventy-two. And when they made music together in concert, with violinist Harrington, new recruit cellist Jeffrey Zeigler, tabla player Debopriyo Sarkar and pipa star Wu Man playing to Asha's tunes, it was magic, the reviewers wrote. The collection, also featuring Zakir Hussain doing percussion, was a hot seller, nominated for a Grammy Award in 2006 for Best Contemporary World Music Album. Asha had great fun, maintaining her own identity throughout. 'I have done many concerts with Kronos Quartet for international audiences, but I still wear a sari, sing my own songs and interact with the foreign musicians and the audience in my special English – and the response has been wonderful!'

It was all because of Ken Hunt, who played matchmaker and consultant. Hunt is a freelance music critic, author and broadcaster who is always listening to, writing about and meeting people involved in music, writing lyrics, conceptualising concerts and more than he will talk about. He is hugely respected and much loved by those in the business and by intrusive journalists who want him to talk about anything and everything in music, but does not suffer fools lightly. He specialises in various aspects of his field, but has an especially soft corner for folk, tribal, popular and art music of the India–Pakistan–Bangladesh region. His repertoire is enormous, uncountable almost. And he has contributed as editor, translator, writer and much more to audio and video releases that cannot be easily listed, including those by Asha Bhosle, Hariprasad Chaurasia, Ravi Shankar – who called his intuition about Indian music 'unique' – Yehudi Menuhin, Vishwa Mohan Bhatt, Ali Akbar Khan and Asha Bhosle, Lata Mangeshkar, Sultan Khan and others.

A fan of Bollywood music – almost any music, really! – and a friend of Harrington et al, Hunt managed to avoid all the usual hurdles and chicanes that may arise when approaching musicians of a certain stature. 'For many decades I'd written about non-Western classical music and, central to this story, Hindustani and Carnatic art music. I had got to know Ali Akbar Khan sahib reasonably well, interviewed him several times, and that professional relationship grew into a friendship, to the extent that he prepared and cooked an entire family meal for his family and my wife Santosh and me at his home in Marin County, California. Khan sahib's and my relationship had gone beyond a straightforward musician–journalist one. A few years after Khan sahib's death, I was talking to Swapan Chaudhuri and he threw into the conversation that Ali Akbar Khan had told him that I was his favourite music journalist. To which I replied (*expletive deleted*), "Well, he never told me!"' So in 1995, when it came to writing booklet notes for the CD of the 1996 release, *Legacy*, 'Khan sahib approached me and naturally I grabbed the opportunity. Ashaji was the other major figure in the collaboration. In order to participate, she had become his shishya. It meant the door swung open immediately when I suggested interviewing Ashaji for the notes. Khan sahib saw how I could do an hour, two hours of interview, mind-mapped without questions and without resorting to paper notes. I imagine he mentioned that to Ashaji. Her guruji had a way with words. Her and my relationship was perhaps underpinned by her guruji's approval of me as a good egg as much as anything.' The interview was done over the phone and 'When we finally met, it was in the spirit of mutual respect. And in my case, in the side-glow of the *guru–shishya parampara* (mentor–protégé tradition).' Hunt had a major advantage. 'I wasn't a *chamcha* like the unnumbered many who wish to get close to her, to touch the hem of her sari. Plus, I'm a charming blue-eyed *gora* (fair-skinned foreigner) with impeccable instincts. I've even passed as an English-speaking

Indian after talking for over an hour with a blind South Indian.' Whatever the spell he cast, it worked.

Hunt knew Harrington well and had been writing about the Kronos Quartet since 1981. The two men started talking about music and musicians and soon got to know each other better and, per Hunt, 'in particular, got to know each other's ears. He is far more musically omnivorous than me. In 1984, I came on board for the album project that became *Pieces of Africa.* It took until 1992 to be released and none of my suggestions made the final album selection. It didn't bother me, but what counted for *You've Stolen My Heart* was that I had first-hand experience of how the Harrington editing process worked. We'd learned to trust our instincts and how to make leaps of the imagination as far as places string quartet music could go was concerned. We could fire off each other.' That was hugely valuable when it came to any collaboration that Hunt and Harrington managed, together or with other people. 'In 2000, when *Caravan* came out, its music was new territory for the Kronos and it was taking the string quartet repertoire to new places with its assortment of music from Café Tacuba, Carlos Paredes and Anibal Troilo. It had the quartet's take on '*Aaj ki raat*' on it. Hard to believe now, but when I wrote its booklet notes we couldn't even conclusively establish R.D. Burman's birthplace!' At the time, Hunt and Asha had never met, face to face, even though the singer would perhaps have remembered the writer from the *Legacy* interview. 'I introduced myself to her at the Nehru Centre in London and handed her a taste of the good Kronos stuff. I remember trying to explain what Kronos had done on the CD she was holding in her hands. I'm sure she found it – and me – frankly bemusing. I mean, how bizarre must it have sounded back then for a bunch of foreigners to have recorded an instrumental version of a Bollywood song! She had no idea what the term "string quartet" meant, so I counted out the instruments. I imagine Ashaji's curiosity was piqued. The proposal came a few days later.' There was, Hunt reveals, another project cooking, involving her and they met a few days later for an exhaustive interview, at the end of which, 'without consulting David, I mooted the project that would grow into *You've Stolen My Heart.* David and I had talked about Bollywood music in the past. Nevertheless, it was a pretty radical thing to suggest, if I say so myself, and I had the chutzpah to suggest it. When I told David, he was beyond delighted.'

It also helped that this wasn't the first time that Hunt had written about Asha. As he said, 'Down the years I had increasingly been called on to write not about South Asian classical or folk music forms, but popular music. I compiled a whole bunch of thematic CDs, one of which was the *Rough Guide to Bollywood Legends: Asha Bhosle* (2003).' He had one more little trick up his musical sleeve to get the family involved and to get better access to the singer. 'I picked my sixteen tracks, but left a lacklustre one in the selection: "Oh perfidious Albion"! But the ruse worked a treat and the family responded. I'm really proud of the selections in that introduction.' Hunt met Asha and her son Anand 'shortly after, whilst they were breezing through London. We did an interview specific to the *Rough Guide* volume's track selections, with Santosh taking photos. At this point I proposed the project that became *You've Stolen My Heart.* I did it on the spot and off the cuff.' Spontaneity became the mother of invention, fortuitously linked to history. 'On an earlier occasion – in 2000 at the Nehru Centre in London – I gave Asha a copy of another project I'd worked on: *Kronos Caravan.* It included a string quartet version of '*Aaj ki raat*' with Zakir bhai accompanying.

What I proposed was that she collaborate with Kronos on an album of R.D. Burman compositions. I hadn't ever discussed the matter with David Harrington!' But Harrington had been well coached, since over the years he and Hunt had 'talked a great deal about R.D. Burman and I'd given him listening tips.' It was a happy ending to the story. As Hunt remembers, *You've Stolen My Heart* worked out beautifully and got a Grammy nomination but (*curses*) missed out at the final hurdle.' The final selection for the album was made at a small hotel in Paris. 'David and I thrashed through the shortlisted Burman compositions – one of the most intense listening experiences I've ever had. We got most of the tracks on first pass, because we had chosen the same ones. *You've Stolen My Heart*'s secret weapon was the Bengali songs – have you heard Pancham's Bengali tracks on the album? I was at the sessions in Marin and Ashaji asked me who'd chosen them. I head-wobbled. David and I wanted a bigger Pancham picture and that's what, I believe, came out of our Parisian days.' Harrington and Hunt were 'on the same alpha wave band when we met in Paris to discuss Burman compositions in November 2003. It coincided with Kronos performing at Théâtre de la Ville. We were all staying in Hôtel Victoria Châtelet, maybe 150 metres from the venue. We'd both agreed to turn up with a bunch of ideas. I brought two burned CDs of R.D. Burman tracks – twenty-two tracks. Aside from the obvious business of bringing compositions to the feast, a good number of the tracks we brought were solely for sonic idea, not to be weighed up for inclusion. That was part of the deal to capture the spirit of Burman's idiosyncratic song visions. The outro of *Rishte bante hain* is Burman meets the Beatles – something he never did, to my knowledge. I don't remember Burman putting a trumpeting elephant on a track, but we wanted to do something in the spirit of Pancham, since he loved effects and David loves SFX. In my own defence, I have to say, I was overruled on elephant calls.' But in between all the chaos, a short list was made, of which 'Four of the compositions that made the final selection were in the first seven I played.'

Harrington was as enchanted by Asha as Hunt right through the recordings. He said in an interview to *The Record*:

> Ashaji is kind of like Elvis! We don't have anyone in our culture in America that has the same role in our society that she has in your society. There's certainly no artiste whose voice is so miraculous like hers is and can take on so many musical colours. She commands one of the biggest vocabularies of all the musicians I've encountered. She has the capability of making her voice like one of the instruments we play, and also of being the quintessential vocalist. It's just incredible! The idea that Kronos could have Asha Bhosle as our first lead singer was just too good to be true. I knock on wood every day when I think about this.

The almost-intuitive bond with Rahul Dev Burman came with the recognition that of all the music from Indian films that Harrington listened to, 'I began to realise that as an orchestrator he's as good as Stravinsky or Debussy or Duke Ellington, and as a melody writer he's on the same level as Schubert or Gershwin or the Beatles.'

He selected twelve songs, with Hunt – eight to be sung by Asha, the others solos by the Kronos Quartet – and then with RDB's original recordings as templates, started working on sound effects, adding layers and instruments, many of which Burman himself would have loved creating. For one, they threw around eight violin bows to make a clicking sound they called 'bow percussion'! Harrington has a favourite song too. ''*Mera kuchh saamaan*' was the song that I absolutely had to have on this album. To me it's one of the most beautiful songs I've ever heard!'

This entire project was something Asha called 'a new experiment'. Perhaps the selling point was the fact that the Kronos Quartet were huge fans of RDB. 'They met me when I was touring the US, and they described him as the Mozart of India,' she laughs. 'They were very keen to reinterpret his music, and I was impressed by their dedication.'

The experimentation was constant. In Paris, Hunt roped in Bapi Das Baul to demonstrate Baul instruments; he had the idea to 're-imagine a Bengali track of Pancham's as if it were a Baul song. It never happened, but it gives you a flavour of how ideas were flying around' he recalls. It was in Paris that they discussed adding more to the album, to add colour and instrumentation to each number they had chosen. 'Sultan Khan playing sarangi was one idea. Zakir Hussain had to be there, as he had been on *Kronos Caravan*. I adored the way Burman's sarod parts were transferred to Wu Man's Chinese instrumentation. David and I had both got to know Ashaji independently of each other; when I heard what she had done with transposing the sarod's voice to the pipa, I was completely floored. At one point during the sessions, Zakir played the cycle as the *taal* proscribed, playing each matra. Ashaji pulled him up: There had to be a missed beat, as opposed to a *khali*, an empty beat. Pancham had missed a beat because it fitted the cinematic action. Zakir had autocorrected.' From the start, *You've Stolen My Heart* was going to recognise Burman as a composer and innovator. As Hunt remembers, 'It took a bunch of Westerners to see his potential beyond remix and rip-off. We knew what we were doing. But it was a huge gamble.' The wish list was endless and never matched. 'The one I'd have really wanted was an instrumental interpretation of '*Pyar hua chupke se*' from *1942: A Love Story* as an instrumental string quartet piece. Its melodicism really excited me.'

What is special about Asha is that her music is at best 'the sound of surprise', Hunt said in an interview. 'That applies particularly to her work with R.D. Burman, and when she voiced Helen. My philosophy is, it's much better to focus on her music that makes your toes curl with pleasure. After all, better to remember the Alphonso mangoes of life that make your taste buds swoon than whatever made you grit your teeth.' Hunt and Asha spoke at length on many occasions, but when they discussed the 'size of her output, she was frank about taking assignments because she had to be the breadwinner. Anyone who had or has had a family or relatives to support can relate to that.' What makes the singer so special is something that goes beyond technique or delivery for Hunt. Instead of talking about either, 'I'd say I wish I could relive the thrill and moment of first falling in love with '*Rishte bante hain*' on the non-film album *Dil Padosi Hai*. The mood of that Burman/Gulzar song is quite different from the epiphany of experiencing Aruna Sairam, for instance, sing the '*Kalinga Narthana Thillana*' for the first time in concert, but both were significant epiphanies.'

Above and beyond anything else, it is the way that Asha conveys emotion that Hunt is caught by, even though, he confesses, 'I may not understand the word-by-word meaning or the intellectual sweep of what she is delivering in, say, Hindi or Bengali. That is probably true of many songs I listen to in English or any other language.' On a musical level, he admires her 'skills in negotiating pace, tempo and melodic shifts. The Indian and Western scales and octaves are very different and it is not often that a musician straddles both worlds, as it were.'

Asha is a vocal actress. She can deliver in character. Who else at the time could have sung for Helen? Listen to her breath control in 'Koi aaya aane bhi de' and you know she's at the top of her game when she made You've Stolen My Heart. *On one occasion during the sessions in* Sausalito *I was next to her as she recorded and saw her switch into character.*

During one of our Parisian conversations David asked me whether I'd ever heard of Indian laughter clubs. As it happened, I had – I'd watched an Indian TV news clip about them. We talked about Ashaji's ability to laugh on cue and the idea for the album's hidden track is the merger of those two ideas. I was standing next to her in the studio for a laughter club take. There were perhaps eight to ten of us waiting to laugh on cue. My laughter was puny beside hers. She just instantly slipped into the role.

If Hunt had to do it all over again would he choose someone else to collaborate on this kind of album? 'Nobody,' he is sure. 'Kronos and Ashaji were of a moment. We knew it was the like of which, concerts included, could never happen again. I mean – as we joked – if you're going to have a lead singer…'

Hunt also made friends with the woman called Asha – as much as that could be possible. He watched her as keenly as he listened to her on that greatly cherished album. 'Her off-stage personality isn't necessarily anything like her on-stage one. One time I was at a concert of hers in Amsterdam and she came to the wings with her son Anand. She was waiting for the stage announcement for her to come on after the instrumental overture. She looked her age, but when the announcement came she shed a decade or two on the spot.

It was a completely different woman who hit the stage. That's nothing unique to her. It's what happens to musicians and actors or public speakers and politicians when the adrenalin kicks in.'

The next year, in 2007, the story moved on to its new chapter. Asha was asked by popstar Robbie Williams, formerly of the boy band Take That and by then a success as a solo artiste, to collaborate with him on remixes of two of his songs, '*Rock DJ*' and '*Better man*'. It took a long time to actually be finished, and Asha was heard to say in 2009, 'I finished recording my part two years ago, but there were some problems from Robbie's side and the songs got stuck. But they will be out soon.' The words were the same as in the originals, but the songs were given an Indian flavour with new instrumentation and Asha's voice. The stars did not sing the remix versions together. With technology playing its part, Asha recorded her sections in Mumbai with instrumentalists from China, Hong Kong and Singapore, after which it was worked on in Hong Kong and the final song put together. '*Rock DJ*' had a distinct masala Bollywood vibe to it, while '*Better man*' was more soothing, spiritual. And in 2010, there were reports of Asha in talks to follow this up with a collaboration she had always wanted – with Carlos Santana. 'I have always wanted to sing with an artiste like him. It will be something new and different. I have experimented with my music a lot and this is going to be a new challenge.'

Even as Asha made music with international artistes, she worked on non-film albums in India and stepped into the controversial realm of remixes. When she was seventy-five, in 2008, she won the Padma Vibhushan and celebrated with *75 Years of Asha: A Musical Journey*. This compilation featured new recordings of her favourite songs as well as new compositions, and was supposed to include a number by one of her own most-loved singers, Miriam Makeba, which unfortunately did not make it to the album. And once she started redoing her own songs, working on remixes was a short step in a new direction. As she said when asked at the time, 'I change with the times. There was a time when ghazals were very popular, but when the fad ended the singers were out of work. I thought, *Baap re!* If I only sang in one style, I'd soon be gone too!' Perhaps that always will reflect in her attitude to her music. She even roped in people she knew from Hindi films to join her in *Asha and Friends*. As she said, 'I can tell who is a good singer. And I need to know, because nobody has had the courage so far to approach me! They respect me a lot and give me a lot of love. So I find out who can sing well and then call them for a recording.'

So when Asha went out-and-out pop with Hindi songs, she was good at it. Consider *Jaanam Samjha Karo*, *Rahul and I* and *Legacy*. At over sixty-four, Asha broke out of the filmi mould and went pop with a vengeance, making it big on the charts. In fact, she won the Indian Viewers' Choice award from MTV with '*Jaanam samjha karo*', even being showcased as MTV's Artist of the Month in October of 1977. The recognition is thrilling for her, even after the slew of trophies that she has garnered over the years: 'It made me feel special that even the third generation across the world loves my voice. It rejuvenated by singing spirit!' And there was more – *Legacy*, an album she recorded with sarod maestro Ustad Ali Akbar Khan, was nominated for a Grammy award. The 1996 *Rahul and I*, a remix of songs she worked on with her then-late husband R.D. Burman, sold over 1.5 million copies in just three months, a record for the time. She sang pop for hit-maker Biddu, Bengali *geet* with Amit Kumar, a new collection of songs with sitar maestro Shujaat Khan called *Naina Lagaike* and a ghazal album with Khayyam. Bryan Adams, Santana and Phil Collins, among others are also on her extensive wish list of collaborations. In June 2015, Paul Di'Anno, a vocalist with the heavy metal group Iron Maiden, announced that he wanted to record a song with Asha, calling her a master of her craft, whose voice he finds deeply soothing. 'I can listen to Asha Bhosle songs the entire day long. Her voice has an amazing quality – it makes the hair on my body stand up. You do come across good voices, but she is in a different league altogether; the bends in her voice are a class apart. I wish I could record even just one song with her before I die.

And she was equal to the task of squashing the wannabes too; in 1995 British-Indian Bally Sagoo tweaked Asha's '*Chura liya hai*' from *Yaadon Ki Baraat* and the MTV generation loved it. She had to retaliate and make sure she stayed ahead of the brat pack that was speeding along and threatening to overtake her. With the support of her children, she set up a collaboration with Lesle Lewis, composer, singer and one half of the musical duo Colonial Cousins with Hariharan. Lewis had already worked with her on remixes for *Jaanam Samjha Karo* and took on the task of writing scores for a new collection of familiar songs called *Rahul and I*. He saw Asha as 'quite ahead of her time. She took a calculated risk and plunged into New Age music, using her experience to her advantage.' It worked. Audiences lapped up the songs that now had a new edge and gave rave reviews to the music videos that featured a sweetly matronly Asha wearing her embellished saris and diamonds. Ken Ghosh, who directed the video for '*O mere sona re*' that was originally part of the *Teesri Manzil* soundtrack (Shammi Kapoor, Asha Parekh) said, 'It was a big challenge to retain the traditional look and still make her seem hip.' But Asha knew what she wanted and how to get it. Maybe it came from what A.R. Rahman describes as 'a voice with a face. She is still 16 at heart.' The album included favourites like '*Chura liya hai*' (*Yaadon Ki Baraat*), '*Dum maro dum*' (*Hare Krishna Hare Ram*), '*Duniya mein logon ko*' (*Apna Desh*), '*Jaane jaan*' (*Jawaani Diwaani*), '*Jai jai Shiv Shankar*' (originally sung by Lata in *Aap Ki Kasam*, 1974), '*O mere sona re*', '*Piya tu ab to aaja*' (*Caravan*) and '*Yeh ladka haye Allah*' (*Hum Kisise Kum Nahin*, 1977). And it was a bestseller.

Even as she gets older and faces some harsh realities in her never-serene life, Asha finds solace in music. She used it to heal after a bad marriage, to escape to when her beloved second husband R.D. Burman passed away, to regain strength on the passing of her daughter Varsha, to recoup after the death of her son Hemant. And she had kept going, her latest international collaboration being at the Womadelaide, the annual world music and dance festival held in Adelaide, South Australia, which featured over five hundred artistes from twenty countries. As she has said, 'Music is like breathing for me. The day it stops, my breath will stop too. There is so much to do and I am afraid there is very little time left. I hope I can continue singing in my next birth too.'

10

Pujo and Marathi Music

Asha has often been compared to Devi, the feminine power incarnate. But Asha is far more human, with all the failings and weaknesses of a mere mortal. She is a devotee of Lord Shiva and rejects the idea of anyone taking on the divine mantle. 'I believe in God and not in humans [as Gods],' she has said. 'Anyone who has taken birth cannot be a God. The only God is the one who is above. I believe in only one God: like Lord Shiva, whom my family worships.' She is known to regularly recite the *Mrityunjaya Mahamantra*. 'We are from the city of Mangeshi, which has a famous Shiva temple – that is how we are Mangeshkars. We worship all gods, but we are big devotees of Shiva. If we are alive today, it is because of Shiva.' By extension, anyone who worships Shiva will pay respects to his consort, Devi, Shakti, Parvati, Durga … whatever her avatar may be.

In 1954, Asha took the devotional route with *Durga Pooja*, a film directed by Dhirubhai Desai and starring Nirupa Roy and Trilok Kapoor, singing numbers like '*Jai hey Durga mata*' for composer S.N. Tripathi. These songs – and many more of the kind, like '*Chalo bulawa aaya hai*' from *Avatar* (1983) and '*Sabse bada tera naam*' from *Suhaag* (1979) – took Asha out of her well-worn groove of sexy dance numbers and made her a fixture in the soundtrack for religious celebrations, be it Durga puja in Bengal or Ganesha *aarti* in Mumbai. In Kolkata, the *pujo* commanded the musical offerings of composers and singers from Hindi cinema, from Lata Mangeshkar, who recorded her first Bengali song in 1955, especially for the puja, to more recent offerings from Shreya Ghoshal. The prerequisites for a special song for Durga puja are simple: it must be original, new; it must be in Bengali; and it must be released during the pujo season, not in a film, but for the festival. So many familiar names added their magic to this genre, including S.D. Burman, R.D. Burman, Hemant Kumar, Kishore Kumar, Manna De, Asha Bhosle, Mukesh and Mohammed Rafi.

One very important element in pujo festivities, be it in Bengal or Maharashtra or anywhere else, has always been music. The significance of Bengal's Durga puja celebrations in this context is rooted in the popularity of Rahul Dev Burman, who composed a number of songs still played at pandals today. Many were sung by Asha Bhosle with characteristic passion and emotion, forming a genre of their own in her repertoire. And RDB brought a new wave of sound and rhythm to a realm that was at the time staider and very obviously locked into the tenets of tradition. There were big names like Salil Chowdhury, Hemanta Mukherjee, Shyamal Mitra and others who had already set the standard and captured the audiences when Pancham made his debut into this quasi-religious world and he had to do some battling for space before his talent was acknowledged. It took time. He started with tapping the already accepted greats like Kishore Kumar, Lata Mangeshkar and Amit Kumar, edging his way on to the scene. R.D.

Burman's partnership with Asha gave them a reputation on the pujo circuit that was on par with the image that Lata–Salil Chowdhury had, the four producing what has often been called 'the best music of modern Bengal'.

Pancham's favourite was always Asha Bhosle. They did an astonishing 87 pujo songs together. The musical couple was made famous in the genre by '*Phule gondho nei*', '*Sandhyabelay tumi ami*' and '*Nach Mayuri nach*', all still considered classics by lovers of Bengali music. But in 1994, that came to a halt. It took Asha fifteen years to release a new puja album, this one dedicated to the goddess Durga, in 2009, a month before the festival began in Kolkata. '*Mono Rekho*' (Remember Me) was her re-emergence on to the puja music scene after her hiatus.

> '*Puja albums have a special significance. I have sung many Bengali songs with veterans like Manna Dey, composed by music directors like Nachiketa Ghosh, Hemant Mukhopadhyay and of course, R.D. Burman – the first puja album. I recorded was for him. Songs like* 'Jabo ki jabo na' *and* 'Chokhe chokhe kotha boli' *became overnight hits, but then when Pancham passed away I decided not to do any more puja albums.*'

Her reasons were emotional, but practical too. 'I didn't feel like doing an album without Pancham. I also knew that it would not be possible to recreate our combination.'

Asha made her debut in Bengali music in 1958. She recorded duets with Binod Chattopadhyay for HMV, with music composed by Manna De. A year later, De and Asha made a puja album for the record company, which was a huge success. There was a flood of requests and recordings and at one time she was told that she had sung the maximum number of songs in Bengali, far more than any other singer. '*Sara pyar tumhara*' became '*Amar swapno tumi*' respectively in the Hindi and Bengali versions of the film *Anand Ashram* in 1977, both with Kishore Kumar, with whom she dueted in '*Adho alo chhayate*' in *Kalankini Kankanati* (1981) and '*Chirodini tumi je amar*', a Bappi Lahiri composition for *Amar Sangee* (1987). By then, she had sung playback in films like *Chhadmabeshi*, *Bandi* and *Mouchak*. She worked with composers like Sudhin Dasgupta, Nachiketa Ghosh and Vinod Chatterjee, but says, 'After singing "*Jabo ki jabo na*" for Pancham, all the Bengali songs I have sung were for him.' Some of these were converted from Hindi, like '*Gunjone dole je bhramar*' from '*Gun guna rahe hai bhaware*' from *Aradhana*, '*Chokhe name brishti*' from *Jaane Kya Baat Hai* and '*Gungun gunje*' from *Pyar Deewana Hota Hai* (2002).

With time acting as the great healer, Asha did indeed get back to working on a festival collection, *Mone Rekho*, and one fine morning she asked Babul Bose to compose eight puja songs. The recording was done under the Asha Audio label, established years earlier by Mahua Lahiri, a friend of Asha's. The team recorded six songs in eight days, the other two a short while later, when Asha returned from a trip to the United States. Then came the process of mixing after which the video was created. *Mone Rekho* was indeed a memory, and a dedication to a great love and a successful collaboration of music and minds. 'You could say that it is a tribute to R.D. Burman, yes. While we were recording, I felt as if Pancham was sitting near me and listening to my songs.' Perhaps he was, because it worked. People loved it.

A few years later, she decided to re-record the music that Burman had sung. 'It has been so many years, the technology of recording has changed, sounds and styles have changed and I wondered, if he were alive, how would he have recorded it? So I selected the songs and got Nitin Shankar, who has lived with Pancham's songs for many years, to rearrange the sound in a way that youngsters could relate to it.' *Pancham Tumi Kothay* was released in 2014 in memory of Rahul Dev Burman, on his seventy-fifth birth anniversary.

Asha's Marathi repertoire is no less impressive. In fact, she started her movie career with '*Chala chala nav bala*' for the film *Majha Bal* in 1943, when she was just ten years old, following it up with more in *Gokulacha Raja* (1950) before moving her focus to Hindi. Over twelve thousand songs and many decades later, she is still going vocally strong, with her performing in Dubai to celebrate her ninetieth birthday in September 2023, and more recently, with the superb rendition of the catchy number '*Tauba tauba*'. On the way, she has sung more Marathi film songs than can easily be counted, along with bhavgeet, natya sangeet, abhangs, aartis and the lokgeet. The awards were aplenty and included the Best Singer trophy from the government of Maharashtra in 1962 for the film *Manini* (1961, director Anant Man; starring Jayshree Gadkar and Ramesh Deo). Other films she has sung for are *Molkarin*, *Jait Re Jait*, *Gharkul*, *Devbappa*, *Sangtye Aika*, *Saamna*, *Nivdung* and *Singhasan*, to name a few. '*Dhundit rahu mastit raahu*' from the 1999 film *Nisarg Raja* also features Mahendra Kapoor with Asha and is still one of her most popular Marathi hits.

11

Remixes and Beyond

Even as Asha Bhosle's musical star shone less brightly by the late 1990s than it had for decades, she was on a new track. It was the time of remixes and remakes, with classic songs being contemporised. After a little initial hesitation, Asha took to the new sound, beat and tempo with as much vim, vigour and verve as she had done the rhythms of the bossa nova and the Rolling Stones. She rocked the live stage too, performing in her glittering diamonds and sparkling saris, swaying and bopping with the enthusiasm of any singer half a century younger than her.

It was Lesle Lewis of Colonial Cousins who coasted to the top of what came to be called the Indi-pop wave. And along the way he brought in memorable voices, from Asha to Sunita Rao, Alisha Chinai and KK. Lewis's father was P.L. Raj (a well-known choreographer in Hindi cinema who gave major hits like '*Khaike paan Banaraswala*' from *Don,* and '*Yahoo!*' from *Junglee*, 1961). Lewis was influenced not just by the film music he was surrounded by, but also by the Western sounds of Eric Clapton, Jimi Hendrix, the Beatles and others. He started writing his own music and sang at hotels, played in bands, composed advertising jingles and created signature tunes for leading television networks, on the way seducing Indians to drink more milk with the unforgettable '*Doodh, doodh, piyo glassful doodh*' jingle!

It was during a jingle recording session in 1992 that the idea of collaborating with ghazal singer Hariharan came up, The duo became known as Colonial Cousins and produced such memorable numbers as '*Krishna*', '*Sa ni dha pa*', '*Feel alright*' and '*Let me see the love*', fusing sounds of the East and the West in a seamless and appealing manner. Bollywood soon called, and Lewis collaborated with music directors like Kalyanji Anandji, Laxmikant Pyarelal, R.D. Burman and Louis Banks.

And then came a wave that was huge, but which subsided fairly quickly: remixes. 'A remix is about taking the original vocals of the singer and re-doing it with new music,' Lewis has explained. It is not just about adding beats or funky loops, but is essentially 'enhancing the original with new sounds, catering to the same emotions'.

Asha and Lewis set off the trend with the album *Rahul and I*. 'It became a hit, so people branded me the Remix King. I consider myself a good composer and love doing remixes, but people started thinking of my original compositions as remixes!' So he backed off and worked on original compositions and Colonial Cousins for a while. He wrote and produced the music for *Janam Samjha Karo* for Asha, worked with pop artistes and composed for Hindi and Tamil films. But his thinking was logical, as he said in an interview: 'There was Hindi film songs on one side and classical music on the other. Then came the age of ghazals, followed by Indi-pop. When that was used a lot in films, there was a vacuum. That is where the remix fit in.' He aimed to take old songs and their melody to the younger generation with a little bit of work on them. 'I tweak the pace, add some rap, make some creative bits of music ... but never let go of the music.'

That was perhaps what made R.D. Burman like the young Lewis when they first met. 'I think I understood RD's vibe and his music, so I could give a new sound to it. One day, back when I was working as a sessions person, during a recording break, I decided to stay back instead of leaving the studio like everyone else, and was playing one of my compositions on the guitar. Suddenly I heard the same composition being played on the piano by someone who was trying to figure out the harmonic shift that I was doing. I looked around and there was R.D. Burman himself playing my tune! He listened to my song and then said, "Very nice music, very good." I was so happy! It was a shot in the arm for a youngster like me who was just starting his career in music.' Lewis already knew Asha, or at least of her as he watched his father choreographing some of the best-known songs in Hindi movies. He started working as a sessions musician. 'I was playing for films. I was in Lonavala and hanging out with my guitar when a car drove up and out stepped RD and Asha. It was very strange. He asked me, "What are you doing here? How is Daddy?" That was a standard line, everyone asked me that. Asha knew of me though she had never met me; she knew my mother better – they shared a birthday, 8 September. She asked, "Daddy who?" RD said, "Raj. This is his son." She asked, "Who Raj? Our Raj?" They were all part of the same gang and would hang out together. RD said, "Yes, this boy is a rock guitarist." It was amazing to see this interaction!'

Soon Lewis was doing something outside the norm of the 'regular music stuff'. He recalls, 'I started Indi-pop and Suneeta Rao's '*Paree hoon main*' was a massive hit that turned a lot of people on their heads in the Bollywood space and the non-Bollywood space and the college space and even the fashion space – it was the first Indian track to be used on the catwalk, where Indo-fusion design had just made its entry.' It was 1994-95. This was the time that the new Asha Bhosle was launched, the persona that everybody could identify with, especially the new generation. 'Apparently RD wanted to redo his old songs with me for that new generation. Why? Because I am good, the best!' Lewis was tickled all shades of the rainbow with this, a project that became *Rahul and I* (1996).

'The whole Indi-pop culture that I brought in then is what Bollywood is now. Everything was tabla–dholak when I brought in the keyboards, the funkiness. '*Dum maro dum*' was probably the funkiest song then in the live space. I was using electronics and computers to create dance music and pop and a very Western vibe, but singing in Hindi,' he remembers.

'The Bollywood people were listening.' R.D. Burman was too, Lewis discovered. 'When we met, Ashaji said that I must do [the album *Rahul and I*] and I said I was very busy, finally doing my own album. She said RD had wanted to work on it with me – he could have picked up anybody, so why did he choose me?' There had to be something special in Lewis, Asha reasoned. 'So I had to do it, but I did it from my perspective as a tribute to Ashaji and R.D. Burman.'

The album kicked off the trend of remixes in the country. Lewis' version of '*Piya tu ab to aa ja*', '*O mera sona re*' and other familiar songs evoked excited response. Everybody started doing remixes and they became a rage. But soon, he found, 'They started getting visually cheap, really atrocious,' so people started losing interest in them.

Good remixes were the perfect new direction for Asha to take, she decided, urged on by her family and her audience's changing preferences. Even as everyone said '... great respect, she is a legend,' they would add, 'but she can't really sing for the younger actors – the new girls are young, her voice will not suit them'. Asha, however, knew that this was not true – after all, she was an artiste and could do more.

It was not an easy progress that Lewis made with Asha. But the work went on. Asha did not like his version of '*Piya tu*', and refused to do it. Lewis put '*Piya tu*' aside and did another song with a higher tempo that did not make him very happy, but they got through the rest of the album. 'And as we did, she got to like me more, got to like the songs more. She hung around with me and realised that I had the ability to break rules, but to keep it sounding good to everybody, to the people who loved good music and those who wanted to party. I break rules, but nothing looks broken.' By the time they finished the project, Asha was comfortable with the concept, Lewis was calling her '*Aai*' (Marathi for mother). 'I was son number two types! She was there, I was there, we had a great rapport; she would talk and feed me. I asked her to sing when she felt good – at sixty-one, as she was then, she was allowed to decide when that was.' By the time Lewis was ready to go off to mix the album in London, Asha was feeling good about it.

> *She got a good vibe out of it and knew it was good, so she said, 'You know that first song I said no to,* 'Piya tu', *what was that? Can you play it again?' I did, she listened, then asked how to sing it. She heard me out and said, 'Chalo, let's record.' We did.*

Lewis left for London the day after that and when he returned to India, they had a meeting at my studio with the recording company – 'Aai's son and daughter-in-law, my wife and me, and the Universal people. It was the first remix ever and a double album. I pressed play. We heard fifteen songs. Everyone was grooving, but she was static. We finished them all, she got up and said, "This album will not be released."' There was a dramatic pause worthy of any movie that Asha may have sung for. 'The background music was missing, but it felt like it was playing loudly! Everybody jumped, because they had been grooving. The record label was upset and asked what happened. She said, "This is not Asha Bhosle's voice, her sound." I knew what she was saying. It did not sound like her familiar self. She was not used to that perspective of voice, where she is softer and the music is louder, unlike with the usual songs. There was this *Oh God!* kind of silence, then her son tried to explain that the music was really cool, perfect for the clubs, the next generation. 'Okay, play it again,' she demanded. We sat through the whole thing again, nobody grooved, everyone sitting quiet, everyone was stressed out.' Lewis wanted the album out, since it had taken a lot of work. He was upset. 'It was my space, something new and she was saying no. Everyone looked at her, waiting, she got up and looked at me and said, "Album hit *hai*!" and gave me a big hug. For a sexagenarian to change her mind like that, just on the dime of fifteen songs, to relook at it so carefully!' He was thrilled. The album was released and sales went through the roof.

'During this process, I would keep singing stuff for her. She realised that I was writing compositionally nice songs, even though on this album I was limited to recreating RDB's songs. Then she said, "The next album we do, you have to do your songs." I said I would love to. She latched on to one and wanted it, even though I insisted that it would not suit her and that I would give her something else. It was a Bossa Nova song, in the South American Latin space. She loved it, because RD loved that sound. I was trying to pull it away.' Lewis turned up the magic and gave Asha *Janam Samjha Karo* instead. The new album had favourites like '*Raat shabnami*', '*Maine dekhi ek pari*', '*Wo na bhule jahan*' and others. Not many know that Asha insisted that Lewis be an audible part of it. 'I sang a duet with her on the album. She asked me to sing this one song with her, a very Punjabi song, '*Oye hoye, oye hoye*'.' The record label believed that this song would be the next video, but the title song '*Janam samjha karo*' was chosen instead.

While Asha may have wanted more such collaborations, for Lewis, it was time to move on. 'I'm one of those who need to put my flag on a new island before anyone else does, and by the time others discover it, I am gone, looking for the next island.'

The reinvention process did not stop there for Asha. A decade later, she worked on a more classical collection with producer music veteran Atul Churamani and the 2004 Grammy nominee sitar player and singer Ustad Shujaat Khan. *Naina Lagaike* is not strictly a classical album, but a collation of folk, ghazals and lighter music based on classical compositions, Khan explained. About Asha, he says, 'When I met her, I thought, let's do an album with her – and I had a great time recording it. The idea was not to give each song much thought, but to meet, sit together and have a great time over music.' But during the recording, there was a problem – Asha had always used a music director to tell her what was right or wrong and how to sing what. Khan was not a music director and Churamani was not a musician. After thinking about it, they decided that they should record live. Asha agreed. That was the turning point. Churamani discovered that Asha's competitive spirit was the secret. 'She thought that since Shujaat is a trained classical singer and I am not, I have to not only keep up with him, but be above him. The tempo was there, the music was there, the lyrics were there. There was no plan.'

The *jugalbandi* began, a kind of vocal contest, a give and take, each singer trying to outdo the other. Churamani enjoyed every moment. 'He would do an *alaap*; she would measure it up and do hers. He would do a *tihai*, a *sargam* … she would respond. The problem was that she would refuse to let go and every track became thirteen or fourteen minutes long. And he was having fun too. It was so enjoyable – like watching a concert, just fun, fun and more fun.' A tour was planned, with Asha's son Anand involved in the scheduling. Khan would 'open a performance with '*Chaap tilak*', and then Asha would come in. We chose songs that worked well in an acoustic arrangement, like '*Aaj jaane ki zid na karo*' and '*Mera kuchh samaan*', ending with '*Chura liya*', in which the tabla player would do that thing with the glass (that R.D. Burman had used in the original). She would dance, get Shujaat to dance – she had the whole audience dancing. It was unbelievable!'

Shujaat Husain Khan also has many memories of Asha Bhosle, many filled with laughter and friendship. Of the Imdadkhani Gharana with its roots in Mymensingh in what is now Bangladesh, and with a musical pedigree going back seven generations, Khan is the son of legendary sitar player Ustad Vilayat Khan. Asha and Khan recorded *Naina Lagaike* in London, and toured the UK together with it. She said in an interview, 'Shujaat's father is someone I consider one of the best sitar maestros in the world – we were close friends and colleagues and I have recorded with him also. When I heard Shujaat's tunes, I was immediately captivated by their simplicity – they are not simple to sing, but the way they have been constructed makes them seem simple, even as they are intricate and beautiful. Shujaat is a wonderful human being and musician. It was great fun working with him and it's going to be fun performing in concert with him.' The results of the partnership between Bollywood and classicism were eagerly awaited since, as Ken Hunt wrote at the time, 'By any standard she is one of the greats of popular music. He is, in my opinion and that of many others, the finest sitarist of his generation, with a work ethic and melodicism drilled into him through studying sitar with his father...'

By the time *Naina Lagaike* was made, Khan had done a lot of background work with R.D. Burman, Laxmikant–Pyarelal, Kalyanji–Anandji and others, playing sitar for their songs. 'I used to see her from afar and knew that she was a big deal, but her humility was obvious – she seemed to be a very simple, straightforward, fun person.' Working with Asha, Khan found 'this wonderful, wonderful singer, a very simple human being who was stuck in the three-minute syndrome (which is the average length of a film song). My first thought was, of course we will do it, but I want to do this live. We both knew the songs, but I made her go through them with me. After that, I thought, we would stand across from each other and just sing. There would be no fixed bars – if I want to sing one line three times and she sings it back three times, so be it. There would be live music and the singing would be up to us. That is what is special about this album.' And they did it the same way when they took it on tour in England. 'Nothing was fixed, so it changed every day.'

For Asha, this was an unusual experience. She had last recorded live about thirty years earlier with Pakistani ghazal maestro Ghulam Ali. 'Here we just sang and if something sounded better, we repeated that part. And we sang our hearts out!' It may have been an unusual experience singing live with traditional instruments, but Asha enjoyed it, since 'The tunes and rhythms were in sync and we could improvise wherever we wanted to. There were no rehearsals, and whatever happened happened in the recording studio.'

Khan had her listen to some songs to understand what he was looking for in terms of feel and melody. 'And she was worried about the *khandaani* ustad people looking down on her and anything to do with Bollywood. It's not easy. They are wonderful musicians, wonderful people and they finally cajoled her into trying, and she gave in.' He explained, *Naina Lagaike* is just two people singing, which is what we do. I can't glamourise it. The flavour of Indian music is that – we take one line and we embellish it.' Asha enjoyed every moment of that, 'because it was a challenge; I don't think she had ever done it before. She was nervous because she knew it was the forte of classical musicians. I told her that I understood that she was afraid, that I knew so many different ways of singing the same line that perhaps she didn't, but she had a much better voice, with so much more control over singing, so it would balance out.'

Before the project was crystallised, Khan and his wife invited Asha to their home in Delhi. 'It was important for her to see who I am as a person: a *khandaani* from a well-known and cultured family, and I have a little realm that I am king of. She understood all that, but needed to understand how much arrogance, ego, pride – which we all have – was there in me. You see, temper, arrogance, ego is good fun, but when it gets out of control, it's no fun.' They spent a lot of time together and Khan wanted to establish in Asha's mind not just how much he respected her, but that he was a great sitar player though not a great singer – just someone who sang for fun and whom people enjoyed listening to. We were together in the studio and it was lovely, a gradual closeness of two human beings, who share a life onstage, share a respect and share each other's reputations.'

Khan and Asha shared a delightful camaraderie in their mischievous natures and would occasionally escape the work environment too. 'We at times snuck out and went shopping at Tesco. I had her taste the flan – they make a lovely flan at Tesco. 'We shared little moments like that. We ate flan and potato crisps. She wanted to know, "*Yeh kya flavour hai?* Rosemary?" I coaxed her to try it, saying that we would buy a small packet. The big one would be expensive, she insisted. Ashaji had reservations, wondering, "How can I stand on the pavement holding packets of chips, in London, where people know me!" I said nobody would know her at Tesco. We were out and about with maybe fifty pounds cash between us. Ashaji budgeted, keeping back what we needed to go back by cab.' The silliness continued in the taxi going back. 'The cabbie recognised her. She insisted that she was not Asha though her face matched. I told the cabbie my aunty did look like Asha and everyone bugged her about it but really, it was not her.

She decided that we would buy small packets of different flavoured crisps and she would come by my room in the evening to 'discuss something' about the music and we would taste the chips! This was the fun of being with her, to just be silly and to explore parts of the city she would not have seen otherwise.

They laughed, they had fun, they were carefree like children and they made memories together. Khan knew that it might never happen again. 'There are so many memories in a person's life that are special, that can never be retold in any medium. But we were two artistes together, running away, having fun. We made up stories of what we were doing outside. Most of the time that we have spent together, I totally enjoyed. It was all about the happy and important parts of our lives together ... my life, at least – for me, it was great. Onstage, she was a legend, people would be clamouring to see her, talk to her, I understand, but I was able to see that she was a little girl too. It was those lovely moments where I saw the little child.'

Naina Lagaike was well appreciated, but it was Asha's film music that always made waves, in the original form or as a remixed version. An always popular song sung by Asha and Mohammed Rafi was '*O mere sona re*', from *Teesri Manzil*. Ken Ghosh made the music video of the remix version using special effects and incorporating R.D. Burman, who had passed away by then. Asha watched the video, got up and left the room. Ghosh recalls with sadness clouding his face, 'I followed her and she was standing outside sobbing. She told me "I love it, but I can never see it again." She watched that video only once.' Ghosh shot other videos with Asha, including a ghazal. 'We had to retain the traditional look – one that she liked and that suited the song – but also make her hipper.' It was easier since she knew exactly what she wanted and how to make it happen. Ghosh, a former break dancer, music and television producer, much later director of films like *Ishq Vishq*, *Fida* and *Chance Pe Dance*, was the right choice for a music video with Asha. His work has been described as 'happy, peppy stuff, sort of popcorn art for popcorn music', or as Churamani once said, 'music to put a glow in your heart'.

Ghosh's stories go back twenty years or so. 'They are wonderful memories. Like when we were shooting a ghazal music video with her, Mickey Contractor was the only one allowed to do her make-up. She was getting ready when Mickey came out and told me that he was trying to convince her to keep her hair loose and would I go in and talk to her. She was sitting there like a five-year-old with a pout on her face, saying that she would not, she never left her hair loose – she looked lovely, grumpy face and all! I will never forget that image. She was like a baby on the set; she threw tantrums – baby ones, not star-sized ones – and you could mollycoddle her out of it.'

For the video of '*Na marte hum*' (from *Aap Ki Asha*), Ghosh decided to shoot in Paris, with actress Dia Mirza being part of the video. *The Great Gambler*'s (1979) '*Do lafzon ki hai dil ki kahani*' was remixed (from *Songs of My Soul*, 2000) and the video was also made at that time in Paris. 'While we were shooting in Paris, the local production manager was asking me, "Who is the lady that we are shooting the video on?" and when I told her that Asha had sung more songs than Elvis Presley, that was when it really impacted! The thing is, you could listen to her music for up to sixty hours non-stop, without repeating any. I also shot three or four songs with her and five or six promotional videos.'

Another director who worked with Asha and has fond memories of the experience is S. Ramachandran, a journalist turned filmmaker, public relations expert, television show director, among other things. He made a series of music videos starring Asha Bhosle and various celebrities, called *Asha and Friends*, which featured music by Shamir Tandon and the star singer with actors Sanjay Dutt and Urmila Matondkar, cricketer Brett Lee and young singers from a television reality show. His connect with Asha was deepened with other videos for her *Precious Platinum*, cited as the thirty-seventh most popular album in the world. 'I first met Ashaji when she was recording a Marathi song, long, long ago, when I was a journalist, in the late 1980s. I had just finished school a year earlier and she laughed, saying, "He is a small child, looks like he has run away from school, what will he do?" She came across as a very nice person.' A while later, Ramachandran interviewed her. And then he worked on *Asha and Friends* with the singer. 'She initially came up with the idea to do it with Ghulam Ali and others, but we knew the PR angle wouldn't work. Coming from a media background, I felt that we needed something more. So we thought of a few people who could sing, but were not singers. Sanjay Dutt, for one. We created a song, and decided to go to him. I dialled his number and gave the phone to Ashatai – it was ringing but he didn't pick up. The next time I called, I told him, "Sanju, Ashatai wants to talk to you." He said, "Ashaji wants to talk to me? Sure! But wait, wait a minute, why does Asha Parekh want to talk to me?" I said, "Not Asha Parekh, Asha Bhosle." He said, "Hey, what does she want with me?" She spoke to him and told him that she was making this album and wanted him to sing with her. He told me that he almost fell off the chair, wondering how he would sing!'

The song '*Aapke dil mein*' was done super-quick. Dutt took all of fifteen minutes to sing his part, which delighted Asha. 'I was stunned when Sanju recorded it so quickly. And his voice is so much like Kishore da's. It has a masculine feel to it,' she said. There was also a surprise in store for the actor. Ramachandran recalls, 'After doing her lip-sync portions, she broke into a dance with Sanju as well. She had rehearsed some steps very shyly with me earlier.' It was a very retro kind of song. 'He heard it, he came, he chatted. She started telling him about how his father Sunil Dutt had also sung a song with her. He had been as shy about it as Sanju was now, she said; in fact, he had pulled his cap over his face so that she couldn't see him when he sang. With her, there is always a lot of nostalgia that comes across. It's so good, because she remembers everything many years later.' The video took about seventeen minutes to shoot – a record!

The other two videos with celebrities were also done easily and quickly. Ramachandran is still somewhat amused at how it happened. 'The next song we shot with Ashaji and Urmila Matondkar: '*Mehbooba dilruba'*. She came, she mimicked me shot by shot, how I walked in, how I would direct, how I pulled at my trouser leg since I had lost weight, how I said "Look here, look there, not like that, look straight!" She was bringing in humour all the while.' Urmila had known Ramachandran from when he was a journalist. 'They both teased me the whole time. I knew what was going on, but went with it to keep them both happy.' The Brett Lee video took a slightly different track. '*Can you tell a girl'* was recorded when the cricketer was at Mohali in India, for the Champions Trophy ODI tournament. 'I was in Goa, but he arrived in Mumbai early and demanded to do it that same day. I flew in. My assistant started setting up and Lee started talking. "How old is this Asha Bhosle?" he wanted to know. I asked why. He said, "Mate, my wife is pregnant, I don't want any link-up stories!" I told him that he was not even thirty and she was seventy-plus then. When the two came together, she started discussing cricket: "Why don't you call him Sachin Lee?" she joked. She has that sense of humour, very childlike, very sweet.'

Ramachandran has rarely seen the singer get upset or disturbed, 'unless it has to do with the music or the sound. She is very specific about all that. So if the technicians or musicians are not up to her standard, they did not deserve to be there at all. If you want her to sing or perform, things have to be right, which every artiste has the right to demand. She does lose her temper and become temperamental, but only if the work is not going right. She is also vain – she has said that her figure could be slimmer, so use Photoshop, she says, she knows it could be done. Or she says, 'My sari is puffy. You will fix it, won't you?' I've seen her get angry with the media, especially when it asks too personal questions. I've seen her walk out of interviews, not wanting to express personal thoughts. You are human, you are allowed to be emotional, it happens. With questions on R.D. Burman or Lata, she gets touchy. There is a way to ask and she will respond if asked properly.'

Remixes, remembrance albums, devotional collections and film songs apart, Asha has also private compilations to her credit. The most notable is probably *Dil Padosi Hai*, a double album with music by R.D. Burman and lyrics by Gulzar. Released in 1987, it was appreciated for its complex melodies and expressive poetry. *Legacy* came from the 'adoption' of Asha by Hindustani classical musician Ali Akbar Khan in 1995, after which she studied the Maihar Gharana. Together, the two recorded eleven *bandishe*s for the album and garnered a Grammy nomination.

Asha collaborated with Pakistani singer Adnan Sami for '*Kabhi toh nazar milao*'. The story goes that she and R.D. Burman had met a ten-year-old Adnan in London and had advised him to take music seriously. The grown-up Sami, a professional musician, sang with Asha on the title track of his album in 2000 and then for another, called '*Barse Badal*' in 2007.

Her ghazals include songs for *Meraj-E-Ghazal*, *Aabshar-E-Ghazal* and *Kashish,* and in 2005, she released the self-titled tribute to Mehdi Hassan, Ghulam Ali, Farida Khanum and Jagjit Singh – *Asha: A Brand New Album*, with music by Somesh Mathur. She is also known for various collections, like the three-album set released on her sixtieth birthday in

1993. EMI India released three cassettes: *Bala Main Bairagan Hoongi* (devotional songs), *The Golden Collection: Memorable Ghazals* (non-film ghazals by Ghulam Ali, R.D. Burman, Nazar Hussain, etc.) and *The Golden Collection: The Ever Versatile Asha Bhosle* (forty-four popular film songs). And of course there are countless songs sung in various languages.

12

Her Songs

A challenging song became a scandalous musical moment in 1956, when Asha Bhosle sang '*Eena meena deeka*' for the film *Aasha*, the senseless patter falling smoothly and joyously from her lips, as easily as it had when Kishore Kumar, the master of musical nonsense, had sung it. This song was the earliest in the collection that music writer–composer Ken Hunt put together for the *Rough Guide* series. It was perhaps the first time that rock and roll was heard on a Hindi film soundtrack, composed by C. Ramachandra. And it is a staple at Asha's concerts. The story goes that the lyrics were inspired by the noises made by children who were playing 'Eeny meeny miney mo' just outside the composer's music room. Ramachandra and his assistant John Gomes together came up with *eena meena deeka de dai daamonika*, with Gomes adding *maka naka* from his native Konkani (meaning 'I don't want') and then the two went a little crazy with the nonsense syllables, singing:

Eena meena deeka
daai daamonikaa
maka naka naka

cheekaa peekaa reekaa
eenaa meena deeka deeka de dai daamonika
maka naka maka naka
cheekaa peekaa rolaa reekaa

They ended the lines with a triumphant *rum pum posh*! The song, which did include words that made sense, speaking of love, was a huge hit, featuring at the fifteenth spot in the Binaca Geetmala final countdown of 1957. While the male version with Kishore Kumar was better received, Asha's rendition – which had a young and spirited Vyjayanthimala dancing around a stage with a chorus line, while Kishore Kumar thinly disguised in a burkha and Minu Mumtaz looking on – was also extremely popular. '*Eena meena deeka*' inspired many cover versions, including by German band Timid Tiger (2010) and the New York-based group Goldspot (2011), both with Indian frontmen. John Mathew Matthan's *Sarfarosh* (1999) used the lyrics at the start of the catchy '*Jo haal dil ka*', while the song became the background music for an advertising campaign for a British bank in 2008.

While '*Eena meena deeka*' was being made, Asha was also trying her hand at other kinds of music. She joined the chorus in the upbeat '*Dukh bhare din beete re bhaiya*' in *Mother India* (1957) and progressed rapidly to vampish tunes like the challenging '*Mera naam hai Shabnam*' from *Kati Patang*, which was done in the talk-sung style that Professor Henry Higgins played by Rex Harrison made popular in *My Fair Lady*. Choreographed as a cabaret with the scantily clad Shabnam (Bindu) aiming to cause trouble for the heroine (Asha Parekh), for the number Asha had to segue seamlessly between speech and song, balancing tempo and orchestration while sounding seductive and secretive. It worked. The song is still remembered.

As difficult was '*Sapna mera toot gaya*', from *Khel Khel Mein* (1977). For this she had to use a key that could rise higher and shine brighter than the male voice, which was unique and in a high register. And when she did, the duet of R.D. Burman and Asha made the song a winner.

> *When I sang, I gave my one hundred per cent to each song; they are like my children. Some became famous, others were forgotten, but I love them all and if I say any one is my favourite, the others will get upset!*

Also challenging was another track that is part of her regular repertoire in performances. '*Aaja aaja main hoon pyar tera*' from *Teesri Manzil* had a rock and roll base, perfect for Shammi Kapoor to display his gyrations even as Asha Parekh played the lady. Sung by Mohammed Rafi and Asha Bhosle, the song was composed by R.D. Burman, with lyrics by Majrooh Sultanpuri. According to film lore, Shammi Kapoor did not think that producer Nasir Hussain had made the right choice with R.D. Burman; Shankarsingh Raghuvanshi would suit his dance style better. And then he listened to '*Aaja aaja*' and was so impressed that he insisted that Pancham would compose the music for this film and many others after it. Asha remembered the way her husband asked, as he often did when he had created something unusual, 'Do you think this song is good? Is it really?' It showed, she said, that he was so shy and self-effacing that he could not assert himself in the way he needed to be more successful, quicker. But the song was not easy for Asha to sing. It needed breath control and precision, since the end – *oh oh aaja aah aah aaja aah aah aaja* – needed a kind of quiver. Asha asked for time, and practised diligently at home. She was worried enough to ask her sister Lata whether she was singing it right. 'You are doing well, just go ahead and see what a great job you make of the song,' Lata said to her.

At first, Asha made her mark with sexy songs, but was a chameleon when it came to changing her voice and the emotions it described. In Ramesh Saigal's 1958 drama *Phir Subah Hogi*, she showed what she could do with Khayyam's composition for lyrics by Sahir Ludhianvi, '*Woh subah kabhi toh aayegi*', in spite of it being a number dominated by Mukesh. In the Muzaffar Ali directed *Umrao Jaan*, she sang lyrics by Shahryar set to music by Khayyam: '*Dil kya cheez hai', 'In aankhon ki masti', 'Justuju jiski thi', 'Jab bhi milti hain'* (which is essentially a *capella* and shows off the pathos that Asha could convey so well, including that crack in her voice made so famous by Begum Akhtar when she sang ghazals) and the plaintive '*Yeh kya jagah hai doston*', which won her the 1981 National Film Award for Best Female Playback Singer. Annu Kapoor, who hosted a radio show called *Suhana Safar*, told the story of how Khayyam lowered the pitch of the songs of *Umrao Jaan* by half a note. Asha was taken aback and protested that she wouldn't be able to do it. She then did it, surprised at her own voice and the difference that lowered half-note made. Asha has spoken of the film and its songs with a certain reverence. 'Jaidevji was originally supposed to compose the music for this film, but later Khayyam sa'ab took over. Director Muzaffar Ali gave me a novel on *Umrao Jaan* to read to get into Umrao's frame of mind before we recorded. Everything about this song was so unique. It was sad, haunting, and I sung it two notes lower than my usual pitch. For '*In aankhon ki masti*', Khayyam tried an Indian classical style and we improvised each line with harkats. Rekha added such magic to it.'

She won the National Award again in 1987, when she sang all four songs for Gulzar's *Ijaazat*, set to music by R.D.

Burman. '*Khaali haath sham aayi hai*', '*Mera kuchh samaan*' – reportedly composed in ten minutes by Pancham – '*Katra katra*' and '*Chhoti si kahaani se*' showed off her classical skills and conveyed a wealth of feeling with every note. Asha perhaps knew that the music was a departure for her and would find her a new and very appreciative audience. 'Pancham made me use the double voice effect – he made me sing '*Katra katra*' twice, one over the other, to get an echo effect. This was much before editing and new forms of dubbing evolved. It was a tough song.' And it was not all happy and peaceful. 'At the recording of '*Mera kuchh samaan*', Pancham would quarrel with Gulzar over the lyrics,' saying that next he would ask him to set newspaper headlines to music! 'When I started humming the refrain '*Woh lauta do*', Pancham caught on to that phrase and composed the tune.' She tweeted in 2010, 'Pancham jokingly referred to the song '*Mera kuchh samaan*' as the *luggage song*; my band members still call it that when we are on concert tour.' The song is not about things, but about the memories that the protagonist wants returned by her former lover. Asha told *The Fader* magazine in 2005 that it was autobiographical, 'This song is my life.' When it was released, it was cited as being one of her best, 'ahead of its time', since it was free-rhyming and had a soft composition that allowed the focus to remain on the lyrics rather than the tune. It was included in various compilations of both – Gulzar's greatest hits as lyricist and Asha's as a singer. More interestingly, '*Mera kuchh samaan*' was re-recorded for *You've Stolen My Heart: Songs from R.D. Burman's Bollywood* with Asha's collaboration with the Kronos Quartet, whose David Harrington said, 'The experience of a lifetime has tinged her voice with even more poignancy when she sings a song like '*Mera kuchh samaan*'.'

Musician Shamir Tandon, who composed the Number One

album of 2006–07, *Asha and Friends*, got his big Bollywood break with Madhur Bhandarkar's *Page 3* (2005). Two songs stood out for the way they illustrated the differences between Asha and Lata. '*Huzoor-e-ala*' by Asha, with Hrishita Bhatt doing what could be described as an 'item number', was peppy, and seductive, while Lata's '*Kitne ajeeb rishte hain yahaan pe*' was more subtle, introspective. Tandon did a lot more work with Asha, but he remembered *Page 3* as the film in which 'Lata Mangeshkar sang in the same film with her sister after many years, though they did not sing together'. After singing '*Huzoor-e-ala*' for him from a studio in California, Asha told him a story that he found very interesting. 'I asked her, "What made you agree to sing this song?" She could have flatly refused, which she did at first, and I then had to convince her to do it. She said, "For me the use of technology is exciting – nobody is there in front of me, I am singing to a wall, to a brief that came on email with a white engineer who understands nothing about it all." That was a revelation for me as well. Asha Bhosle is all about experimenting, novelty, exploring, changing with the times – that's what makes her what she is today.'

But there was much more that made Asha unforgettable. Consider her almost childlike tone in sections of '*Bhawra bada nadaan haai*', depicted in the film *Sahib Biwi Aur Ghulam* (1962) as sung by a young Waheeda Rehman as Jaba. It was a secondary role to Chhoti Bahu played by Meena Kumari, but an important one. The actress makes the song work with her gestures – she scratches her head and sticks her tongue out as she sings *Bhawra bada nadaan haai* ... She told Nasreen Munni Kabir in *Conversations with Waheeda Rehman* (Penguin, 2014), 'She brought that song alive. If you hear it again, you will notice how she stresses each syllable. I had to make exaggerated facial movements to match her singing and intonation. She sang the words like that because in the scene Jaba is making fun of Bhootnath, whom she thinks is foolish. Ashaji understood Jaba's character and the situation in the story totally.' The actress also is all praise for 'How beautifully she sang '*Nadi naare na jaao shyaam*' in *Mujhe Jeene Do* (1963) and '*Paan khaaye saiyyan hamaaro*' in *Teesri Kasam* (1966).'

But she is not infallible. As she told Sonu Nigam in a special interview for *Stardust* magazine, 'I am a human being, not God. *Sur* is such that *aapne ek bar sur lagaya, uske baad tum nahi keh sakte ke phir main waise ke waise hi lagaungi. Sur ek aisi cheez hai jo ek bar nikal gayi haath se toh usse pakadte pakadte jaan nikal jaati hai.* Yes, there is a possibility that I haven't sung few songs well. For '*Sona re sona*' *(Teesri Manzil),* I felt that I hadn't done it well, so I told Pancham. He asked me to wait until the song was heard. The song did very well, but I still believe I could have done a better job.'

Her output was varied, from the plaintive '*Ab ke baras*' (*Bandini*), in which a sister yearns for her brother, to the celebratory '*Maang mein bhar le rang sakhi re*' from *Mujhe Jeene Do* and the more seductively sweet '*Abhi na jao chhod kar*' from *Hum Dono* (1961) – this one had lyrics by Sahir Ludhianvi and music by Jaidev, 'whose tunes were like him, simple and pure'. The aching feeling and the Sadhana–Dev Anand magic only added to the song's appeal. 'Rafi sa'ab's nuances helped me as a singer too,' Asha said. Of course there was the unforgettable '*Aaiye meherbaan*', which made Madhubala look so much more come-hitherish than she had ever been. The club number from the Shakti Samanta-directed *Howrah Bridge* was composed by O.P. Nayyar, with lyrics by Urdu poet Qamar Jalalabadi, and had as its competition in the same film, '*Mera naam hai Chin Chin Chu*', sung by Geeta Dutt and picturised on a very young Helen. In contrast was '*Kaali ghata chhaye*' from the 1959 film

Sujata, with Nutan playing the title role. Composed by S.D. Burman, with lyrics by Majrooh Sultanpuri, 'It is a deceptively simple tune,' Asha found at first, 'but each line unravelled to show a new complexity as I discovered. Nutan's simplicity and longing for love heightened the mood of the song.' Director Bimal Roy obviously knew what he was doing!

Then there was '*Jhumka gira re*', which set a kind of trend for earrings from the town of Bareilly, the place made contemporarily famous by actress–singer Priyanka Chopra. From *Mera Saaya* (1966), a film directed by Raj Khosla and starring Sunil Dutt and Sadhana, the number Asha made her own had a playful and siren-ish vibe, in contrast to the more sedate '*Naino mein badara chhaaye*' and '*Tu jahaan jahaan chalega*', both sung by Lata Mangeshkar. With music by Madan Mohan and lyrics by Raja Mehdi Ali Khan, the movie reprised the success of the Marathi *Pathlaag* on which it was based. Surprisingly, this was not the first time the *jhumka* had fallen off in the *bazaars* of Bareilly – it earlier happened in 1947, in the film *Dekhoji*, in which Shamshad Begum, Asha's rival at one stage, sang it. '*Jhumka gira re*' is a traditional folk song that uses a concept often found in Hindi poetry to depict a woman who has abandoned her inhibitions, who has submitted to a lover, who has found a certain satisfaction in her own femininity. Bareilly is referenced often as a town famous for its zari work, rugs, jewellery – especially *jhumkas* (chandelier earrings) – and *surma*, or kohl powder. And it came back in the 2023 release *Rocky Aur Rani Kii Prem Kahaani*, with Ranveer Singh and Alia Bhatt doing a version as sung by Arijit Singh and Jonita Gandhi. Did it match up to the original? The jury is out...

While they voiced separate moods in *Mera Saaya*, the Mangeshkar sisters came together for '*Jabse laagi tose najariya*' in *Shikar*, a 1968 film by Atma Ram. The murder mystery had songs composed by Shankar–Jaikishan and written by Hasrat Jaipuri. A standout was '*Parde mein rehne do*', for which Asha won a Filmfare award as Best Female Playback Singer. In 1970, she was the female voice for all the songs for Raj Kapoor's ambitious but unsuccessful *Mera Naam Joker*, including a solo '*Ang lag jaa balma*'. Before that, in 1965, *Waqt* showcased her talent with '*Aage bhi jaane na tu*', one of the few songs she sang for director–producer Yash Chopra. The film was one of the first multi-starrers and had Sunil Dutt, Shashi Kapoor, Raaj Kumar, Sadhana, Sharmila Tagore, Balraj Sahni and other luminaries in the story of a family torn apart by time and its subsequent reunion. It is perhaps best known for the ever popular song: '*Ae meri Zohrajabeen*', sung by Manna De.

From the late 1960s to the early 1980s was Asha's time to shine. Almost everything she sang became a hit, and '*Aao huzoor tumko*' was no exception. From *Kismat* (1968), it was composed by O.P. Nayyar and written by Noor Devasi and is often ranked as one of Asha Bhosle's top five songs. The situation was a party where Babita gets very drunk and starts singing to invite the hero to join her in a dance. In spite of its various connotations, it was chosen to be part of the Shaan-e-Pakistan celebrations in New Delhi on 10 and 12 September 2015. A far more sober number was '*Do lafzon ki hai dil ki kahani*' from *The Great Gambler*, which, while not considered to be one of R.D. Burman's best, has always found fans. With lyrics by Anand Bakshi, it begins with Italian voiced by Sharad Kumar, and then fluidly segues into explanations in Hindi, sung onscreen by Zeenat Aman to Amitabh Bachchan. The action takes place on a gondola being poled through the canals of Venice, and Asha has often said that it is her favourite song. In fact, she told veteran journalist Khalid Mohammed that she ranks it Number One, followed by '*Aaiye meherbaan*' (*Howrah*

Bridge), '*Jaaiye aap kahaan jaayenge*' (*Mere Sanam*), '*Deewana hua baadal*' (*Kashmir Ki Kali*), '*Aage bhi jaane na tu*' (*Waqt*) and '*Yeh kya jagah hain doston*' (*Umrao Jaan*).

A young and voluptuous Mumtaz sang '*Yeh hain reshmi zulfon ka andhera*', on the big screen as she tried to entice Biswajeet in *Mere Sanam*, a Hindi film remake of *Come September* (1961), with Asha Parekh reprising Gina Lollobrigida's role. It was a box-office hit, and the nine songs composed by O.P. Nayyar with lyrics by Majrooh Sultanpuri had much to do with its popularity. '*Jaaiye aap kahaan jaayenge*' (Asha Bhosle), '*Pukarta chala hoon main*' (Mohammed Rafi) and '*Yeh hain reshmi*' (Asha again) are considered game changers in the history of Hindi film music. As popular, or perhaps even more memorable was '*Chura liya hain tumne jo dil ko*', a lilting tune from *Yaadon Ki Baaraat* (1973) sung by Asha and Rafi, with R.D. Burman's music and Majrooh Sultanpuri's lyrics. It was inspired by '*If it's Tuesday this must be Belgium*' by Dutch folk-pop vocalist Bojoura. A funny story about this song is that Pancham added the tinkling sound by tapping on glasses, cracking quite a few in his quest for that perfect '*ting ta ting*'! '*Lekar hum deewana dil*' and '*Meri soni meri tamanna*' are Asha–Kishore duets from the film, which starred Dharmendra, Zeenat Aman, and incidentally, was also the debut of Aamir Khan (as a child artist).

And then there was '*Dum maro dum*', an iconic Asha number from *Hare Rama Hare Krishna*. As she remembered, 'Sachin Dev Burman didn't want to compose for this film because it dealt with drugs and hippies, so Pancham took over. He gave the song '*Dum maro dum*' some really interesting bass notes and *harkats* (vocal twists).' The song, written by Anand Bakshi, was the highlight of the film, which had director–actor Dev Anand and Zeenat Aman playing brother and sister. Interestingly, it was originally designed to be a duet with Lata Mangeshkar and

Usha Uthup, (then Iyer) the former singing for the heroine and the latter for the vamp. Changes were made, presumably due to personal dynamics, and it became a solo by Asha, winning her a Filmfare award, with Usha adding a dash of *masala* with the aa ... aa ... aa sounds at the end of each verse and joining in the chorus. Usha has fond memories of her star co-singer, and saying, 'Asha Bhosle is a singer with a focus on the sky!' '*Dum maro dum*' was a huge hit, so hugely popular that Dev Anand decided to use only a small portion of it in the film so that the song would not overshadow the story. It topped the annual countdown in the show Binaca Geetmala and went on to become a Sartaj Geet by staying in first position for twelve weeks and on the list for over eighteen! Kishore Kumar called it a song that was 'powerful enough to bring a dead person to life', while American reviewer and radio show host Daniel Shiman described it as a 'Montage of creaking synthesizers, psychedelic guitars and, of course, vocals nailed by Asha Bhosle in an ear-piercing exposition of sound'. There was a riposte to the track later in the film, when Dev Anand sings (in Kishore Kumar's voice, of course) '*Ram ka naam badnaam na karo*'.

There were lots of other songs that the singer herself has spoken of with fondness. Take '*Duniya mein logon ko*' from *Apna Desh*, directed by Jambu and starring Rajesh Khanna and Mumtaz. R.D. Burman composed the music for the afro-jazzy number and sang in his characteristic gruff tone, while Asha sang high notes that kept pace with the driving rhythm. The stars are heavily disguised in the song that takes the story forward, hinting of underhanded dealings and plenty of action. '*Hungama ho gaya*' from *Anhonee* is still as magical as it was when the Laxmikant–Pyarelal composition with Verma Mallik's lyrics was first heard. The club lights, the insistent beat, Asha's voice and Bindu's sexy dance brings in a much more modern context that it was then. Amit Trivedi recreated the song for 2013 Kangna Ranaut film *Queen*, setting it is a dimly lit strip bar in Paris. And it worked as well. As did the far more subdued and moodier '*Chain se hum ko kabhi*' from *Pran Jaaye Par Vachan Na Jaaye* (1974), directed by S. Ali Raza, with Rekha and Sunit Dutt in the lead. Composed by O.P. Nayyar with lyrics by S.H. Bihari, this song was a kind of epitaph to the Asha–Nayyar relationship. It won her an award that she refused to collect, and she never acknowledged her former mentor/rumoured lover's role in creating it for her. But Asha has said, 'In sad moments, this song is a balm. I'm always asked to sing it at my shows. S.H. Bihari told me that the song reflected the pain and turbulence I was going through at that time.'

Romance was given a voice with songs like '*Roz roz aankhon tale*' from *Jeeva* (1986), a Raj N. Sippy film starring Sanjay Dutt and Mandakini. With lyrics by Gulzar and music by R.D. Burman, this number is still well-liked; as Asha commented, 'Pancham's biggest misfortune was that his best songs never got their due or were only recognised after his time.' The couple also did '*Tumse milke*' from *Parinda*, the Vidhu Vinod Chopra film with Jackie Shroff, Madhuri Dixit and Anil Kapoor. The simple yet emotional words by Khurshid Hallauri were set to music by R.D. Burman and sung by Asha and Suresh Wadkar. It has a waltz-like rhythm and a sweetness that is in contrast to the story that showcases the murky Mumbai underworld. In a departure from Pancham's music, Asha also sang for her brother Hridaynath Mangeshkar's brilliant composition for director Gulzar's lyrics in '*Jhoote naina bole saanchi batiyaan*' from *Lekin* was much lauded by Hema Malini, who played a guest role as a Kathak dancer in the Dimple Kapadia-Vinod Khanna film.

The song, which begins with a *alaap* by Satyasheel Deshpande, was based on raga Bilaskhani Todi and shows Asha's versatility as a classical singer, well matched to her sister's voice in the other songs of the film. Asha said about the song, 'My brother Hridaynath Mangeshkar is a tough taskmaster. He tricks you and challenges you with his experimentation with form. We recorded this song late into the night. It is a classical tune beautifully composed and was a challenge to sing. It's also Hemaji's favourite.'

Then, of course, there was A.R. Rahman, the composer who challenged Asha to push herself in unexpected directions and produce superhit songs. *Rangeela* (1995) marked a comeback of sorts for her after a hiatus, earning her a Filmfare Special Award for '*Tanha tanha*', long after she and Lata had announced that they would no longer accept any trophies for their work. The Ram Gopal Varma film starred Urmila Matondkar, Jackie Shroff and Aamir Khan and included seven songs with lyrics by Mehboob. Asha also sang '*Rangeela re*', with a young Aditya Narayan for company. *Daud*, also a Ram Gopal Varma film that released in 1997, was another experiment for Asha, who sang '*Zehreela pyar*', '*O bhaware*' and '*O! Sai yaiye*' for Rahman, who once again composed out-of-the-box tunes for Mehboob's words. While the film didn't do too well at the box office, it was noted for its music, and the rather risqué picturisation of '*Zehreela pyar*'. But, perhaps the number that Rahman assigned Asha that pushed her the most was '*Rang de*', from Govind Nihalani's *Thakshak* (1999). With lyrics by Mehboob, the song was 'difficult. I felt breathless, as the lyrics and the tune coiled and overlapped,' Asha said. It was reportedly as challenging for Tabu, who had to dance at high speed in the classically coloured track. Interestingly, the song was used in the 2008 Griffin Dunne film *The Accidental Husband*, featuring Uma

Thurman. Rahman and Asha worked together again in '*Kahin aag lage lag jaave*' in Subhash Ghai's *Taal* (1999), a showcase for the dancing talent of Aishwarya Rai and the drama that Anil Kapoor brought to the big screen. The soundtrack of the film was a huge commercial and critical success, earning Rahman, lyricist Anand Bakshi and director Ghai appreciation in India and internationally. The same happened with the songs from the greatly lauded *Lagaan* (2001), a historical fiction drama by Ashutosh Gowarikar that starred Aamir Khan and Gracy Singh. Asha sang '*Radha kaise na jale*', which won lyricist Javed Akhtar a National Award. The song tells the story of the *maharaas* – a dance that Lord Krishna did with the *gopi*s on the full moon night of Sharad Purnima, transforming himself into many forms to make all the women equally happy. The song is a dialogue between Radha, his beloved, who is jealous at the affection he showers on everyone, and Krishna's playful reassurances that there may be many stars in the sky (the gopis), but there is only one moon (like Radha is to him). Asha managed to convey all the emotion as only she could have in the song.

For novelist, writer and music lover Madhulika Liddle, favourites by Asha are classified mood-wise. In her blog 'Dustedoff' she writes:

> At the risk of being labeled an iconoclast and inviting censure (and possible debates?), I have to admit that I tend to prefer Asha to her sister Lata. Unfortunately, most people tend to associate Asha Bhonsle only with the sultry 'cabaret' songs that she sang for umpteen songs picturised on vamps, all the way from Helen to Parveen Babi. Few remember that Asha's was also the voice of the hauntingly beautiful '*Yehi woh jagah hai*', or the bhajan '*Tora man darpan kehlaaye*'.

For Liddle, the madcap '*Daiyya yeh main kahaan aa phansi*' (*Caravan*) 'has to be one of the most "unlikely to be filmed on a heroine" songs made in Hindi films … because the heroine is neither being romantic nor come-hither, neither maternal nor sad, but an utter clown. Asha Bhonsle, singing to R.D. Burman's music, called [it] the most difficult song she ever sang – this is a tough song to sing, very fast-paced, the notes going low, high, and through the roof, while the lyrics are mostly nonsensical enough to make it even more difficult to sing them correctly. Yet, Asha is flawless. She sings this with a panache and a nuttiness that does not, however, detract from the sheer skill of her performance.'

Another favourite is the patriotic '*Saare jahaan se achcha*' (*Bhai Bahen*, 1959). With lyrics by Jaan Nisar Akhtar, it uses the first two lines of Iqbal's original poem and goes a completely different way after that. The music by N. Dutta is more melodious, making it less of a 'marching song'. The icing on the cake is Asha's rendition. While older sister Lata may be credited with the more well-known patriotic songs – like '*Vande mataram*' or '*Ae mere watan ke logon*', this one works just as well. Her voice is very sweet and handles the twists and turns of the music perfectly.'

And then there is the teasing '*Dekhne mein bhola hai*' (*Bombai ka Babu*, 1960). Liddle says:

> What makes this song especially likeable for me is the way Asha sings it, the little bits of emotion that show in her voice at different stages. Besides the generally teasing air of the song, there's the momentary soulfulness of when she sings …*Gali-gali gaon ki re jaagi hai sote-sote*, as if ruing the past loneliness; there's the sudden, almost sultry twist to …*Gaon hai yeh pariyon ka, dil ko bachaana*, and there is

> the almost flirtatious playfulness of ...*Haseenon ka shahzada hai, hansi na udaana ji.*

And for Liddle, no list is complete without '*Yehi woh jagah hai*' (*Yeh Raat Phir Na Aayegi*):

> It is, in my opinion, one of her very best ... The misty atmosphere, the lyrics, the relatively subdued music (which swells only in the interludes) – all contribute. But most of all, there's Asha's voice: serene, melodious, and hauntingly beautiful. '*Yehi woh jagah hai*' gives me gooseflesh like few other songs can.

Composer–singer–producer Lesle Lewis, who has worked extensively with Asha, said, 'Before, you had to be an Asha Bhosle to be able to make a mark as a singer. The Asha Bhosle level is single malt, a high level of sophistication which the average listener was being subjected to all the while. That is why the older listeners are much better listeners, who expect a certain level of art in the singing, the music, the composition. In the olden days, they would rehearse for nine or ten days, travelling miles to get to the place, making the song theirs. You sing from the heart that way – that is why those songs are eternal.' He was in part responsible for Asha's more contemporary image, music-wise, creating remixed songs for her and composing new Indi-pop numbers. But he kept her in traditional clothes, since, he says,

> *Imagine Asha Bhosle in jeans and a T-shirt walking around – that does not work. Wear that sari, put on those diamonds, stick on that bindi, walk the way you do and rock the house ... that is what she does. Don't lose the mummy–daddy crowd, but also lock in the younger generation.*

'I think that is what I did with the remix album *Rahul and I.* A lot of people listening to it now say hey, this is good! For a lot of people, these are the originals. For some, both work.' But there is a special something about Asha, Lewis has always known. 'For me, Ashaji is a killer, she has killer instincts. If she wants something, she will attack it, work at it until she gets it, if she believes she needs to have it. She is quite an artiste at heart. Probably that's what has kept her in the limelight. Ashaji never stopped, always latched on to the right ahead of the race composers. The best singers in the world need the songs to make them happen.' And Asha found them.

13

Asha the Actress

31 January 2013

Crowds gathered outside the Cinemax movie theatre complex in Versova, Mumbai, for the grand premier of a new film: *Mai*. The occasion was indeed a special one. After all, it marked the acting debut of a woman known all over India and the world for two things – her music and her cooking. *Mai* featured singer Asha Bhosle, then seventy-nine, in the lead role, her first appearance on the big screen in a role perfect for her, suiting her age, her sensitivity and her voice. Directed by first-timer Mahesh Kodiyal, *Mai* tells the story of a sixty-five-year-old woman, played by Asha, who lives with her son, who puts her in an old-age home when he decides to move to the United States for work. Mai's eldest daughter, Madhu (Padmini Kolhapure), refuses to allow this to happen and takes her mother home with her. But Mai, who is slowly slipping into the bewildering haze of Alzheimer's disease even as she is helped by a specialist (Anupam Kher), has problems fitting into a family where her son-in-law (Ram Kapoor) is antagonistic towards her and her granddaughter (Shivani Joshi) is uncomfortable having her in the house. It takes time, effort and many tears before Mai finds acceptance and affection. The music for the film was composed by Nithin R. Shankar, with songs by Manoj Tapadia and Sahil Sultanpuri, a few sung by Bhosle herself and one by her real-life granddaughter, Zanai. This song, '*Dhakku makum*', with Amit Kumar as the male voice, is special since it depicts Asha dancing in the first rain of the season with all her neighbours, young and old. The title song, '*Mai*', and the lullaby, '*Chanda ki bindiya*', were sung by Asha herself. The movie did not do too well commercially, but Bhosle's performance was acclaimed by the critics, one well-known magazine saying that she 'weaves magic'. When asked, Bhosle explained that she had always been interested in acting, but never wanted to be an extra – albeit a famous one – or play a small part in a film. She wanted to be the star that she was off screen. *Mai* was her chance to do just that.

But she was not the first choice for leading lady, director Kodiyal said. Filmmaking was not his originally chosen career. 'I started my professional life working on an oil rig, then went on to the merchant navy.' Then serendipity stepped in. 'When I came to Mumbai during a vacation and met a childhood friend, he said to me, "You are a creative guy" – I play the tabla, do photography, etc. – "you should be in that field".'

Kodiyal loved writing, and did it all the time. 'I told Shamin (Desai, producer) that I was thinking of coming out with a book of short stories. I had written plenty of them. One of them was actually the story of *Mai*, which was originally called '*Maaee*'. I had always thought that the first film I would do would be serious. The ones after that could be commercial, without a head or a tail, for the public, to make money. But my first would be for self-satisfaction.' The story was almost self-generating, growing organically from reality.

Kodiyal wrote it, discarded it, rewrote it, threw it out again and when he was done finally, he was sure that nobody would finance it. So he took the decision to start with a Marathi version of it. 'That was the start of my struggle, going around the industry with my script. People wanted *naach gaana*, not something deep and meaningful.' But all along, though he knew what he wanted, the idea of Asha Bhosle playing the title role never entered his mind. 'For the Marathi version, it was the late Sulabha Deshpande that I was thinking of casting. I spoke to her at length on the film and the story. After enacting one of the scenes, Sulabha – undoubtedly a fantastic actress – said that I had written a beautiful script and she would do it: "The day you find a producer, come to me, give me ₹11 and I will do it," she said. I was in tears, because I could see one small bit of my film actually happening!' Kodiyal thought at the time that if the film were to be made in Hindi, he would choose Shabana Azmi and Tabu. 'After all, at the end of the day, one needs to look at the commercial aspect of a project.'

'One day, out of the blue, I was told that there was a man from Surat called Subhash Dawar who wanted to produce a film. I met him and told him a more commercial story, but he wanted a family drama. I told him about my story that I had written for a Marathi film – he and his wife started crying as I narrated it. Dawar wanted to make it in Hindi, and I had no problem as long as he could meet my budget. He left soon after and I had a feeling it would not work out with him. But he called me back.' Kodiyal decided he could be cautiously optimistic, and started the process of casting for the film. 'I was trying to get in touch with Shabana to rope her in. It was then that Nithin Shankar called me – he was a producer and a music composer, who also plays an instrument for Asha Bhosle. It was around Navaratri and he wanted to record the first song just after Dussehra – we did that with Sukhvinder Singh.'

Formalities done, contracts signed, money banked, the film was on the way to being made. Another song – a lullaby – needed to be composed. 'I wanted Ashatai to sing it, no matter what language – Hindi or Marathi – it was in.' Kodiyal was sure that Asha's was the perfect voice for the job. 'We fixed a date and Ashatai was there. It was the first time ever that I saw her in a non-glamorous avatar; she was wearing a simple sari and had her hair in a bun. I sat with her and told her what the song was all about and how it would be picturised.' The 'Aha!' moment came in a flash to me then. When she was recording, I mentioned to my partner that Ashatai would be the perfect *Mai* ... the quintessential warm, positive and strong mother. So, at the end of the day, when she was leaving the studio, 'I approached her, "Tai, I wanted to talk to you about something, if I may." I explained my idea to her that as the film was called *Mai,* the central character would ideally be someone like her.'

My little plea was met with silence. She asked if work was done for the day, whether the song had been recorded – did anyone want any changes? When I said yes, we were done, she still did not react to my proposition. She asked her man Friday to fetch her car and left. I felt awful. Nithin said he would talk to her.' Kodiyal had his fingers firmly crossed. 'Ashatai went to Pune for a show and Nithin spoke to her there. And she said okay! Her son Anand then called and asked me to come over. We spoke at length. I'd never been so scared! I knew the lady I was going to meet had heard narrations galore from the best filmmakers ever. I was trembling. I thought she would catch me on the first line! I was sweating, drinking lots of water. This was a different level of celebrity – it was film history incarnate sitting in front of me. I fumbled for the first five minutes; then I saw the body language of mother and son and launched into my speech in full flow. When I was done, Anand said to me, "Mother has always wanted to do a feature film. She has done every variety of music and singing that she possibly could – she was the first woman to sing with a pop star, the first to do a music video. She has wanted a full-fledged film to be made with her as the pivotal character, and not to be cast merely as one of the characters." Asha had liked the story and Kodiyal had his lead actor, but there still was a lot of work to be done. 'I said we would do a workshop; I would train her for a month. But she did not need any training. I guess this was because so much emotion goes into singing that a singer is an actor anyway. Facing the camera was not a problem either, neither was dealing with crowds. She said that the first thing that struck her was the title of the film – *Mai*. This was what she used to call her mother. That is what touched her heart.'

It was not her acting debut strictly speaking. When she was twelve years old, Asha had played a small role in *Badi Maa*, and as a child, Asha did a tiny role in the Marathi *Te Maze Baal*. Her father had died three years before and she and her sister Lata were working to support the family. 'Since then, I have been scared about acting and standing before the camera. Perhaps I did not like the hardships faced during outdoor shootings. But in *Mai*, there is nothing like that,' she told the press.

Asha spoke to the media about her new 'job'. In an interview with IANS she said, 'When I heard about the role, I knew that I would be able to do it because the acting bug runs in my family. My father was a drama artist. Also, when we sing, we also act. If we don't put some acting in a dance song, no one would be able to dance to it. We have to put expressions in a song when we sing it. So many times there are dialogues in songs too. So I realised if I can do that, I can act on the screen as well.' It was not an instant decision, and when Nithin Shankar told her about the project, as he had promised Kodiyal he would, she had listened half-heartedly. And then, 'He told me that the name of the film is *Mai*. I felt really nice, because I used to call my mother that. So it really touched me. Then my son and everyone else there said that no one else could do this role except me.' Talking to IANS, Asha recalled that 'I was shocked and I told them to stop joking, but they said they were serious. So I asked for some time to think about it. I discussed it with my son Anand who said, "You have always tried so many different things, sung all types of songs, done shows around the world, even sung English songs. You have tried so many new things in your career and you always have the hunger to do more and more new things; so why not this?" It needed some thought, but Asha knew her son had a point. 'I realised he was right. I have tried so many new things, but acting on the big screen was something I have not done, so why not try that too? So I said yes.'

Asha was signed on. *Mai* was a small film, Kodiyal a first-time director, and the story was not the usual Bollywood fare. The other actors were ready. 'Padmini Kolhapure was suggested by Ashatai, who wanted someone she was comfortable with. Padmini is an amazing actor; it was a pleasure working with her. She had to play the daughter, so had to be seen as a daughter – my USP was Asha by then.' Also, there was already a deep familial bond between the two women, so the role playing came naturally. 'With Ashatai, it didn't matter whoever was there, as long as they were good actors. Ram Kapoor as the daughter's husband was someone who I had suggested.

He was not perfect physically, a normal middle-class guy with a paunch, a typically husband-like character. Ram agreed immediately, since his grandfather had Alzheimer's. But he is also loud, as a Punjabi and a soap star, so I had to actually stop him doing his usual acting and dampen his expressions, demanding underplaying and softness – "Think that you are at a funeral," I would tell him.'

Workshops were held at R.D. Burman's house in the Western suburbs of Mumbai. Kodiyal was stunned at Asha's easy style and the way she became the character he had written. 'The first day, I had taken two scenes and told her that we would just read out the dialogue. I would do some characters; she would need to do hers. 'Let's see how that goes,' I said. I gave her a scene, an emotional one. The way she read it, she floored me totally. Her voice modulation, her pauses … she was 70 per cent there already. My work was to get that finishing touch, the last 30 per cent.' Every actor is different and has a different perception of and reaction to the camera, which captures the smallest of movements, just like a professional singing microphone captures every nuance of sound, even the breathing. 'I shot in 35 mm. The slightest movement of the face changes emotion and mood, since the face is what you are, and there are very few who can actually maintain a poker face.' For a film like *Mai*, everything needed to be subtle, the expressions restricted, the hamming curbed. Kodiyal explained to Asha that 'The whole idea was to film this in a very candid way. The audience should not believe that there is a camera filming everything, but that they are looking into a window of a house. I told her, 'You are not enacting for a camera, but just naturally, as if you are at home with you and me. Imagine that there is no filming equipment here, that you have just come to visit, but do it the way you want to. If you want to scratch your head, please do. People should relate to you, so be real, be natural.' That is where I had to work hard with her. Her expressions are naturally loud, dramatic, but she did it, especially on the sets.'

Asha told *IANS* in an interview, 'I wasn't anxious while acting because I knew that people would help me do my job and I could look to them for advice. The one time I got really nervous was while doing scenes with Anupam Kher, but he made me feel comfortable. Everyone was cooperative.' Producer–director Yash Chopra did the *muhurat* shot for *Mai* – he had sent Asha four or five scripts over the years and she had refused them all. 'He wondered what she had seen in me to agree to do the film, especially after she had refused so many others, all more famous than me. I think somewhere at the back of her mind she knew that it could have been better, but she was happy being the focus of it.' She was now not just a singer, but an actor as well!'

There was one day that Asha was furious with her director. A scene has her sitting on the terrace in the rain. It involved showering water on Asha from pipes connected to tanks. A much younger and more practiced actor would perhaps have hesitated, if not objected, but 'She was willing. I didn't want retakes, so it had to be done in one shot. Someone said that it had to be warm water, or else she would fall ill. She heard that and decided that she wanted hot water to avoid any problems later.' But Kodiyal had a very tight budget and limited time, so he used one tank with hot water, the rest being cold. The shoot started and the water showered down on Asha. 'She was actually shivering – but she did it, never mind if she was not comfortable. After the take, she was furious and blasted us. I explained, but it didn't make any sense, because she couldn't feel the warmth.' But she played the consummate actor and stayed in character right through, chattering teeth, anger and all!

Kodiyal assessed Bhosle's thespian skills. 'She is a very good actor, a director's actor. She will do exactly what you ask of her. There is no inhibition of "No, I am Asha", not beyond a point. Even her crying scenes are all natural.' A sticking point was wardrobe. 'As far as her costume was concerned – in the initial days, when she was given a cotton sari, she protested, saying that she never wore them. We had to tell her that she was not Asha Bhosle here, she was Mai!'

Asha's reputation of being ready and willing certainly showed itself during the shoot of *Mai*. 'She would be there long before everyone else – one day she was due only at 11.30 a.m., but at 7.30 a.m., she called from the sets to ask where everyone was, since everything was locked! She was willing to sit and watch the shoot, since she was awake at 5 a.m. We all scrambled to get there and not keep her waiting too long. That kind of energy and enthusiasm is beautiful.'

This was the norm for the singer. 'Even during rehearsals – she would come from Pedder Road. We would be doing our thing and she would sit quietly and hum to herself. One day, when I looked up, she was looking at her watch. She insisted, "Finish this quickly. I've brought some fish, marinated, and I need to fry it – we have to eat, right? We won't get food from outside, we will eat home cooked food, my maid will make rotis." She is a fabulous cook, and insisted on feeding us all. Some days she made mutton curry – she would bring it from home early morning and heat it up just before serving. She told us, "We will work until lunch, eat and then go home, because we will not be able to work any more." I asked why and she said that she had made mutton curry and rice, which is quite filling and leaves you not wanting to do anything but take a nap!' The motherly instinct expressed itself too. 'We were eating, and she stood next to me, selected pieces of meat and served them to me. She insisted that we eat first, before she did.' After all this, throwing a tantrum about a sari was okay, Kodiyal said. 'She was Asha Bhosle, after all! I expected much more ... She actually hugged me at the end of the shoot saying she was satisfied.' The only time that she needed time out was after the shoot, when the film was ready; and even then, she did not demand it. Her daughter had died one week before the release of the film. 'We postponed it. It was a matter of respect; she did not ask it of us.'

But the project was not without hurdles, some of them fairly major. The film was critically acclaimed, but had not turned out to be the product that its director had envisaged. For one, there was little publicity, even though it marked the debut of a renowned singer as an actor. And there were edits made that did not please the director. 'One particular scene that was cut would have been the most shocking and perhaps most real – in the middle of the night everyone is startled to into waking up to hear Mai singing an old romantic song. She has made herself up, draped over a grand sari and is standing by the window alone, singing a beautiful tune. That would have made such an impact!' And then there was a vignette when Mai, descending into a vortex of memory loss, enters a party hosted by her daughter and son-in-law wearing just a blouse and petticoat, without a sari. Kodiyal's realism was too much for Asha's children to bear. 'When her family saw it, they were horrified and demanded it be removed. After all, they said, this was Ashatai, her image could not be sullied, her fans would not like it! She was very sporting about it all, but the family objected. She understood the point that it was not a biopic on Asha Bhosle, but a film about a mother with Alzheimer's disease. So that disturbing scene was required. She did it, and as she did, the set was dead silent, with very few people present. The first time she walked in dressed like that, everyone froze. Nobody expected to see her that way. She did it!' But the scene was deleted.

The whole family watched the film and reacted emotionally. 'She cried the first time she saw it – that was the best part. Her son asked her, "Mummy, it's you on the screen, why are you crying?" Her sister Meena cried, saying, "It was just like our mother!" Hridayanath Mangeshkar, Asha's brother, asked if I was the one who had made his sister do all this! Asha loved it and said she would love to do it again. She wanted to talk to producers in the South and make a version there, since she had sung many Tamil songs and could manage the language.' All that excitement was more than justified, since the singer had made her debut as an actress at eighty. But Asha herself told *IANS* that this would be a one-time attempt, however successful it may be.

> *I won't do any other film after this. I just wanted to try something new. I don't want to become a full-time actress. I'm happy being a singer.*

The reviews for her performance were guarded, most lauding the singer's debut for her personal charisma rather than her thespian skills.

Kodiyal regrets that *Mai* did not garner the attention he believed it deserved. 'Recognition should have been given to her. It would have been apt. I told everyone who was involved that whatever happens, remember that with *Mai* we are making history – this is the only film with Asha Bhosle as an actor. And whenever her name is mentioned, mine will be too – I am the only director who has made a film with her!'

14

Her Culinary Skills

Asha confesses that if she had not found success as a singer, she would have become a cook. 'I'd have cooked in four houses and made money,' she once said in an interview. Ask any of the celebrities from the film world who have worked with her and they will all talk about at least one culinary favourite she has cooked for them, apart from a song that they can never forget. Her forte is Indian cuisine and it is said that the Kapoor family still requests Asha to make her famous *paya* (trotters) curry, Goan fish curry and dal for them. The *kadhai gosht* and biryani have a huge fan club too. Ask the singer to make something special and she will rarely refuse, people know! At ninety-plus, she is still willing and able to spend a few hours on her feet cooking up the proverbial storm. 'I have people who cook for the family – I don't cook daily meals any more – and my daughter-in-law supervises. But if there is a special dish to be made or people are coming over to eat, I cook everything in two or three hours.'

She once said in an interview: 'Happiness is a medicine for life's sorrows. We all get stuck in negatives like anger and desire.

I prefer to be positive, to find happiness in small things like a blooming flower in the morning, good music, cooking, etc.'

Her way of sharing is not just singing, but cooking and feeding her friends, family, visitors, even those who come to interview her. 'I find cooking de-stressing. Like with music, I love experimenting with flavours and ingredients. Like I sing all kinds of songs, I also cook all types of food. But I believe in being traditional – I like traditional clothing, traditional food,' and tends not to go beyond what she does best, which is Indian vegetarian and non-vegetarian cuisine, she says. Journalist-filmmaker S. Ramachandran has been a guest at Asha's table. 'It was a pleasure to sit with the entire Mangeshkar family to eat – she is a fabulous cook! At Asha's, her restaurant in Dubai, she actually cooks and trains the chefs. My meals with them were moments to enjoy and cherish personally. I am strictly vegetarian and she would say, "*Tum ghaas phoos khaate ho* – you eat grass and shoots!" and Lataji would respond with "He is a boy, don't tease him!" Those were memorable times.'

Long-time friend, actor Poonam Dhillon is a frequent visitor to the Bhosle home. She says, 'Ashatai is a great cook and host. She knows I like prawns and fish and always makes sure these are on the menu when I visit. Her favourite thing to do undoubtedly is cooking. There is nothing else that relaxes her as much and gives her as much happiness – after all, she's not doing it for herself! She's cooking for her grandkids or her family or her friends. Other than being with her grandkids, that would probably be the most important thing for her.'

Actor Randhir Kapoor suggested Asha give up music and concentrate on cooking. The singer always knew her ability to make magic with good food; in fact, it bound her to her second husband R.D. Burman and to the poet, Gulzar. She explained in an interview, 'I love to cook. And the two men love to eat. Gulzar bhai loves my *karela gosht* and Bengali *kheer.* They would argue with me sometimes, but it would always be okay in the end because I had the deadly combination of *khana* and *gaana* on my side!'

The businesswoman in Asha – encouraged by her children, especially her son Anand – spurred on by her love for food, and cooking drove her to invest in a chain of restaurants in the Middle East: *Asha's,* specialising in traditional North-western Indian cuisine, with chefs trained by the singer herself over a six-month period in specialities she is known for, from Goan fish curry to biryani, which also happen to be her favourites. 'If a restaurant is to have my name, then it has to be successful, so I want the food to be exactly the way I cook it.' Asha once told a journalist:

> *Ever since I was a child, I have asked my mother to teach me how to cook. I wanted to learn how to prepare my favourite dishes – like shrimp curry. I probably learned how to cook before I started singing, but both are passions that will last forever!*

The menu is inspired by the preferences of the singer's family. Kebabs came from the admission Asha's grandson made to her – that he preferred kebabs to more elaborate fare because they suited his need for food that was not rich or too filling. As she has described it, 'It is like *ghar ka khana* from all over India. What I don't like to eat, I have not put on the menu. And most of what I know is what I learned from my mother and grandmother, and my friends: my mother's prawn curry cooked in coconut and turmeric gravy; boneless chicken cooked in ginger, garlic and almonds to be eaten with coconut gravy that I learnt from Majrooh Sultanpuri's wife, Begum; the Peshawari biryani that Raj Kapoor showed me how to make; *maa ki dal* cooked for three days over a coal *sigri* (Indian griller). There is also the paya that is simmered in its own gravy for three days, *raan* marinated overnight with the masalas ground by hand on a *sil batta*, Goan fried fish with *hari mirchi tadka* in ghee and RD's favourite fried prawns.' The Maharashtrian flavours sing the loudest, but 'When I cook rice with brinjals, the masala is different. I make tomato chutney, Bengali style; the *chana dal* is cooked just like my mother did; the *aloo sabji* is Haridwar style.'

Asha herself has varied tastes in food. As she has said, 'When I was young, I had different favourites. I like Thai food – it is very similar to South Indian cooking with its coconut-based sauces and similar ingredients. I also like Chinese cuisine and some Italian food, but I dislike fast food.' Her favourite meal is a simple one: plain rice, dal and chilli pickle. She prefers Indian food, with Bengali specialities like *Shorshe bata maach* (mustard fish), *parshe maach* (mullet) and *ilish* (*hilsa*, a kind of herring). 'When you fry the ilish, squeeze some green chillies into the oil left over in the pan, add salt and eat this with rice – delicious!' She eats everything, but in small portions, with sweets being her only indulgence, ice-cream being a favourite … but only if she is not on a concert tour. 'I rarely go to bed without having a sweet. But I take care not to stuff myself. If I eat too much in the day, I skip dinner.' Exercise, to Asha, is a strange concept: 'Music is my yoga.'

Even as she works on her *alaaps* and *bols*, Asha plays with food.

> *As a singer, I improvise; in this sense, I like to do that in the kitchen too. When I am creating a new dish, I think of the healthiest ingredients that will not upset the one who is eating. I have always cooked with my children's best interests at heart – the same way, I always cook what is best for everyone's health.*

Asha said some years ago, 'My daughter and sisters follow me into the kitchen and write down what I cook – they record it, because my recipe changes each time I make a certain dish.' She collects recipes from everywhere she travels to and whoever she meets, like a hugely popular menu of Lucknowi specialities acquired from music director Majrooh Sultanpuri's wife, or traditional Bengali *chingri-maach* (prawn curry) from R.D. Burman's grandmother – even Peshawari biryani from Raj Kapoor. 'I just remember recipes from experience. Even if I don't recall all the details and end up adding something new, that becomes a new dish. Which, I would say, is better. A bit like a remix!'

The love for food and cooking and the wicked mischief that she was known for snuck into the equation with music writer Ken Hunt too, as it always has done where Asha is concerned. 'Outside of music, the subject I've found her most passionate about is cooking and cuisine. After a studio wrap in Sausalito, she cooked a meal from scratch, including – her daughter-in-law told me – going off herself to buy the vegetables. Food is my passion too., so when she and I were discussing a Maharashtrian recipe, I asked her about the ingredients. She asked me what all I could taste in it. I started listing the ingredients randomly. There came a point when it dawned on me that her 'ji's' and head wobbles had stopped. and her beautiful brown eyes had narrowed. There was still an ingredient in the masala I couldn't quite place or name. I blew it deliberately by mentioning something foolish: *methi*. Her eyes lit up with triumph and the intensity lightened. And no, she never told me what the missing ingredient was!'

The triumph she found while teasing someone has always been mirrored in that which she finds in cooking something her family relishes. As she once told Shekhar Gupta, who was then with the *Indian Express*, 'If you want something from the heart, you will always find the time – if you wake up and go to the kitchen, you can cook food in time!' And all good things take time. After all, people say that she spent three months creating the menu for Asha's, picking up 'something from Punjab, something from Maharashtra and bits and pieces from many places'. Some of Pancham's favourites are included. 'Since we could both cook well, we often had competitions at home. He would relax by cooking, after thinking about music, composing tunes and experimenting with sounds.' Describing her late husband as 'an impromptu chef', Asha once told a reporter, 'He would cook with anything he could find in the kitchen and make it taste amazing. Like when he added beetroot to mutton curry, or when he made chicken with peas – his recipes were almost always a success.' And they made plans, most of them castles in the air, with food being the foundation. 'When Burmanji, Anand Bakshiji and I travelled to perform at concerts and stopped at a dhaba to eat and rest, we would talk about starting a restaurant of our own. "*Chalo ek dhaba shuru karte hai. Do koyle rakh denge aur us ke upar khana pakayenge!*" (Let's start a dhaba. We will install two tandoors and start cooking on them.)

Deenanath Mangeshkar was a stage artiste and classical singer, but also a foodie. 'My father liked to eat good food,' Asha told a reporter a few years ago. 'Every morning, he ate chicken and every evening fish, so we also ate that with him. Now I don't, but I like to cook good food.' There is a sad thought attached to this too. 'I started cooking at the age of ten,' a year after my father passed away. 'For our father's first-year death ceremony, my sister and I started cooking at eleven at night and finished at eleven the next morning, making a variety of Indian foods like pakoras, *puranpoli* and lots more.'

Cooking is also a way for her to deal with trauma. When her daughter Varsha passed away in 2012, Asha dived into her music and her cooking. As a relative said at the time, 'Ashatai has always loved to cook and feed family and friends. Now, cooking has also become her way of dealing with the pain.'

Along with her family, her children and their friends, others would also throng the house, people that Pancham would casually invite for a meal. 'He was a great foodie; he loved to entertain.' Often, her husband would phone her to tell her that he was bringing a few guests over and Asha would need to feed forty or more people! Amitabh Bachchan, Shashi Kapoor, Sanjeev Kumar – they were crazy about my *kaali* dal and Goan fish curry. Dev Anand, Yash Chopra, the entire Kapoor *khandaan* loves paya. Jeetendra, Zeenat Aman, Rajesh Khanna, Dilip Kumar … Every week, twice a week, Burman sa'ab would request me to cook for them. He was so proud of my cooking!'

According to Asha, 'One day after a dinner, RD said to me, "Did you know that I am very proud of you?" I laughed and said, "Proud of my singing or my cooking?" He replied, "I am proud of your presentation in both. Just as you know how to sing each song, you prepare and present your cuisine in the same meticulous and delectable way."'

She has talked about a dinner visit from then-superstar Rajesh Khanna, who came into the kitchen to watch her at work. She was wary about adding too much ghee which, she has often said, is the secret to her youthful spirit and glow, but Khanna insisted she be generous. 'Why just one, add three spoonfuls of ghee!' Dhillon attested that 'She is a fabulous cook – she isn't ever satisfied until she has cooked with her own hands and fed you properly. Sometimes I tell her, "You've made the whole thing – a kebab, for instance – let the maid fry it on the tawa! You've done it already, now let them take over!" But no, she has to fry it, turn it, and serve it on a plate herself. That only happens from the heart. Over the years I have come to believe that it is the affection and involvement that makes her food truly delicious – *Maa ke haath ka swaad*, the taste that only a mother's touch can give to the food!'

At home, she does have a long-time cook that she has trained to follow her directions. But she will shop for ingredients if she can, walking through Mumbai's Prarthana Samaj for spices and condiments, Citylight Market in Mahim, Mumbai, for fish, Crawford Market for vegetables, arguing with vendors, bargaining, exchanging friendly insults and gossip alike and choosing the best to take home. There will be the rare instance when she is not recognised; most of the time, people will clamour for a song, a photograph, even a handshake. Asha once told Farzana Contractor, editor of *UpperCrust India*, 'I can cook everything that I like to eat. My menus at home are mixed. Don't expect typical Maharashtrian food here. It might be Bengali fish, Lucknowi shami kebab, Peshawari biryani, Goan prawn curry, South Indian chicken fry, Maharashtrian pathare Prabhu bhaji, Parsi mutton *dhansak*, Hyderabadi *salan* pulao. There is not much that is vegetarian. I learned from when my children Anand, Hemant and Varsha were very small, to have plenty of non-vegetarian food at home. That way they did not go to restaurants to eat it. Or to other people's homes.' Radio producer and host Hrishikesh Kannan, who is a friend of Asha's grandson Chaitanya, aka Chintu, remembered how 'When I went to her house what I remember most is that aroma – she is a fantastic cook. She cooked *bombil* (Bombay duck) and offered me some. I am not a fish fan, but if Asha Bhosle has made it, you bloody well eat it! She can rustle up a mean meal. All her restaurants' recipes are hers.'

Her minced chicken, or *murg kheema* has hand-chopped

fowl, and came to be made when her children refused to eat meat with bones. It is cooked with potatoes, onions, tomatoes and garam masala that Asha makes herself. The singer dished out some easy-to-follow advice: 'You can create different preparations of food by thinking about all the ingredients that would go into it. You think of exactly what you want to do, whether you are going to use more of one ingredient and less of another. Don't count or measure too much – I don't think anybody who's cooked with numbers in mind has ever cooked up a great dish. Observe how a dish is made, contemplate about it and cook with all your instincts and your best gut-feel. And last but not the least – always feed with love!'

ASHA'S NASHEELI RAAN

Ingredients

Leg of lamb 4 × 850g
Kashmiri chilli powder 200g
Shahi jeera 50g
Malt vinegar 1-2 litres
Ginger garlic paste 100g
Green cardamom powder 30g
Mace powder 30g
Salt 70g
Cinnamon sticks 20g
Bay leaf 20g

Method

Trim and marinate the lamb in all the ingredients, cook up to about 95 per cent on a slow fire. Let it cool in same stock. Put the lamb in the tandoor at 270°C. When the meat acquires a colour, take it out, cut it into pieces and baste with butter. Add lemon juice and chaat masala. Serve with mint chutney.

ASHA'S VEGETARIAN SHAMI KEBABS

Ingredients

Portion size 8
Yam 750g
Banana (raw) 250g
Potato 250g
Kabab chini 20g
Salt 5g
Ghee 200g
Turmeric powder 20g
Chana dal, roasted and powdered, 350g

For the stuffing

Onion (chopped) 500g
Mint leaves 50g
Green chilli 50g
Yogurt 500g

Method

Boil the yam, raw banana and potatoes with turmeric and salt. Grate, add salt and kabab chini powder and roasted chana dal powder. Set aside. Mix yogurt (curd), mint, onion and green chillies and add to the yam-banana-potato mixture. Shape into small patties and fry in ghee until crisp and brown. Serve with mint chutney.

CHINGRI CHAAP

These crumb-fried prawns were a favourite of Asha's late husband, R.D. Burman.

Prep time: 30 minutes; Serves: 1

Ingredients

White shrimps 3 large
Breadcrumbs 300g
Concentrated lemon juice 3 tsp
Fresh eggs 2
Red onion 60g
Ginger 30g
Garlic 30g
Chopped coriander for garnish 10g
Red chilli powder 10g
Oil for frying

Method

Peel and devein the prawns. Clean them in cold water and cut each into a butterfly shape (slice through the middle as far as you can, without cutting them into half). Flatten with the side of a knife and set aside.

Make a paste of garlic, onion, ginger, lemon juice, red chilli powder and chopped coriander. Adjust the seasoning by tasting it. Add the prawns and marinate in the refrigerator for 2-3 hours.

When ready to serve, beat the eggs and dip each prawn into the mixture, then dip into the breadcrumbs and deep fry until golden brown.

MURG RASAM PATTI

Ingredients

Chicken, boneless, 350g
Red chilli, small, whole 1
Fennel seeds 5g
Mustard seeds 4g
Cumin 2/5 tbs
Onion, small, chopped 1
Onion seeds 5g
Coriander seeds 2/5 tbs
Curry leaves 3g
Vinegar, white, 50ml
Yoghurt 60ml
Red chilli powder 1 tsp
Salt 1 tsp
Turmeric powder 2/3 tsp
Coriander leaves, chopped, 1-1/5 tbs
Mustard oil 60ml

Method

Grind all the ingredients into a smooth paste, except the onion, red chillis yoghurt and mustard seeds.

In a sauté pan, heat the mustard oil, crackle mustard seeds, add chopped onion and cook for 2-3 minutes until golden brown.

Add curry leaves and red chilli, followed by the ground masala and chicken pieces.

Cook on a low flame for about 45 minutes, until the chicken is done. Serve with steamed basmati rice.

MALMALI DAAR BOTI

Ingredients

Mutton, fresh, 400g
Ginger-garlic paste 1-1/5 tbs
Lemon juice 1-1/2 tbs
Salt 1 tsp
Red chilli powder 2/5 tbs
Cumin powder 2/5 tbs
Garam masala powder 1tsp
Ghee 2-1/2 tbs
Papaya paste 2 tbs
Yoghurt 4 tbs
Brown onion paste (medium onions, slow fried) 3-1/5 tbs
Coriander, fresh, 4/5 tbs
Cinnamon powder 3/5 tbs
Turmeric powder 4/5 tbs

Method

Wash the meat and cut it into cubes.

Grind garlic, ginger, browned onion, coriander, cumin, red chilli, turmeric powder, papaya paste and curd to make a mixture. Mix all the spices together.

Marinate the meat cubes in this mixture for an hour.

Cook in a pan for 45 minutes on medium heat.

Garnish with onions and chopped coriander and serve.

Acknowledgements

Thank you to everyone who became part of this, willingly or not.

Most of all, to my father, Nataraja Sarma and my mother, Vimala Sarma.

To Naman Ramachandran, who started it off, and Jayapriya Vasudevan, who pushed me into it.

To Amaryllis and the unflappable Bidisha Srivastava, editor, friend, publisher, and to Mriga Maithel.

To everyone who added value – Aman Arora, Ameen Sayani, Anjali Mathur, Atul Churamani, Boy George, Brahmanand Singh, Hariprasad Chaurasia, Hrishikesh Kannan, Ken Ghosh, Ken Hunt, Kumar Sanu, Lesle Lewis, Longinus Fernandes, Madhulika Liddle, Mahesh Kodiyal, Mandar Bichu, Manish Purohit, Manohar Iyer, Mukesh Batra, Narendra Kusnur, Parveen Khan, Poonam Dhillon, Rajan Shahi, Rajeev Masand, S. Ramachandran, Satish Chopra, Shamir Tandon, Shujaat Khan, Sonu Nigam, Sumit Dutt, Usha Uthup and Yogen Shah.

To everyone who helped – Aditya Raj Kapoor, Ananth Padmanabhan, Dhiren Trivedi, Dominic Ferrao, Indu Mirani, Krithika R, Letty Maria Abraham, Neeta Kolhatkar, Nina Rao, Prathamesh Jadhav, Rachana Parekh, Ritu Ferrao, Rocky Mohan, Roshmila Bhattacharya, Smita Khanna Bajaj, Suresh Gopale and Vivek Kapoor.

And to the many who soothed, scolded and made bad jokes so that I would not take myself so seriously, many thank yous!

www.ingramcontent.com/pod-product-compliance
Lightning Source LLC
LaVergne TN
LVHW090543110826
845146LV00003B/1244

9789355436818